Environmental law and citizen action

Alan Murdie

Earthscan Publications Ltd, London

Dedicated to my Grandparents
Mr Frederick Mann and Laura Mann (1904-64)
– and –
Mr Robert Murdie and Elsie Murdie (1905-92)

First published in 1993 by
Earthscan Publications Limited
120 Pentonville Road, London N1 9JN

A catalogue record for this book is available from the British Library

ISBN: 1 85383 156 5

Typeset by Meta Publishing Services, Southfields, London
Printed and bound in Great Britain by
Biddles Ltd, Guildford and King's Lynn

Earthscan Publications Limited is an editorially independent subsidiary of
Kogan Page Limited and publishes in association with the International
Institute for Environment and Development and the World Wide Fund for
Nature.

Contents

Preface

Environmental law has become an increasingly important topic in recent years. Every week stories of controversial planning developments and prosecutions for the release of toxic substances feature in the news. Growing numbers of books and journals are devoted to explaining environmental law and seminars, conferences and courses on pollution control and the legal protection of the environment are held regularly. Usually these are designed for an audience comprised of business, industry and various governmental and professional interests. Welcome though these developments are, ordinary citizens have largely been left behind. All too often, the public have been relegated to the role of bystander, not included in the decision making process, even though they may be the people most directly affected by environmental problems. Few publications and events have been aimed at informing the ordinary citizen about environmental law and the new environmental rights which have come into existence in recent years for the benefit of individual citizens. As a result most people remain unaware of their rights, and trying to obtain information on environmental law in the UK remains an exceedingly difficult task for ordinary citizens. This is despite the fact that probably more people than ever before are now seeking such information.

This is an unsatisfactory situation for two reasons. Firstly, although it may be trite to say, the environment affects everyone and legal information should not be monopolised by a relatively small number of groups and individuals. Secondly, it has been the concern shown by public opinion and pressure which has brought many pieces of legislation onto the statute book. Having put the environment onto the political agenda and into law, ordinary citizens should now be in a position to see their wishes put into practice.

It is hoped that this book may play some small part in supplying information on environmental matters to a wider public and make the legal system and the rights we enjoy more accessible to the ordinary person. Each of us has many more rights than may be popularly imagined, both to obtain information and to use the legal system to protect the environment. In my own view - based on experience - non-lawyers are fully capable of using the law and the legal system as effectively as many lawyers - providing they have access to the right information. Providing such information and thus extending the choices available to the ordinary citizens concerned about the fate of their environment is what this book aims to do.

Many people seeking information on environmental law – whether private citizens, students or even public officials – often experience difficulty with specialist text books designed for professional lawyers. Such books while suitable for professionals and students, usually assume a background knowledge of the court system and legal procedure on the part of the reader. As a result such texts may seem almost incomprehensible to non-lawyers at first perusal. This book hopefully supplies some of this vital background information which lawyers may take for granted but which is crucial for understanding and for practical use of the system by the non-lawyer. With recent suggestion in May 1993 to reduce the numbers of people employed by the Government in pollution control, the role of the citizen in enforcing environmental law may be of growing significance in the next few years.

Apart from the ordinary citizen seeking preliminary information on a specific environmental topic, it is hoped that it may be of use to enforcement officers taking pollution cases to court who often feel themselves to be at the mercy of defence lawyers and the formalities of court, and also for busy solicitors and advisers already burdened with heavy work loads. It is also hoped that it will be of assistance to the busy professional in the environmental field who does not have the time to study law or the resources to afford a lawyer on every point that may arise.

Because of the breadth of the subject, each of the topics mentioned can only be approached in outline. Such is the size of the field that in many areas this book can provide no more than a pointer to finding further sources of information. As with any other books, the selection of material reflects the perceptions, concerns and priorities of the author, and some areas, such as legislation covering the control of radioactive substances have been omitted entirely. Whole books could be devoted to almost all the topics discussed, and it is hoped that many such works may appear in the future.

It should also be appreciated that this book is exceedingly

parochial in character, and concentrates almost exclusively on the law in England and Wales but with little on Scotland or the EC. This is not to denigrate either the status of Scottish or EC law but reflects the constraints of size of text and the knowledge of the author, combined with the fact that it is with domestic courts and tribunals that a citizen is likely to come into contact at first instance, rather than the structures of the EC, and because the majority of polluting industries are situated in England and Wales.

Three people are due mention and particular thanks for giving me help in writing this book, for having provided both information and encouragement. I am particularly grateful to Mr Stuart Maclanaghan BEng (Hons), MSc, AMIMech for many valuable technical and scientific comments and observations made throughout the preparation of this book. Warm thanks are also extended to Mr Richard Halliday for allowing me access to his research and thesis on development plan control and Sites of Special Scientific Interest (SSSIs) referred to in Chapter 11, and for many useful insights on the planning system. Thanks are also due to Mr Jonathan Hewett BA (Hons) who gave great assistance with tracking down a number of recent pieces of legislation as soon as they emerged and in answering a number of important queries on EC law.

Finally, it should be pointed out that the law changes quickly – and environmental law is one of the best examples of the speed of change. As a consequence it is necessary to point out that the law stated in this book is as believed correct on 10 May 1993.

Chapter 1

The Environment, the Citizen and the Law

ROLE OF THE INDIVIDUAL CITIZEN

In the face of global environmental problems, it is all too easy to feel powerless. Even in their own neighbourhoods many people feel there is little they can do to stop the relentless pace of environmental destruction or force the authorities into taking action to prevent pollution. 'Think globally - act locally' has long been a slogan of environmental and 'green movements' - but how can the individual citizen take action to stop environmental harm? One option, as this book seeks to show, is through the law. An oft quoted phrase, used in many contexts, is 'There ought to be a law against it'. When it comes to harming the environment there frequently is.

This book seeks to provide a guide to those laws which exist to protect the environment and to outline ways in which the individual citizen can use them. Far from being powerless, every citizen may invoke a wide range of laws - providing they have access to the right information and a knowledge of the practical steps involved.

The rights that are available to individual citizens are an increasingly important part of the growing body of environmental law. Recent legislation, introduced by the British Government and arising from the UK's membership of the European Community, gives every citizen new rights of access to environmental data held by public bodies. Much hitherto secret environmental information is now made open to public scrutiny for the first time.[1] There are also extensive new opportunities for the public to become involved in local decisions which cover a whole range of environmental issues, going far beyond voting in local elections. These are major developments which would have seemed unimaginable a decade ago [2] when the environment was likely to be dismissed as a fringe issue and largely the preserve of eccentrics, cranks and victims of the NIMBY - not in my back yard - syndrome.

The notion that ordinary citizens should use the law to protect the environment is no longer even a radical one, having been endorsed at the highest level by the British Government. In *This Common Inheritance - A First Year Report* (a summary of progress on environmental goals first set out in 1990), Prime Minister John Major expressed the view that the protection of the environment is not a matter for the State alone but one in which citizens are to become partners.[3] Nor is this mere political rhetoric by government, since it is backed up by legal changes which place individual citizens in a better position than ever before to have an influence in matters ranging from town and country planning to genetically modified organisms.[4]

These developments build upon a body of existing constitutional and legal rights which, though in many cases originally devised to cover non-environmental matters, may nonetheless be taken up by the individual citizen and used to protect the environment. These include a system of private rights (part of the civil law) by which an individual can protect his/her person and property, and various parts of the criminal law covering anti-social activities normally controlled and punished by the State, but which may also be utilised by private citizens. A third category is a body of administrative rules under which the individual can challenge the decisions and actions of public bodies and Government Ministers through the courts.

THE SCOPE OF THIS BOOK

In this book the 'citizen' of the title includes not just the ordinary citizen but any person employed as a local authority environmental health officer, an inspector with Her Majesty's Inspectorate of Pollution (HMIP), the National Rivers Authority or any other person engaged in enforcing environmental legislation. The main bodies and their role in the creation and enforcement of environmental law are discussed in Chapter 2.

Constitutionally, the status of public officials in law is that of ordinary citizens who are paid to carry out certain functions which anyone with the time, resources and inclination might undertake.[5] Whilst the law gives wider powers, such as rights of entry, search and seizure to such officials, those carrying out their tasks must nonetheless act within the framework of existing law and are subject to the same limitations and rules when enforcing legal obligations through the courts as anybody else.

This book primarily covers legal rights that may be used through the court system in England and Wales, although the basic provisions of many pieces of legislation, such as the Environmental Protection Act 1990, will apply with minor variations in both Scotland and Northern Ireland, as will measures which originate from the EC. Some rights – such as those for access to environmental information – can actually be used by non-UK citizens resident anywhere in the world (see Chapter 2). Furthermore, there is normally no restriction on a non-UK citizen commencing an action through the UK courts.

WHAT IS ENVIRONMENTAL LAW ?

This book does not set out to define what constitutes or should constitute environmental law, not least because it is a developing area. The subject cuts across so many fields and disciplines that ultimately no two experts – not only in the law but in other fields – are ever likely to agree at any one time. For the purposes of this book, environmental law is treated as laws and rules of law which exist to prevent or reduce harm to the natural environment.

From section 1(2) of the Environmental Protection Act 1990 comes a legal definition of the environment as

'all, or any of the following media, namely, the air, water and land; and the medium of air within buildings and the air within other natural and man-made structures above or below ground.'

Under section 1(3) 'pollution of the environment' is defined as

'the release (into any environmental medium) from any process of substances which are capable of causing harm to man or any other living organisms supported by the environment'.

Environmental law in English history

The laws which protect the environment have not suddenly appeared from a legal vacuum. Measures to curb pollution of water, air and land have been around since well before the Industrial Revolution. Twentieth century problems such as water pollution and excessive water abstraction (see Chapter 9) were recognised problems in medieval times. Locally enforced laws, operating on a village level, limited the abstraction of water by individuals from common streams and rivers in order to preserve the flow level in the interests of the whole community.[6] Persons guilty of fouling common water supplies were subjected to fines. The dumping of waste in common streets could also attract a fine – one notable offender being Shakespeare's father, prosecuted for allowing a dung-hill to accumulate outside his house in Stratford in 1584.[7] The private right of a citizen to take action against what are today classed as environmental nuisances has been recorded from at least 1607 when Aldred's Case (see Chapter 6) endorsed a traditional right to enjoy clean air.

Attempts to control smoke pollution are recorded from at least 1307, and both Queen Elizabeth I and her successor James I had to issue ordinances prohibiting the burning of sea-coal while Parliament was sitting. By 1661 the subject of air pollution in cities could even boast a book, *Fumi Fugium* by John Evelyn, covering possible solutions to diseases arising from smoke and fumes.[8]

Varied though the pollution problems facing communities prior to the Industrial Revolution may have been, they could largely be tackled through a system of private rights – some of which still exist to this day in civil law. State intervention was only an occasional necessity, but with the rise of industrial society from the eighteenth century onwards, new systems of pollution control became necessary. Increasing urbanisation and overcrowding in towns and cities generated problems that could not be kept in check by a system of private rights. From the early Victorian era onwards specific legislation had to be passed by Parliament to protect the human environment. Thousands were dying from typhus and tuberculosis arising from overcrowding, unsanitary conditions and polluted water supplies. Pollution from smoke had become increasingly worse, with the French Ambassador recording in 1822 the 'immense skull-cap of smoke which covers the city of London,' and of 'Plunging into the gulf of black mist, as if into one of the mouths of Tartarus....'.[9] The increased use and production of chemicals added many new and noxious compounds to the already filthy air, often with damaging effects on the landscape and human health. In particular, chemical production of soda generated acid as a by-product, giving rise to acid rain in its most simple form. By 1862 large tracts of country had been blighted by acidic deposits.[10]

In an attempt to tackle these problems, various Public Health Acts were passed from the 1840s onwards and the 1860s saw efforts to control smoke and industrial discharges under the Alkali Works Act 1863. The Rivers Pollution Act was introduced in 1876 and law on the pollution of water had already become sufficiently complex by 1897 to warrant an entire text book.[11] Unfortunately, the Rivers Pollution Act was seldom used having been weakened by political lobbying over the 80 years until its repeal in 1951, so that Prime Minister Attlee could describe river pollution as a national scandal in 1946. [12]

The main aim of this legislation was to preserve human health: pressure from public opinion (such as it existed) did not demand the protection of the wider environment as is the case today. But it is from this point in history that one can discern people beginning to consider the natural world as worthy of legal protection in its own right. As early as 1810 William Wordsworth argued that the Lake District should be considered '....a sort of "National Property" in which every man has a right and interest who has an eye to perceive and heart to enjoy it.' However, such far-sighted sentiments had to wait until later in the nineteenth century when the interest in natural history gained momentum.

However, it is only since the end of the Second World War that it has generally been considered wrong in itself to damage the environment and that a variety of legal areas such as pollution control, planning law and nature conservation might all be part of a wider but unified discipline that can be termed 'environmental law'.

In the past, the lack of any common perspective meant different pollution controls were never connected with each other in either their design or practical operation. Different enforcement bodies such as environmental health officers, planning authorities, the Alkali Inspectorate and water authorities tended to operate quite independently without any reference to each other and ignoring pollution which did not fall within their remit. [13] It is only with the passing of the Environmental Protection Act 1990 (EPA) that this fragmented system of controls has now begun to be properly rationalised and integrated. The Act clearly defines which State bodies are responsible for controlling particular forms of pollution and for preventing harm to the natural environment, laying down the basic framework for pollution control which is intended to operate in Britain well into the next century.[14] The new system of regulation covering potentially polluting industries came into force on 1 April 1991 and is outlined in Chapter 3. A complex system of licensing and authorisation is established, administered by local government and State bodies with many details contained in a system of public registers where individual authorisations can be consulted, supporting the rights to environmental information detailed in Chapter 2.

In addition to the EPA, there are a number of other Acts passed over the years and particular rules of law operating today to achieve a number of important environmental goals.

Functions of the law

The law currently exists to:

- set standards and safeguards which individual persons, corporations, and governments must observe and adhere to regarding emissions and releases of substances into the environment.

- provide rights of access to environmental information held by public bodies.

- give rights to citizens to participate in the decision making process concerning pollution and the environment.

- give rights to challenge and review decisions by public bodies including national and local government (eg planning decisions).

- fix criminal sanctions and penalties for those who damage or pollute the environment. These measures seek to curb and control activities which harm humans, animal and plant life, the soil, water resources and the atmosphere in its capacity to support life.

- provide private rights to individuals to tackle, on an individual basis, environmental pollution which harms his/her personal welfare, and the enjoyment or exploitation of rights.

The measures may operate independently or in combination in achieving the goal of environmental protection. What is common to all of these areas is that no one need rely upon the State or State enforcement bodies to apply or enforce the relevant laws. The individual citizen is entitled to invoke all these measures and may even enjoy a greater flexibility and freedom of action than State-backed enforcement agencies. In the case of civil remedies, the individual involved may be the only person able to invoke the law.

Each of these legal measures can be broken down into a further body of laws and rules of law, many of which are not generally recognised as 'environmental law' but classified under headings such as 'evidence' and 'procedure'. Few books covering environmental law currently give any consideration to these related topics. However, in order to actually use the law to take action, the citizen must have an awareness and understanding of these other areas of law and a way of obtaining information on them. In practice, it has always been very difficult for citizens to obtain the relevant information, even when they are employed to enforce environmental law.

To give but one example, section 85 of the Water Resources Act 1991 (see Chapter 9) makes it a criminal offence to pollute water. But this information alone will be effectively useless to a citizen who discovers a river being polluted by a factory. If a citizen wishes to use the law to prosecute the offender, the citizen will have to know in which court the offence is prosecuted, how to begin criminal proceedings, what evidence is admissible at law to prove the offence and how to present that evidence in court. In practical terms, a knowledge of environmental law alone is not sufficient to be able to put that law into action.

THE APPROACH OF THIS BOOK

The approach of this book is to combine both relevant rules of evidence and procedure with specific pieces of legislation designed to protect the environment. Because of the complexity of the law, particularly in civil cases, it is only possible to give a brief outline of much of the relevant law or point readers in the direction of specific sources of legal information used by lawyers (see Chapter 3 and the appendices to this book). Details of the prosecution structure for the enforcement of criminal law by enforcement agencies or individuals are set out in Chapter 4. The way in which government ministers and enforcement agencies exercise their discretion and their legal powers is considered in Chapter 5. This important area comes under the heading of administrative law (really a branch of the civil law) regulating the behaviour of public administration and State bodies to ensure that the authorities themselves observe certain standards and fulfil their responsibilities.

Administrative law issues may arise when citizens seek to exercise their rights but come into conflict with the authorities or where State bodies act unlawfully when making decisions with environmental implications (eg planning matters). For example, a public body which denies a citizen the right of access to environmental information provided at law may be challenged in the High Court through a process of judicial review. Similarly, a decision making body such as a court or a local authority which behaves in a perverse or unlawful manner may have its decisions challenged in the same way. Chapter 5 deals with the role of judicial review – the control of public bodies by the High Court.

Chapter 6 deals with civil law and the private remedies. Here only the barest outline of evidence and procedure can be given because of the complex nature of civil law. These are remedies which are limited not only to private persons, but in practice will only be available to those particular citizens whose rights, as recognised by the law, have been adversely affected.

Frequently, civil law matters will overlap with criminal ones. For example, if a noxious substance pollutes a river contrary to section 85 of the Water Resources Act 1991, the National Rivers Authority or a private individual may bring a prosecution against the polluter responsible. In addition, the legal owner of the water (see Chapter 9) may also bring a private claim for compensation by way of damages for any harm caused. However, only the owner is entitled to bring a civil claim.

Chapters 4, 5 and 6 in Part I outline the three basic rights that a citizen is entitled to use: the right to prosecute for crimes independently of State bodies, the right to challenge unlawful actions of public bodies and the right to take action to protect private rights which neither the State, nor any other person, may take up. In Chapters 7–11 in Part II, specific areas of law are considered – those provisions which have been designed to protect the various media and living organisms defined as constituting the 'environment' under section 1(2) of the EPA. Some are governed by the EPA, others are taken from a wide range of statutes.

Chapter 7 gives an outline of Britain's complex planning

legislation and the new provision which has been made under the Town and Country Planning Act 1990 and the Planning and Compensation Act 1991. For the first time the environmental considerations play a key part in planning decisions and wider provision is made for participation by the public.

Chapter 8 looks at the protection of the atmosphere and the legal controls which exist to curb air pollution and global warming. Water pollution and the protection of Britain's rivers and seas is considered in Chapter 9, and Chapter 10 outlines the control of waste and hazardous substances. Chapter 11 deals with conservation of habitats and the protection of certain species by the law.

Together these areas add up to a wide range of legal measures and sanctions to which text books could be devoted, and no doubt will be in the future.

One form of social control

As mentioned earlier, modern environmental law did not emerge from a vacuum and nor does it operate in one. Legal measures are only one of a wide range of possible methods through which society can protect the environment. The law provides a framework within which other control mechanisms can operate and citizens may use many tactics, short of court action, to ensure companies and public bodies avoid causing environmental harm and comply with the law. Other methods of persuasion include letter writing, lobbying, protest activities and publicity. The law is a tool that may be used where no other mechanism is likely to succeed in curbing polluting activities. Prior to the passing of the EPA, this was very much the approach of local government environmental health officers and enforcement agencies concerned with water pollution.[15]

The law can also be seen as a means of employing economic sanctions as a method of protecting the environment. One concept much discussed by economists and environmentalists has been the so-called 'polluter pays' principle.[16] This principle increasingly exists in law, even if it is not directly recognised as such. Fees are charged for the authorisation of persons wishing to carry out potentially harmful processes (see Chapter 3) and to obtain consents to discharge pollution into rivers (see Chapter 9). In both criminal and civil law, polluters can be forced to pay for the cost of rectifying the damage they cause and compensating individuals who have suffered harm.

Limits of the law

Had the law alone been effective in restraining pollution, much environmental damage could have been prevented generations ago. Since the law does not exist in isolation there are also a number of limitations on what it can achieve.

As long ago as 1904 the naturalist R. Bosworth-Smith commented of bird protection

> '....to pass a Bill into law is, unfortunately , not the same thing as to see it carried out, especially when the means of evading it are comparatively easy, and when the permanent forces of ignorance, of selfishness, of laissez-faire or of indifference to animal suffering – as is the case with some game preservers and many gamekeepers – are arrayed on the other side. Much must depend henceforward, on the zeal and energy of the county magistrates, of the county councils, of the county police, if the law is to be properly carried out.' [17]

This remains true today. Environmental law can no more make people respect or revere the environment and the natural world than child protection laws can make bad parents love their children. But it can do something to prevent the harm currently occurring, set standards which no one should fall below and punish those who fail to observe those standards.

One problem is the pace of technological change. Technology and the development of new products and processes have leapt ahead of the piecemeal development of environmental legislation. Sometimes environmental harm or damage is only discovered many years after it has been caused, too late for any legal measure to be of any use. In some cases, even where harm is recognised, society does not take effective steps to control it – such as the vexed area of pollution from cars.

Political factors also affect the development of environmental law. A marked feature of environmental regulation in the UK has been the disproportionate influence that special interest groups have had on shaping the legislation designed to regulate them. Selective lobbying by commercial and industrial sectors may even prevent environmental law coming into force. A recent example is the delay in implementing section 143 of the EPA to establish registers listing contaminated land in the UK. These were due to come into existence in 1992, but plans were postponed by the government following lobbying by commercial and industrial sectors in the sensitive period during the run up to the 1992 General Election.

Short of failing to implement legislation, it is entirely possible for government to restrict the enforcement of the law by containing the size of enforcement agencies and the resources made available to them.

Drawbacks facing the individual citizen

While the above mentioned are general difficulties, the individual citizen faces more specific problems in using the law.

Despite presumed equality at law for all citizens, the costs which can be incurred with an unsuccessful legal action often deter individuals from taking up their rights. New restrictions on legal aid from April 1993 mean that even fewer people will be entitled to assistance with costs, affecting the potential use of many of the rights in this book.

Even the cost of obtaining preliminary advice may deter citizens from taking action – whether private individuals or inspectors working for State enforcement bodies. If litigation is commenced, hiring representatives will be even more expensive: few lawyers are prepared to waive their fees for environmental campaigners, and the loser in a case is generally expected to pay the costs of the winner. For example, an appeal through the High Court against a decision to route the East London River Crossing through Oxleas Wood in South London, was reported to have cost six local residents £30,000 for both their own legal fees and those of the government after the appeal failed.[18]

Complexity of the law is another factor; even lawyers find the legal system complicated and unfortunately there is no national up-dating service on new developments in environmental law. Although a growing area, relatively few lawyers specialise in environmental law. Those who do operate from a small number of solicitors' firms and barristers' chambers, mostly based in London and usually concentrating on planning or local government matters. Large manufacturing corporations will also have in-house lawyers, some specialising in environmental law. Generally they will undertake advice work to banks, property developers and industrial concerns as to their rights on how to actually keep within the law – and what to do when they step outside it. Unfortunately there is little assistance for the ordinary citizen and, in many areas, this book can only be a starting point from which to find more information.

Advantages enjoyed by the citizen

Fortunately, the nature of the law will seldom require going as far as court action. Much may be achieved by involvement of cost-free procedures such as tribunals and public hearings. Citizens who are informed as to their rights will also be in a better position to negotiate with public bodies and private developers in such situations. Neither public bodies nor private companies have any wish to risk even the threat of litigation themselves because of the costs and adverse publicity. The possibility of an appeal through the High Court, which could take 18 months, may be enough to deter a developer from even commencing an environmentally harmful development.

One advantage is that private citizens may be able to devote far more time to legal research for a particular case than a lawyer representing the government, a local authority or a commercial interest, as it is likely to be only one of many which a lawyer will be engaged upon. In some cases a private citizen may be more motivated than a lawyer who may well be only acting for money. More importantly, the developers, local authorities and government departments have no wish to become involved in litigation themselves – the problem of costs cuts both ways, particularly at public inquiries. Such inquiries are free to the citizen but developers, corporate interests and the government who seek legal representation will have to pay.

As yet, many of the rights outlined in this book and much of the legislation described largely remain untested. These rights, however, are there to be used, despite the drawbacks outlined. The choice now available is whether environmental law remains the exclusive preserve of State bodies and serves limited interest groups or becomes a tool for achieving effective environmental protection in the interests of all. Far from being powerless, the individual citizen, if armed with determination and a certain knowledge of environmental law, is now in a position to undertake public action with a greater chance of success than ever before.

NOTES

[1] See the Access to Environmental Information Regulations 1992, discussed in Chapter 2.
[2] North, R., (1990), *The Freedom of Information Handbook*.
[3] *This Common Inheritance - A First Year Report* (1991), Cmnd 1655 p.3.
[4] Town and Country Planning Act 1990; Environmental Protection Act 1990.
[5] See for example The Royal Commission on Police Powers and Procedure of 1929, Cmnd 3297.
[6] See Rose, C. , (1989), *The Dirty Man of Europe,* Simon & Schuster.
[7] Garner, J.F., 'Environmental Law - a real subject ?' in *New Law Journal,*(1992), 1718.
[8] See Garner, J. and Crow, B., (1976), *Clean Air - Law and Practice,* Shaw & Sons.
[9] See (1966), *The Memoirs of Chateaubriand,* Penguin, p.141.
[10] *The Dirty Man of Europe,* ibid.
[11] Haworth, Charles, (1897), *The Statute Law relating to River Pollution.*
[12] McCormack, J., (1991), *British Politics and the Environment,* Earthscan Publications, London.
[13] See Bell and Ball, (1991), *Environmental Law,* Butterworths, for a useful discussion.
[14] Chris Patten, then Secretary of State for the Environment, *Hansard,* H.C., vol. 165, col. 50, 15 January, 1990.
[15] See Richardson, G., Ogus, A. and Burrows, P., (1982), *Policing Pollution,* Clarendon Press; Hawkins, K., (1984), *Environment and Enforcement,* Clarendon Press.
[16] Pearce, D., Markandya, A. and Barbier, E., (1989) *Blueprint for a Green Economy,* Earthscan Publications, London.
[17] Bosworth-Smith, R., (1904), *The Life and Lore of Birds,* James, London.
[18] *The Independent,* 20 February, 1993.

Chapter 2

Enforcing Environmental Law

The creation of environmental law in the United Kingdom is the responsibility of the British Parliament and the European Community. The task of enforcing these laws is, at present, largely undertaken by a variety of State bodies operating under powers that have either been specifically granted to them or which are recognised as existing generally in law. Some knowledge of the functions that these agencies perform is necessary to gain an understanding of the system of environmental law regulation and enforcement which presently applies in the UK. The new rights of access to information, also discussed in this chapter, provide a practical way for citizens to obtain information held by these bodies.

THE GOVERNMENT

The Government is the prime source of environmental law; it is responsible for creating most legislation, in the form of Acts of Parliament. The Government inherits a large body of legislation from previous governments which may be altered from time to time and is also entrusted with putting European legislation into effect in UK law.[1]

The Government sector concerned with environmental protection is, as its name suggests, the Department of the Environment (DoE) created in 1970.[2] Direct political responsibility for the DoE lies with the Secretary of State for the Environment to whom wide powers are given under the Environmental Protection Act 1990 to create environmental legislation. Such legislation is known as subordinate or delegated legislation and has the full legal effect of any Act of Parliament, even though it is made by a single Minister. In practice, much environmental law is now made by regulations (see Appendix 1). These are laid before Parliament – a process simply of displaying them – but seldom debated. After this formality they enter into force, in some cases before they are actually printed by Her Majesty's Stationery Office.[3] Law making by way of regulations has become increasingly common in recent years. It is a practice that has long been open to criticism, not least because Parliament will not have had a proper opportunity to scrutinise the legislation and because of the power it places in the hands of one Minister.[4]

The Secretary of State for the Environment, it must be remembered, is only the present and temporary holder of an office of State. He or she has a number of responsibilities and duties and must act in accordance with a number of constraints. The Minister must operate within the framework of the existing law, even if enjoying wider powers than any other citizen. Merely because the Minister would like to see certain legislation emerge or certain changes occur, does not necessarily mean that he has the power to order them, since the Secretary of State's powers have to be exercised within the existing law. If the Minister exceeds the powers given by the Act, the regulations will be *ultra vires* and can be challenged. Similarly, if the Minister makes a decision which is contrary to the principles of administrative law, such a decision may be challenged by an aggrieved citizen through the courts (see Chapter 5).

In addition to creating legislation which has the full force of law, the Department of the Environment publishes guidance notes for enforcement agencies, codes of practice and circulars to assist with the administration and day-to-day running and enforcement of pollution control by regulatory bodies. Ultimately, the government is answerable to the electorate, but in its day-to-day running is susceptible to persuasion and pressure from lobbying groups and the public and the efforts of individual Members of Parliament to amend existing laws and introduce new legislation.

The Secretary of State also has the power to make many final decisions in disputes arising from the implementation of pollution controls, determine planning appeals and to make certain nature conservation orders.[5] The only way such decisions can be challenged is through the courts, as outlined in Chapter 5.

THE EUROPEAN COMMUNITY

In recent years the European Community has had an increasing impact on environmental legislation, not just in Britain but throughout the territory of its Member States. The EC has been developing its own environment policies since 1972. Although it is 20 years since Britain entered into the EC, there is still a wide misunderstanding about the Community and other institutions, such as the European Court of Human Rights in Strasbourg. [6]

Since the EC began developing environmental policies, the UK has suffered a reputation of being the 'dirty man of Europe' [7] and has fallen foul of EC legislation, most recently in November 1992 over nitrate content of water.[8] Many legislative changes in UK law have been made to enable Britain to comply with the environmental standards set by the European Community, standards with which Britain is *obliged* to comply. There are three EC institutions – the Council, the Commission and the Parliament, the latter body containing a substantial 'green lobby' of members elected from different European countries.

Although legislation from Brussels has helped accelerate and, in many ways, set the pace of change in UK environmental law, one should beware of assuming that the EC always acts as a progressive institution in achieving environmental goals. It did, after all, operate for 15 years without having any environmental policy at all. The EC also endorses schemes which can have a harmful effect on the environment - in the areas of transport and agriculture. It should be remembered that the EC is primarily an economic institution with the aim of furthering the free movement of goods, but one which has legislative and treaty making powers. However, in a landmark case *Commission* v *Denmark* (1989), (54 CMLR 619) (known as the *Danish Bottles* case), the European Court ruled that measures to protect the environment could override the aims of establishing a common market in certain instances. The case arose from laws in Denmark which required beer and soft drink bottles to be returnable. The Commission argued that this restriction amounted to a barrier to free trade under Article 30 of the EC Treaty and took the case to the European Court. However, the Court disagreed, stating that protection of the environment was a 'mandatory requirement' of the Community which could justify interference with the free movement of goods in some cases. [9]

The forms of EC law

EC law takes three forms – regulations, directives and decisions. Regulations are of 'direct applicability' and operate as a valid part of the law in the UK and other Member States without any further national legislation being passed. In practice, few regulations cover environmental measures, and those which do usually implement international treaty obligations. An example is Council Regulation 594/91 on substances which deplete the ozone layer, adopted on 4 March, 1991. This applies to the production, consumption, import and export of CFCs, halons and other ozone depleting substances. Decisions are only binding on those to whom they are addressed – specific groups or Member States – and are little used in environmental law.

Of much greater importance are directives. Directives are made by the EC but are left to Member States to put into effect in their own legislation. A directive is normally cited with a reference number giving the year it was issued and its position on the list of Directives issued in that particular year. These Directives are brought into force either by a statutory instrument under the 1973 Act, a special Act of Parliament, or amendment of existing legislation. Examples range from Directives covering the protection of wild birds, the dumping of waste, the packaging of products and the important right of access to environmental information discussed below. (See p.28).

Where a Member State fails to implement directives, a complaint may be made to the Commission and action commenced against them. Britain has not been the only offender in this regard. Ultimately, however, there is no way to compel a Member State to follow EC directives other than through moral and political pressure.

At present there are in excess of 200 EC directives, resolutions and recommendations which set standards for environmental protection and at least another 60 are currently being developed by the EC. Points of EC legislation which arise in court cases in Britain may be referred to the EC Court for a ruling on the direction of the Court, further to Article 177 of the EC Treaty. An international environmental body, the European Environmental Agency, is also being established to monitor and investigate the state of the environment throughout the EC. All Member States were represented at a meeting held by the Commission in March 1992 to discuss issues relating to enforcement, including the establishment of a network of enforcement agencies and the possible creation of an audit-type inspectorate. However, these ideas have yet to go beyond the planning and discussion stage.

In a book of this size it is not possible to do justice to the full range of measures affecting environmental law arising from the EC and the reader is referred to works such as Nigel Haigh's *Manual of Environmental Policy, The EC and Britain.* [10] The short space in which the EC is covered here does not in any way reflect the continuing importance of its impact on domestic law. However, since most EC legislation takes effect in UK law and is enforced, in the vast majority of cases, through the British courts, it is on domestic law which this book concentrates.

THE COURTS

No special 'environmental court' exists through which environmental law and environmental rights can be upheld. One may yet be established as a specialist tribunal necessary to deal with increasingly complex environmental issues.[11] Special hearings and inquiries may already be convened for the new system of pollution control under the EPA (see Chapter 3) and for planning issues (see Chapter 7). Unfortunately, at present any case brought involving environmental law will be heard by the ordinary civil and criminal courts. While in some cases this will not pose a particular problem (eg simple pollution cases or prosecutions for failure to hold a licence for certain prescribed processes), many cases could raise complex scientific and technical issues which criminal courts may be ill-equipped to assess properly. In civil courts, the complexity of procedure and length of time are major drawbacks.

Criminal Courts – the magistrates' court

A large number of criminal offences exists which the State seeks to restrict and deter by means of punishing the offender, be it an individual or a company. Criminal cases are dealt with through the magistrates' courts and the Crown Courts.

Enforcement of the criminal law takes place initially through magistrates' courts which deal with 98 per cent of criminal actions and their remit is wide. Magistrates' courts sit at some 500 locations in England and Wales. The more serious cases are committed to the Crown Courts. The majority of criminal offences involving the environment will be heard by magistrates' courts, and certainly in the early days of enforcement under the EPA, this will be the usual starting point for most prosecutions, at least until prosecutors and the attitudes of the courts become clearer.

Matters which magistrates' courts can deal with include breaches of the Environmental Protection Act 1990, any other criminal statute and any provision of EC law which is enforceable as though it was the law of this country. The maximum penalties in the magistrates' courts are six months in prison or in the case of certain environmental matters up to £20,000. In certain cases involving oil pollution, fines may rise to £50,000.[12]

There are a number of drawbacks with magistrates' courts. Under their judicial oath, magistrates are required to swear faithfully to observe the law without fear or favour.[13] Unfortunately, although many are well-meaning, the people who sit as magistrates do not have formal legal qualifications and are dependent on advice from the Clerk, which naturally puts the Clerk in a powerful position. The only exceptions are professional Stipendiary Magistrates who are qualified barristers or solicitors of at least seven years' standing.

As many who have prosecuted through magistrates' courts will verify, much can depend on the attitude of the Clerk, [14] on whom the justices rely for advice, in most cases, and courts can vary in policy and attitudes. Penalties and acquittal rates may vary dramatically from court to court even though justices are applying – or meant to be applying – the same law. While in one sense this gives perhaps justified local flexibility – a pollution offence may be more serious in some areas of the country than others – there is a risk that magistrates' will judicially express their disapproval over some activities and not others. This makes the enforcement of the law something of a gamble.

Appeals from magistrates' courts lie to the Divisional Court (part of the High Court) on a point of law, discussed in Chapter 4. A further appeal may go to the House of Lords.

The Crown Court

More serious cases will go to the Crown Court. The Crown Courts are held at some 120 locations [15] and cases are heard by judge and jury. Offences triable in the Crown Court are known as offences triable on indictment (basically a formal listing of offences). The differences between magistrates' courts and Crown Courts are considerable, not least in the penalties. The maximum penalties will be imprisonment up to the statutory maximum and an unlimited fine. (For example, Shell were fined £1 million for a pollution incident in the Mersey).[16]

Civil Courts – County Court and High Court

Civil claims are essentially private disputes between parties. The civil courts do not seek to punish but to apply the law to determine the rights and liabilities of the parties concerned – the only people who can be involved in the dispute. Most civil actions are claims for compensation. The size of the claim will determine which court proceedings are commenced: claims for sums of up to £50,000 go through the county court. Claims exceeding £50,000 go through the High Court, which sits in the Strand in London and a number of other cities.[17]

Another important class of orders are injunctions which restrain a party from doing certain acts. They may be obtained from both the High Court or county court and can be acquired by private individuals, local authorities and enforcement bodies such as Her Majesty's Inspectorate of Pollution.[18]

The review of administrative action

The High Court also has the task of deciding upon what are called 'inferior tribunals' - ie whether courts and tribunals, lower than the High Court, have acted according to the law.

The High Court can rule on whether public bodies and Ministers of State have acted in accordance with the law. In addition the remedy of judicial review is available from the High Court and is discussed at length in Chapter 5.

The doctrine of precedent – the importance of court decisions

Arguments exist in all fields of law as to the precise meanings of particular words and phrases used in both Acts of Parliament and in statutory instruments. It is to the courts that the problems of interpreting statutes – settling disputes as to what the law actually means – will fall. Environmental law is likely to be a ripe area for appeals on interpretations, restrained only by legal costs. For example, the word 'causes' as used in the phrase of 'knowingly causes pollution' in section 107 of the Water Act 1989, (now section 85 of the Water Resources Act 1991) has been taken to be a positive act, rather than failing to do something - as in the case of *Wychavon District Council* v *NRA* (1992) (see Chapter 9). The interpretation of one word made all the difference in the outcome of the case.

Where a court reaches a decision as to the meaning of a word or term contained in a piece of environmental legislation, a precedent will be set. Effectively, the definition given by the court will enter into the law itself (known as 'case law') and the decision must be followed by courts and tribunals faced with the same facts or circumstances in the future. All courts must follow the decision until Parliament or an appeal to a higher court changes the law. The case may be raised as authority for the meaning of the law: in future cases, prosecutors will look at the definition of the law in the case and decide whether it can apply to the behaviour of a polluter. If it does, a prosecution may go ahead and the polluter will be liable to conviction. It is to such decisions that lawyers will look when giving advice as to where a party may stand at law.

Not all courts make a precedent with their decisions – only the superior courts. These are the High Court, the Court of Appeal and the House of Lords. Thus, magistrates' and Crown Courts may reach different decisions on different points, providing they do not go against a decision of a higher court. If a party to a case disagrees with a view taken by the magistrates' or the Crown Court, an appeal may be made to the High Court (or sometimes the Court of Appeal) for a ruling on the point. The ultimate court to which appeal may be made is the House of Lords, which binds all courts below it. The only route beyond this is an appeal to the European Court on a point of EC law, but this is likely to have been commenced at an earlier stage. As noted above, a UK court may refer a point to the EC Court. When the EC has ruled on the case it may then return to a UK court, which interprets the law in light of the view of the EC Court and reaches a final decision.

Until such precedents for the EPA are set, only older cases where the same words or circumstances may have arisen can give guidance. Early cases under the EPA will tend to be 'test' cases. Binding decisions are written up in law reports, many of which are published each week or month or annually in volume form. For more information see Chapter 3 and Appendix 1.

ENFORCEMENT BODIES

Certain statutory bodies have been set up to control pollution and protect and conserve the environment. They have the daily task of policing pollution and putting environmental legislation into effect. Historically there have been a range of bodies undertaking the control of pollution in different forms, often without reference to each other or any coherence. [19]

Since the introduction of the EPA there have been moves to rationalise the system and integrate the functions of different bodies within the scheme of what is termed 'integrated pollution control' (IPC) discussed in Chapter 3. Eventually they may be consolidated into one enforcement body, provisionally entitled the Environmental Protection Agency. [20]

Her Majesty' Inspectorate of Pollution

Her Majesty's Inspectorate of Pollution (HMIP) was established in 1987, bringing together a number of pollution control bodies such as the Alkali Inspectorate, the Health and Safety Atmospheric Control and certain aspects of the work of environmental health departments previously administered by local government.

HMIP (known as Her Majesty's Industrial Pollution Inspectorate in Scotland - HMIPI) is the major pollution control body in the UK, being responsible for the system of integrated pollution control. It has local offices around the country, and is responsible for granting authorisations to industry to carry on processes which have the potential for harming the environment, investigating cases of pollution and enforcing control. It is to HMIP that the public can report cases of industrial pollution.

HMIP has the initial power of granting and overseeing

authorisations for potentially harmful processes; any process which is carried on without such an authorisation will be illegal (section 6 (1) and section 23(1) EPA). HMIP Inspectors have wide powers to take action to control pollution and enjoy immunity from civil or criminal proceedings providing that they act in good faith. [21]

A number of problems have faced HMIP since its inception due to insufficient funding and resources. Under section 4(9) of the EPA, both HMIP and local authorities are under a duty to follow developments in technologies and pollution control techniques. A similar duty is placed upon local authorities with regard to air pollution.

National Rivers Authority

The National Rivers Authority (NRA) is the public body responsible in England and Wales for investigating and preventing water pollution and a range of other duties – the 'guardians of the water environment' as they style themselves in their annual reports.[22] (River Purification Authorities cover Scotland.) The NRA was formed in 1989, is sponsored by the Department of the Environment and has links with the Ministry of Agriculture, Food and Fisheries. Since the privatisation of water authorities there has been an increased concern about the quality of water. Like HMIP the NRA has regional offices and may carry out investigations into cases of water pollution reported by the public.

Many decision making bodies must consult with the NRA in cases where there is possibility of water pollution; for example, HMIP must consult with the NRA when granting authorisations to carry out potentially polluting processes. The NRA must be consulted by local authorities when drawing up plans for waste disposal. This reflects the capacity that water has for absorbing and dispersing pollution and the obvious implications for human health and the whole ecosystem.

The Nature Conservancy Councils

Originally one unified body, the Nature Conservancy Council has been split into three by the Environment Protection Act 1990, forming English Nature, Scottish National Heritage (under the Natural Heritage (Scotland) Act 1991) and the Countryside Council for Wales. These bodies are referred to as Countryside Councils for convenience. Funded by the Government, they are responsible for habitat protection, the designation of Sites of Special Scientific Interest (SSSIs) and advice and research on nature issues. However, because three bodies are now involved instead of one, it is possible that nature conservation might not be as effectively co-ordinated as in the past.[23] These organisations sit under the umbrella of the UK Joint Nature Conservation Committee, a statutory body, which is consulted on national and international conservation issues by decision making bodies.

Local authorities

Protection of the environment is not the sole preserve of Central Government, the EC and various State agencies. Local government, in the form of local authorities, also plays a major role in regulation and enforcement of environmental controls. Whilst local government has been given extra responsibilities in curbing harm to the environment (for example duties to control waste and litter), they have simultaneously been faced with tighter controls on spending by Central Government, reducing their ability to fulfil such responsibilities.

Unfortunately, they are also limited by financial considerations. For example, few local authorities can afford the risk of appeals where they become involved in court cases and lose. Changes to local government legislation seem to have become an annual feature of the legislative calendar since 1979, which has made the task of local government all the more difficult. Hit by financial restrictions and difficulties in collecting their own revenues in terms of outstanding rates, poll tax and a new council tax system from April 1993, the task of local authorities is becoming an increasingly difficult one. Scattered throughout the Environmental Protection Act 1990 are signs that Central Government wishes to have the power to curb local authorities further and increasingly shift the balance of power towards other statutory agencies such as HMIP and the Department of the Environment itself. For example, under section 4(4) of the EPA the Secretary of State may direct that functions on air pollution control carried out by a local authority may be carried out by the HMIP – one of a number of signs which do not bode well for the future of local government as a major influence for environmental protection.

Nonetheless, local authorities still have widespread powers to curb environmental harm. The local authority is still the first port of call for many members of the public, because of the widespread knowledge of environmental health departments and what they do. Actually these have only a discretionary existence following the wording of section 112 of the Local Government Act 1972, but many of their duties are compulsory under law for every authority.

Local authorities have responsibility for the following:

• Maintaining public registers under the EPA (see Chapter 3)

• Controlling air pollution (see Chapter 8)

• The control of statutory nuisances (see Chapter 6)

• Planning responsibilities and tree preservation (see Chapter 7)

• Waste regulation (see Chapter 10)

• Controlling litter

• Responsibilities involving highways

Various other powers and duties are available, and there is no doubt that authorities could do more – budgets and political willpower permitting. As large purchasers of products and services, users of energy and employers, they could have a major influence on the consumption of environmentally friendly products. A number of local authorities have already made 'green' plans but a good deal more remains to be done.

Where local government does not take such steps on its own initiative, a citizen can make contact with local councillors, although the likely response and ability of the councillor can vary.

The local authority is also the repository of public registers containing information on the environment. These include registers to be kept under the EPA for integrated pollution control, planning registers, waste registers and registers detailing the storage of hazardous substances.

Making local government accountable

Since 1991 there have been in operation various Citizen's Charters which have had the stated aim of making local government more accountable to citizens and provide good service. There has been some scepticism over these charters since they are hard to actually enforce by law but, leaving them aside, local authorities are accountable by law in a number of ways.

The ballot box is a direct method of control – the members of local authorities are democratically elected by people. They have powers to influence policy, though much of the day-to-day operation of authorities is in the hands of non-elected executives and officials – and power is increasingly shifted towards them. The Local Government and Housing Act, section 2, specifically prevents elected members being officials where salaries exceed £19,500.

Members must act on behalf of their electorate and within the law. Councillors are not entitled to use their role in the local authority to pursue their own financial interests. The Local Authorities (Member's Interests) Regulations 1992, made under section 19 of the Local Government and Housing Act 1989, require each elected member of a council to give the proper officer of the council a notice about his direct and pecuniary interests (or state that she/he has no such interest). Members must keep this information up to date and require the proper officer to keep records of this information. The records are open to public inspection so anyone suspecting an elected councillor can inspect it.

A member who fails to disclose an interest or fails to comply without a reasonable excuse risks prosecution. Where powers are exercised and a claim of bias can be sustained, rights to judicial review may arise from a person affected.

Local Government (Access to Information) Act 1985

This Act provides for public access to local authority meetings, reports and documents (certain exemptions are provided). It amends section 100 of the Local Government Act 1972 to ensure publicity for meetings of at least three clear days. Meetings of the full council, its committees and sub-committees are made open to the public and rights are established for access to committee reports, except in cases involving confidential or exempt information – including matters relating to employees, magistrates' courts' committees, certain matters involving children and matters relating to contracts. There may also be exclusions as to information obtained, advice received or action to be taken in connection with legal proceedings either by or against the authority or the determination of any matter affecting the authority. A determination would probably include any matter that goes to a public inquiry.

Judicial review is available in appropriate cases to compel councils to carry out their obligations under this Act. Open documents to be discussed at meetings must be available to interested members of the public at least three days before the meeting at which they will be raised, under section 100B. If the proper officer of the Council concerned thinks fit that any extract should be excluded, this may be done, but again any exercise of such powers may be open to legal challenge.

After meetings, minutes and resolutions of the authority should be open to inspection under section 100D. Where exempted matters arise, a summary must be available instead. Under section 100F elected members of a local authority are given an additional right of access to council documents held by the authority concerned.

Local councillors and public officials are also subject to various acts making it an offence to accept bribes or indulge in corrupt practices. The prosecution of these offences requires the permission of the Director of Public Prosecutions.

Monitoring Officers

The post of monitoring officer was established by section 5 of the Local Government and Housing Act 1989. The task of the monitoring officer is to ensure that the council, its committees, sub-committees and officers act within the law.

Section 5(2) provides a duty to prepare a report where it appears to the monitoring officer that 'any proposal, decision or omission' has or is likely to give rise to a contravention of 'any enactment or rule of law or any code of practice made or approved by or under any enactment' or constitutes maladministration under the Local Government Act 1974 or the Local Government (Scotland) Act 1975.

Maladministration

Where an authority acts negligently or is biased, legal rights may exist to take action. Unfortunately costs are often a bar to proceedings. However, a complaint to the commissioners for local administration – the Ombudsman procedure – provides an alternative which is free. The aggrieved person must first seek to settle their claim through the normal channels, not by writing first to the Ombudsman. This means complaining to the department and then to the councillor. If unresolved, the complaint may then be passed on to the Ombudsman to investigate.

Record numbers of complaints have been placed with the Ombudsman in recent years and the system may take a long time. Planning is a matter which has frequently given rise to complaints. The Ombudsman may award compensation, but these are only guidelines and the local authority may choose not to pay out. Local authority departments and their staff certainly do not enjoy investigations by the Ombudsman.

Administrative law

The right to a judicial review has already been referred to in connection with access to information. Not only does it extend to access to information but also to any specific duty placed upon local authorities to do certain tasks, eg enforcing Clean Air Act legislation or carrying out waste disposal functions. Local authorities can thus be made accountable through the legal process. Orders of mandamus can be obtained from the High Court to compel local authorities to carry out their legal duties and obligations through judicial review (discussed in Chapter 5).

ACCESS TO ENVIRONMENTAL INFORMATION HELD BY PUBLIC BODIES

Perhaps the most significant move towards making public bodies accountable to the citizen are the rights of access to environmental information.

The Environmental Information Regulations 1992 S.I.3240 establish a positive right for any person seeking environmental information to obtain it from any public body which holds it, subject to certain exceptions. These regulations bring about the aim of EC Directive 90/313 with which all Member States were expected to comply by 31 December 1992. Effectively, these regulations amount to a freedom of information policy but only upon environmental matters.

It should be noted that there are no limits placed upon the purposes for which the information is supplied. As a result, information may be used for openly political purposes by political parties, lobbying groups and campaigning organisations in order to achieve appropriate changes in the law

Information and records covered

Under regulation 2(4) the term information covers anything contained in records. The term 'records' is given the widest possible definition, including registers, reports and returns, and maps, as well as computer records and other records kept other than in a document. Presumably this could be extended to photographic, film and video records and records kept on audio tapes, discs or sound track.

In terms of use for civil legal proceedings admissible in the High Court or county court, a 'record' means a document which either gives effect to a transaction or which contains a contemporaneous register of information supplied by those with direct knowledge of the facts. On this test, it would not include summaries of the results of research or articles and letters published in professional journals: *H* v *Schering Chemicals Ltd* (1983). The term 'record' has been considered in *R* v *Tirado* (1974) 59 App R 80 and *Re D* (1986) 2 FLR and a solicitor's notes did not constitute records. However, this restriction is imposed for the purpose of admissibility of evidence in court. Given that the basis of these regulations is the provision of information to the public, there is arguably no reason why a definition of records should not be wider.

Meaning of environmental information

Under regulation 2 any information to be made available to the public is information which:

(a) relates to the environment

(b) is held by a relevant person in an accessible form and other than for purposes of judicial or legislative functions; and

(c) is not (apart from under the regulations) either

   (i) information which is required already to be available on request;

   (ii) information contained in records that must already be available to any person under some other particular law.

Information relates to the environment if, and only if, it relates to:

(a) the state of any water or air, or the state of any flora or fauna, the state of any soil or the state of any natural site or land;

(b) any activities or measures (including activities giving rise to noise or nuisance) which adversely affect anything mentioned in (a) or are likely to do so;

(c) any activities or administrative or other measures (including environmental management programmes) which are designed to protect anything in (a).

There is no geographical limitation to the information covered; it will cover any environmental data held relating to any part of the world.

Nonetheless, there may be many grey areas as to what may constitute environmental information that lawyers are likely to argue over. For example, do crime statistics relating to criminal offences committed under the waste regulation provisions of the EPA amount to environmental information for the purposes of the regulations? The criminal record of a person is relevant to licensing of waste but do the statistics held by the Lord Chancellor's Department amount to environmental information? Such issues will only be resolved by the courts or the provision of better definitions in new regulations.

Public bodies affected

Bodies and persons covered by these regulations include Ministers of the Crown, Government Departments, local authorities and other persons carrying out functions of public administration at a national, regional or local level, including the Department of Transport, the Ministry of Defence, the Scottish and Welsh Offices, County Councils, District Councils and parish councils. It would include organisations such as the Countryside Councils, HMIP, the National Rivers Authority, and all other relevant public bodies.

It does not extend to private companies, organisations or associations, although the prudent and forward thinking businesses may already be making more information about their activities available for public scrutiny.

The right to information is contained in regulation 3(1), which provides that a relevant person who holds any information covered by the regulations shall make the information available to every person who requires it. Any legal restrictions or prohibition imposed on the release of the information at law will be deemed not to apply. There appears to be no reason why the duty to supply information should not extend to data gathered or acquired before these regulations came into force.

How the information is made available is at the discretion of the body or organisation holding it; it could be made available through a written request or correspondence or alternatively by inspection. Regulation 3(4) permits the body holding the information to make a reasonable charge for supplying the information. Where there is an existing right to environmental information which is not covered by these regulations (through being exempt) the duty and obligation of supplying are brought into line with these regulations.

The word 'person' is not only restricted to physical human beings but also covers bodies such as limited companies and members of consultancies who also could obtain the information. There is no requirement that the person who requests the information need be a UK national; a person from any other EC State or any other country may request it. The inclusion of the word 'shall' indicates that the person holding the information must provide it; there is no discretion to exclude, providing that none of the recognised exceptions apply.

A further duty is that any person holding the information must make the information available as soon as possible and, in any event, within two months of the request. If the information is not supplied, a written statement of the reasons specifying the grounds for refusal must be given. This will form the basis of any legal challenge that a person aggrieved would be entitled to bring.

Information need not be supplied if the request is worded too broadly or vaguely or where it is 'manifestly unreasonable'. What is manifestly unreasonable would include cases where there would be major administrative difficulties in providing the information.

Exemptions

A number of important exemptions to the duty to release information are made in regulation 4. Some information is subject to a discretion to refuse to be supplied under 4(2) and certain categories of information *must* be refused under regulation 4(3).

Nothing in the regulations compels the release to the public of information which is capable of being or must be classed as 'confidential'. Regulation 4(2) states that information is to be treated as confidential 'if, and only if' it is information relating to any of the following:

(a) information affecting international relations, national defence or public security;

(b) information relating to, or to anything which is or has been the subject matter of, any legal or other proceedings (whether actual or prospective);

(c) information relating to the confidential deliberations of any relevant person or to the contents of any internal communications of a body corporate or other undertaking or organisation;

(d) information contained in a document or other record still in the course of completion;

(e) information relating to matters to which any commercial or industrial confidentiality attaches or affecting any intellectual property.

Nothing prevents a body from releasing this information if it so wishes; its discretion should be exercised reasonably.

Confidential information

Further guidance to confidentiality is given in the regulations in that information will only be confidential if:

(a) it is capable of being so treated and its disclosure would contravene a statutory provision, a rule of law or would involve the breach of any agreement;

(b) the information is personal information contained in records held in relation to an individual who has not given his consent to disclosure;

(c) the information is held by the relevant person in having been supplied by a person who

    (i) was not under, and could not have been put under any legal obligation to supply it (eg volunteered statements, reports from the public etc);

    (ii) did not supply it in the circumstances such that the person is not under a duty to supply it apart from the regulations;

    (iii) has not consented to the disclosure or the disclosure of the information in response to the request.

(d) the disclosure of the information in response to the request would, in the circumstances, increase the likelihood of damage to the environment affecting anything to which the information relates.

Authorisation cannot be given under the regulations to release information that must be treated as confidential. One such example of information that could fall under this heading was illustrated by the refusal of the Secretary of State for the Environment to supply information in response to a Parliamentary question concerning the nesting of rare birds. To make some information public could result in the unwelcome attentions of egg collectors and others to a site of special interest.

These exceptions put a number of potential restraints on information which can be obtained, perhaps the most serious being the restriction on legal proceedings. These are further defined by regulation 4(5) as

> 'any proceeding including any disciplinary proceedings, the proceedings at any local or public inquiry and the proceedings at any hearing conducted by a person appointed under any enactment for the purpose of affording an opportunity to persons to make representations or objections with respect to any matter'.

This is an extremely wide definition and would catch controls for pollution authorisation, town and country planning matters, inquiries over water – indeed practically every aspect of environmental law. Much will depend on how the courts interpret the words 'actual or prospective' since it will always be open for a public official to suggest that proceedings on some matter may be prospective and anticipated all along! It is suggested that more than a vague anticipation would be necessary to bring this section into play, but it could, for instance, pose problems where citizens ask a public body for information to be used at any public inquiry, even if the body concerned is not involved.

The wording of the regulation also prohibits any evidence which has been used in a successful prosecution or a public decision by the Secretary of State being automatically available to enquirers. This is certainly a peculiar situation when one considers that much of the information will already have been raised in public (nearly all inquiries and court proceedings are held in public).

However, much information will already be contained in the Public Registers established under the Environmental Protection Act 1990. For example, discretion may be exercised not to supply details of convictions of a company as this information would be 'relating to, or anything which is or has been subject-matter of any legal proceedings' but can be obtained from the register (see Chapter 3).

Further provision is made for existing rights to information so that with every request for information that is already publicly available, a public body must respond as soon as is possible, or at least within two months. In the event of a refusal, written reasons must be given and any charge imposed must be reasonable.

What if requested information is not supplied?

If a public body does not supply the information requested when it would reasonably be expected to do so, or fails to respond at all to enquiries within two months, the person requesting the information has a right to commence legal action to challenge the decision or inactivity of the body concerned. Where written reasons are provided for the refusal to supply, these should be analysed closely to examine whether one of the statutory exceptions entitles the public body to refuse to co-operate.

If there is no justification under the regulations to refuse to supply the information, the person affected may commence judicial review of the decision concerned under Order 53 of the Rules of the Supreme Court. This procedure is considered in more detail in Chapter 5, since it enables a citizen to challenge a wide range of administrative decisions. The person affected would have to commence proceedings within three months of the refusal to supply, and would seek what is known as an order of mandamus through the High Court. Such an order would require the information to be supplied, or for the public body to consider the request properly, depending on the circumstances of the refusal or failure to supply.

Whether this remedy will prove adequate is debatable, not least because of the time taken with judicial review procedures. Given that a public body has two months before it need reply, and even if judicial review is commenced immediately there could be 12 to 18 months delay before a case is heard, delays in obtaining information may be considerable. With a rapidly changing area such as the environment, such delays could easily render useless or irrelevant the information requested. The political potency of any information may be diffused by public bodies manipulating the system to avoid the release of politically sensitive or embarrassing information when it is considered expedient to do so. Nevertheless, there is no doubt that the citizen is now in a better position to scrutinise the environmental record of public bodies than ever before.

Should any body or authority withhold information on the basis of political partisanship or simple prejudice, such decisions may be challenged through the High Court.

Arguably, the requirements of the regulations to supply environmental information could be extended to cover specific pieces of UK legislation affecting the environment and the regulations could open the way to the individual obtaining useful information on environmental rights and guidance as to how they are enforced.

These problems aside, it is to be hoped that public bodies will fulfil their obligations. As well as being of assistance to persons charged with official responsibilities, to business representatives, journalists, researchers of all kinds, consultants and students, the new rights to information provide an opportunity for any citizen concerned with environmental matters to obtain access to hitherto unavailable data.

NOTES

1   European Communities Act 1972, c.68.
2   McCormack, J., (1991), *British Politics and the Environment*, Earth-scan Publications.
3   See *R* v *Sheet Metalcraft Ltd* (1954) 1 QB 586; *Johnson* v *Sargant & Sons* (1918) 1 KB (statutory instrument did not come into effect until it became known).
4   Hewart, Lord, (1929), *The New Despotism*, pp. 96–97, which sets out the traditional objections.
5   eg Wildlife and Countryside Act, 1981 (see Chapter 11).
6   For further guidance see for example Budd, S. A. and Jones, A., (1991) *The European Community: A Guide to the Maze*, Kogan Page, London.
7   See the book of the same title, Rose, C., (1990), *The Dirty Man of Europe: The Great British Pollution Scandal*, Simon & Schuster.
8   *Environmental News*, December 1992.
9   See also *Commission of the European Communities* v *Council of the European Communities* (1991) Case 300/89. For a discussion of this case see 'The Legal Basis of EC Environmental Law', *Journal of Environmental Law*, vol 4, No. 1, pp. 109-120.
10 Haigh, N., (1989), *Manual of Environmental Policy, The EC and Britain*, Longman, looseleaf.
11 For a useful discussion see Carnwath, Robert, *Environmental Enforcement: The Need for a Specialist Court* (1992) JPL 799.
12 See Chapter 8.
13 Promissory Oaths Act 1868, sections 2 and 4.
14 Hutter, Bridget M., (1988), *The Reasonable Arm of the Law*, Clarendon Press, Oxford, p. 73.
15 (1993), *Shaw's Directory of Courts*, Shaw & Sons Ltd, London.
16 Environment Law Brief, vol. 1, No 3, 1990.
17 *Shaw's*, op. cit.
18 See Chapter 5.
19 See Ball and Bell (1991), *Environmental Law*, Butterworths.
20 *Environmenal Law*, February 1992.
21 EPA, section 17.
22 *NRA Annual Report, 1991.*
23 *Reorganisation of NCC Policy and Science Issues*, NCC (1989).

Chapter 3

Sources of Legal Information

Simply obtaining information about the state of the environment may not be enough to ensure the necessary action to protect it. A citizen may discover that environmental harm is occurring but find that enforcement agencies are unwilling or unable to do anything. They may leave it to the individual citizen to take the necessary legal action to prevent such harm or to take steps to remedy it.

In order for the public to be able to use the legal system to protect the environment they must have information about their legal rights, and how to enforce them. Unfortunately, while environmental information is now widely available, there are very few corresponding provisions to make legal advice and information available to the public.[1] This Chapter sets out sources of the law that the citizen can use in practice and summarises the major provisions of the Environmental Protection Act 1990 and pollution control legislation made under Part I.

LEGAL INFORMATION FUNDED BY LOCAL GOVERNMENT

On paper at least, local government could provide information on legal rights to a greater extent than ever before, following changes under section 38 of the Local Government and Housing Act 1989. This section inserts a new section 142 (2A) into the Local Government Act 1972 to enable a local authority to assist voluntary organisations to provide for individuals:

(a) information and advice concerning the rights and obligations of individuals; and

(b) assistance, either by the making or receiving of communications or by providing representation to or before any person or body in asserting those rights or fulfilling these obligations.

Such a power could, if authorities had the funds available, provide a tremendous opportunity to inform and assist local citizens in enforcing environmental law. It could provide advice and assistance in planning matters, pollution control, public inquiries and possibly include legal representation before courts. Unfortunately, at a time when many councils are cutting grants to Citizen's Advice Bureaux (see below) and, where they exist, law centres, there currently is little chance of such services developing in the foreseeable future.

For the citizen concerned about using the information available and taking legal action where breaches of the law are revealed, the problem largely comes down to obtaining relevant information on the rules of court procedure and the admissibility of evidence. A person may have accumulated evidence on a variety of environmental crimes or uncovered potential damage to the environment from a whole host of sources but is faced with the problem of successfully putting such evidence before a court in the correct way.

This problem, it must be said, equally afflicts those who have responsibilities in 'policing pollution', be it the local authority environmental health officers or the Inspector from HMIP or the National Rivers Authority. Unless they have received specialised legal training they have to depend on the advice of hard-pressed in-house lawyers or pay for the services of external lawyers which can, needless to say, be very expensive. Although experienced inspectors and health officers will be armed with some basic knowledge of which court to commence proceedings in and the approach adopted, they may, nonetheless, be thwarted by procedural and technical challenges where a defendant has hired representation.[2]

With higher penalties than ever before, many companies are likely to try and fight cases brought against them to avoid the consequences of a court appearance. With HMIP and other agencies increasingly trying to recover costs through prosecutions, the prospect of taking on a company or organisation which is likely to mount a substantial defence in court may influence the decision to prosecute in the first place. There may be a built-in tendency in the enforcement system to encourage statutory enforcement agencies to go for relatively simple cases and even for those sectors of business and industry less able to defend themselves at law.

For the citizen, the main problem will be obtaining legal advice or access to legal materials. While lawyers have access to books held in their own firms, chambers or certain law libraries, citizens will have to depend on the adequacy of their local library services and sources such as the British Library, or even purchase the materials themselves. Those employed in universities and colleges may have access to student law libraries.

KEY SOURCES

There are many books on law, and any citizen seeking information and advice may be daunted by the wide range of material in existence. Fortunately, there are certain key books which anyone contemplating legal action through the courts can refer to. They are: *Stone's Justices' Manual* (3 vols.) – criminal law as it applies in the magistrates' court; *The County Court Practice* – civil law as it applies in the county court (known as the Green Book); *The Rules of the Supreme Court* – practice and procedure for the High Court (known as the White Book).

It is curious that these essential books are hardly known outside the legal profession and those who have direct involvement with the day-to-day running of courts. *Stone's Justices' Manual,* the *White Book* and the *Green Book* contain a mass of information on all aspects of the law and procedure, including extracts of statutes and regulations currently in force. They also set out the details of standard court forms and procedural tables which should be referred to if any legal action is commenced. Vital though these works may be, practically no advice books for the non-expert ever make any reference to their existence at all. It should be said at the outset that the size of these books is likely to be off-putting to the uninitiated (and to the initiated). Much of the content, however, is irrelevant to environmental matters.

It is worth noting that, with the exception of these three works and a small number of academic textbooks such as *Cross on Evidence,* [3] statements of law contained in text books are not generally to be relied upon by courts (as opposed to advice, negotiations and guidance outside court). The reason is that statements contained in textbooks will be merely the opinions of authors and will not be binding as precedents. Most law books are thus insufficient for the purposes of court proceedings where a court is expected to reach its own independent conclusion on the matters before it. When quoting the law to a court, it should be done by reference to the relevant law as stated in Acts of Parliament, regulations and judgements, not from text books. A citizen presenting a case will need to refer the court directly to a copy of the Act, instrument or case report concerned. Photocopies are acceptable.

Acts of Parliament and Regulations

Authoritative texts and copies of legislation are available through branches of Her Majesty's Stationery Office (see Appendix 1) and some bookshops. Regulations can be particularly hard to track down; the best thing is to contact the Department of the Environment for the current list .

The texts of all Acts of Parliament passed each year are contained in *Halsbury's Laws of England* which are published each year, often with a detailed commentary on the likely interpretations and the meanings of each section of the Act. Acts are divided into sections and schedules. The schedules set out the details to be made in regulations and the repeal or amendment of existing legislation. Lists of regulations are included in Appendix 1 of this book.

EC Law

Authentic English texts of the Community Treaties and Community secondary legislation can be obtained either from the Royal Courts of Justice or the Central Criminal Court in London, from the Crown Court in Manchester, and from the county courts in Birmingham, Bristol, Cardiff, Exeter, Leeds, Liverpool, Newcastle-upon-Tyne, Nottingham and Sheffield. Photocopies can also be obtained from the Home Office by request over the telephone.

Other sources

In reported cases where a point of law falls to be decided by the court, that decision is then followed in subsequent cases where the same facts or circumstances are repeated. In order to be aware of these cases, access has to be found to the sets of reports or journals in which they are carried.

Decisions by judges may be updated in the *Stone's* , the *White Book* and the *Green Book* depending upon the opinions and concerns of the editors. Failing such inclusion, there is no other source available than the law reports and various respected journals which are listed in Appendix I.

Law centres and citizen's advice bureaux

Help can be obtained from law centres and advice bureaux. Unfortunately, they are often overloaded, suffer from financial restrictions and cover only restricted areas. In 1991 there were moves to establish a working group among law centres covering environmental law.[4] As well as these, sympathetic Members of Parliament may also obtain information through the means of Parliamentary questions and obtain copies of DoE guidance.[5]

Legal aid and representation and assistance

Legal aid to enable citizens to take court action has been heavily cut in recent years[6] and, in any case, does not extend to a wide range of matters. Only persons on low incomes such as student grant levels and State benefit are likely to qualify for aid without some kind of contribution.

Whilst this may appear to be a major obstacle to citizens wishing to pursue a matter of law, in practice there are many legal procedures in which citizens can become involved without receiving professional advice or representation. Examples include the different types of fact-finding tribunals and public inquiries which are largely designed to dispense with the formalities of courts, although parties can be represented before them.[7] However, problems will generally arise for the unassisted person when it comes to mounting a legal challenge to a tribunal or inquiry decision. (Methods of appeal are outlined in Chapters 5 and 7).

One provision within the legal aid scheme is the 'Advice By Way Of Representation' - known as the ABWOR scheme – which allows a person to receive their 'advice' in the form of a solicitor appearing for or with them in court.[8]

AN OUTLINE OF THE ENVIRONMENTAL PROTECTION ACT 1990

The main source of environmental law is contained in the Environmental Protection Act 1990 and regulations made under it. Part I of the EPA sets out the duties of enforcement agencies and describes the way in which various types of environmental harm may be controlled and prosecuted. The EPA gives wide opportunities to citizens to be consulted about releases into the environment which are permitted under the schemes introduced by the EPA. These include the right to make representations to enforcement bodies and to participate in public inquiries.

The EPA provides definitions of the environment and what constitutes 'the environment' (see Chapter 1) and what amounts to pollution of the environment as a result of any 'process'. By section 5 a 'process' means 'any activities carried on in Great Britain, whether on premises or by means of mobile plant, which are capable of causing pollution of the environment'. A 'prescribed process' means a process prescribed by the Secretary of State for the Environment under section 2(1) of the Act.

Sections 6 to 12 set out the provisions to make regulations covering the authorisation of prescribed processes. These are industrial and manufacturing processes which can cause harmful pollution. After specified set dates these processes can only be carried on with an authorisation granted by HMIP or the local authority. Sections 10–11 set out the conditions for varying such authorisations.

Sections 13–19 set out enforcement provisions and the powers available to HMIP inspectors. These include powers to issue enforcement notices where an inspector considers an authorisation is being contravened, for example where the operator of a process has exceeded an emission limit prescribed in the authorisation (section 13). Additionally, an enforcing authority is under a duty to take preventative steps where it believes that there is an imminent risk of serious pollution of the environment. This is done by serving a prohibition notice which details the authority assessment of the risks and requires the operator to take certain steps to counteract that risk. Such a notice may be served even where the operator of a process has not been in breach of an authorisation.

The powers to issue enforcement and prohibition notices are not available to ordinary citizens, although the enforcing authorities may act on the basis of data supplied by members of the public. However, it might be possible for an ordinary citizen to take legal action to compel an enforcing authority to issue a prohibition notice where the authority unreasonably refuses to do so. This possibility arises because under section 14(1) enforcing authorities are placed under a duty to issue prohibition notices where appropriate. This renders the decision of the authority open to judicial review for an order of mandamus, discussed in Chapter 5.

Appeals

Under section 15, provision is made for appeals to the Secretary of State against the variation of authorisations, enforcement and prohibition notices. Public hearings may be held in connection with such appeals, allowing citizens to contribute to the decision-making process (see below).

Section 20 sets out publicity to be given to statutory registers which are to be compiled to provide the public with information.

Sections 23–27 list offences (section 23 – see Chapter 4), enforcement by the High Court (section 24) and powers of the Chief Inspector to remedy harm (section 27).

PRESCRIBED PROCESSES – THE BASIS OF POLLUTION CONTROL UNDER PART I OF THE EPA

Part I introduces two parallel systems of control: Integrated Pollution Control (IPC) (or central control) and Local Authority Air Pollution Control (shortened herein to APC), allocated for local control by the local authorities.

IPC covers all effluent streams, air emissions, liquid effluent and solid waste onto land. All listed pollutants are controlled by Her Majesty's Inspectorate of Pollution. The system of IPC brings polluting processes under the scrutiny and control of one enforcement agency, whereas in the past a range of different agencies would need to be involved where the emissions ended up in different media.[9]

APC covers only emissions into the air and is administered by environmental health officers through a local authority. Local authorities are already under a duty to enforce Clean Air legislation, (considered in detail at Chapter 8) and may also investigate emissions which fall into the air known as statutory nuisances.

To carry on a prescribed process after 1 April 1992, a company or organisation must have an authorisation from either HMIP or the appropriate local authority. If a person or organisation does not have such an authorisation an offence will be committed and they will risk prosecution.[10] The authorisation may set conditions on the processes to be carried out, the scale on which they are permitted and the control of any releases. Businesses are expected to use what is known as 'best available techniques not entailing excessive costs' (BATNEEC) – the best available techniques for preventing or reducing the harmful effect of emissions. Those carrying on prescribed processes are expected to keep up with new developments in technology and apply them as is considered necessary.

This is no light requirement, being implied into every authorisation – whether clearly stated in it or not – by section 7(4) of the EPA. If the operator of the process fails to keep up with developments, a criminal offence is committed. For example, an operator could be prosecuted for having out-of-date equipment or an inefficient system. The definition of BATNEEC is a wide one, under section 7(10), and includes references (a) to the number, qualifications, training and supervision of persons employed in the process and (b) to the design, construction, layout and maintenance of the buildings in which the process is carried out. Unusually, for a criminal sanction, the person operating the prescribed process bears the burden of proving that BATNEEC has been used. Prosecutions for BATNEEC will probably be rare since HMIP are likely to give an operator an opportunity to introduce new technology or re-train staff. Prosecutions may also require a great deal of technical evidence and expert evidence which courts may find problematic. A BATNEEC condition also extends to authorisations granted by local authorities concerning emissions into the air.

Processes which must have authorisation

Processes are listed in Schedule 1 of the Environmental Protection (Prescribed Processes and Prescribed Substances) Regulations 1991 S.I. 472 made under the EPA. These came into force on 1

April 1992. They cover:

- the production of fuel and associated processes
- metal production and processing
- mineral industries
- the chemical industry
- waste disposal and recycling

Where an industry operates a number of different processes which fall into more than one of these headings (for example one for metal working and one for the chemical industry) a separate authorisation will be required for each.

Processes listed under these headings in the regulations are further sub-divided into different processes, being allocated as either Part A processes and Part B processes. Those in Part A are covered by IPC and those in Part B come under APC. Industries and businesses carrying out these prescribed processes must obtain authorisations from either HMIP or the local authority, as the case may be. The details of the authorisations will be based in part on guidance for particular processes issued by the Secretary of State, and from information supplied by certain public bodies and from members of the public.

PARTICIPATION BY OTHER AGENCIES AND THE PUBLIC

There are wide opportunities for public consultation and involvement in the granting of authorisations. Opportunities exist for the public to make representations both on the initial grant of an authorisation or with regard to any variation or alteration. Individuals have a right to make representations about prescribed processes and any pollutants which are to be released into their local environment or the environment as a whole. Anyone who is likely to be affected directly or indirectly is free to make representations. The right for the public to be consulted is a safeguard to ensure the granting of an authorisation for a process does not infringe the legal rights of others, laying open the enforcement authority or the operator of the process to legal action from a citizen adversely affected. Such inquiries may also give an opportunity to assess public opinion and reaction.

Schedule 1 of the EPA contains a regulation requiring that any consultations when granting such authorisations must, in certain instances, be made at public hearings. The details for the consultation and hearings are contained in the Environmental Protection (Applications, Appeals and Registers) Regulations 1991 No. 507.

Procedure on applications

The basic procedure for applying for a consent is set out in the regulations. The first hurdle faced by the would-be operator of a prescribed process is to put forward an application in writing in the correct form to HMIP or the local authority. In the early stages of granting authorisations, HMIP have rejected a considerable number of applications because companies have not completed the forms in the correct way.[11] Under regulation 2(1) the application must contain information about:

(a) the identity of the business, telephone number, and in a company the address of the principal office;

(b) the description of the prescribed process;

(c) the proposed substances to be released;

(d) a list of prescribed substances which will be used or result from the process;

(e) details of any other substance that may be released which could cause harm to the environment;

(f) techniques for preventing or reducing the effects of substances released;

(g) details of any proposed release and an assessment of the likely consequences;

(h) proposals for monitoring releases;

(i) how the objectives to prevent or render harmless emissions will be achieved (EPA, section 7(2)); proposals for best available technique not entailing excessive cost (EPA, section 7(4));

(j) and monitoring of the process and releases and techniques of control. In addition, HMIP may send out a questionnaire to businesses to obtain further information.

The application is placed on a public register and the application is advertised in the press. Public comment is sought within 28 days, after which the enforcing authority may consider the application in light of the representations and may then either grant the consent or refuse the application.

Any notice given to an enforcing authority with a proposal to alter the authorisation must also be made in writing and there is a requirement that there is consultation over the application with the following parties:

• The Health and Safety Executive.

• The Minister of Agriculture, Fisheries and Food.

• The Secretary of State for Wales (with regard to processes in Wales).

• The Secretary of State for Scotland (for processes in Scotland).

• The National Rivers Authority (for releases into controlled waters).

• Sewerage undertakers.

• The Nature Conservancy Council in cases of substances which may affect a site of special scientific interest in the Council's area.

• A harbour authority.

It will be interesting to see to what extent these bodies will actually be able to make representations or participate in hearings, given the wide range of responsibilities and functions that many of them will be having to exercise simultaneously.

Public advertisement

As mentioned above, applications must be advertised and Schedule 1 of the EPA and regulation 5 require that an advertisement must be published locally in one or more newspapers circulating in the locality in which the prescribed processes will be carried out. The procedures which are in force bear a broad resemblance to those which have existed for many years in planning appeals.[12] Similarities may grow as the EPA procedures become more established. In most cases an advertisement for an authorisation must be published within 28 days, beginning 14 days from the day on which the application or the application for variation is made. The advertisement must under regulation 5(3):

• state the name of the applicant,

• state the address of the premises,

• describe the process briefly,

• state where any register which contains particulars of an application or action to be taken may be inspected and that inspection is free,

• give the enforcing authority's address and explain that any person may make representations in writing within 28 days beginning with the date of the advertisement.

The advertisement enables the decision making process to be opened up to representations from any individual, any corporate body, and any other local authority who all have the right to contact the enforcing authorities. There is no reason why this should not include other businesses or companies or the members of environmental organisations (a group or organisation need not be incorporated – with legal status – to make representations). Of course, it may include not only those who are opposed to the authorisation but also those who are in favour of it being granted. There is no restriction on the place from which individuals may write; presumably anyone with a view, or with an interest which may be affected, may be involved since pollution may take effect many miles from where it is produced. Participation at the preliminary stage may also be an important factor in determining who may exercise legal rights to challenge any decision ultimately made through the High Court. However, not all who make representations at this stage may be able to pursue a right of challenge, but an early involvement will certainly help.

The persons who make representations at this stage become 'statutory parties' to the proceedings under regulation 11(1)(b) and may be notified of the result.

Representations to the enforcing authority

Representations should contain sufficient details of factors to be taken into consideration by the authority in making its decision and to identify objections to the authorisation being granted. Details should be as specific as possible; wherever possible anyone making representations should seek to put forward any details or documents corroborating the representations. Persons making representations should ensure that they keep file copies of any details or material submitted.

Factors that an enforcing body must consider

In considering an authorisation and any conditions to be imposed, the enforcing authority must consider achieving a number of objectives under section 7(2) of the EPA:

(a) to ensure that best available techniques not entailing excessive cost will be applied for

    (i) preventing the release of prescribed substances, or reducing and rendering them harmless where possible,

    (ii) for rendering harmless any other substances which might cause harm if released;

(b) compliance with directions from the Secretary of State for the implementation of matters in EC treaties or international law (for example international treaties on ozone depleting substances);

(c) guidance from the Secretary of State on quality standards and objectives;

(d) compliance with requirements from the Secretary of State under any plans for authorisations.

In seeking to achieve these objectives, the enforcing authority may confirm, refuse or impose conditions on any authorisation. It may also revoke or vary authorisations which have already been granted.

Rights of appeal

Where applications for authorisations are turned down, or where the authority takes steps against the operators and would-be operators of prescribed processes, a number of rights of appeal are available to the applicant or the operator involved. Rights of appeal under section 15 of the EPA are given against the following:

- refusal of a grant of variation of an authorisation,
- revocation of an authorisation,
- conditions attached to an authorisation,
- variation, enforcement and prohibition notices,
- a decision that information is not commercially confidential and should be included on the public register

The person wishing to carry on the prescribed process may appeal to the Secretary of State. Where such an appeal is commenced, all persons who made submissions at the representation stage must be notified that the appeal is going ahead. Those who have made representations have the right to a hearing or to deal with the matter by written representations. The Secretary of State may decide on a hearing where a prescribed process has proved particularly controversial or where it would be in the public interest.

The notice sent to a person who has made submissions must state the following under regulation 11(2):

(a) that an appeal has been lodged;

(b) the name and address of the appellant;

(c) the application or authorisation concerned;

(d) that such representations that have been made will be considered unless within 21 days the person concerned requests that they are disregarded (this is a chance to withdraw comments or objections);

(e) that further representations may be made within 21 days (this is a chance to introduce new information).

Appeals dealt with by written submissions

Under regulation 12, an appellant may elect to have an application dealt with by written representations. The enforcing authority shall submit any written representations received to the Secretary of State not later than 28 days after initiating the appeal. The appellant then has a further 17 days after the representations have been received to send in further comments. The Secretary of State also has to send to applicants copies of statements from any members of the public or interested parties and allow 14 days for representations.

Applicants are particularly likely to seek appeals which will be dealt with by written procedures because of the saving in time and public scrutiny. On the other hand, they may suffer from adverse press and public attention if the impression is given that they have something to conceal.

Hearings

As mentioned above, in certain cases a hearing may be required for a section 15 or 22(5) appeal. At least 28 days' written notice should be given to the appellant and the enforcing authority unless they agree otherwise.

Any hearing must be publicised in a newspaper circulating in the locality at least 21 days before the date fixed for the hearing. This provision also applies to processes carried out on mobile plants.

Every person who has made representations must also be served with a copy of the notice given to the appellant and the enforcing authority. A failure to make representations at any earlier stage will not necessarily prohibit a person making representations at the hearing. In practice, the hearing will represent an opportunity for local people to express their views on the issue.

There is a right to be heard given by regulation 13(7) which provides that nothing in the regulations shall 'prevent the person appointed to conduct the hearing of the appeal from permitting any other person to be heard at the hearing and such permission shall not be unreasonably withheld'.

This effectively gives a right for 'last minute objectors' to participate in proceedings and express their views. It is an entirely sensible suggestion since it allows those who missed the original advertisements or relevant deadlines as a result of holidays, illness, etc to take part, along with those who have only just moved into an area.

Hearings are likely to be of a relatively informal nature; no strict rules are laid down as to how an inspector should deal with the matters which may arise. Persons participating in a hearing should be advised that much complex scientific information and technical evidence may be raised. While rules of evidence (as applied in civil and criminal cases) will not apply, any evidence as may be introduced must be relevant to the application concerned and the inspector will have to consider the weight to be attached to it. The more expertise behind a representation, the more weight it is likely to be given. An inspector should certainly be reluctant to exclude any scientific or medical evidence which purports to show damage to the environment or health in the past arising from the prescribed process either on the site in question or at another location which is comparable.

If statutory consultors do not participate, it may be up to members of the public to raise pertinent and relevant environmental information. Ultimately, this will depend on how much detailed local environmental data is available, together with any details about the site and the type of business involved. Information from the public register could be raised to assess how a company had performed in the past or to reveal any previous convictions.

As the person determining the hearing is under a duty not to unreasonably deny an opportunity to any person to be heard, any discretion will have to be exercised within the principles of *Wednesbury reasonableness* as laid down in *Associated Provincial Picture House* v *Wednesbury Corporation* (1948) 1 KB 223 and the principles of natural justice. This means that decisions may be challenged by judicial review if they have not been fairly or properly made (see Chapter 5).

The type of hearing envisaged, and seemingly preferred by the Department of the Environment, appears to be a relatively informal approach, lacking the formal atmosphere of a court. While there is much to recommend such an approach in making inquiries open and accommodating to all-comers, situations will undoubtedly arise where a more formal type of proceeding is required and special rules may have to be developed.[13] It remains to be seen whether hearings will be empowered to take oaths and require sworn evidence from witnesses.

The decisions made at hearings and by enforcing authorities are likely to vary from area to area. While this may draw complaints from industry, such a result is entirely appropriate since environmental circumstances between different sites may vary considerably. The environment and how pollution of it may be controlled under IPC or APC will to some extent vary from place to place according to geographical features, existing facilities, population density, existing land use and so on.

Getting information on IPC and APC authorisations – the registers

The EPA puts an onus on enforcing bodies to maintain registers which are open to the public, containing details of authorisations for prescribed processes. The registers should be available for public inspection at reasonable hours and copies of the information contained may be made. Regulation 15 sets out the information that public registers must contain. The following should all be included:

(a) all particulars of any application for an authorisation made to an authority;

(b) all particulars of any notice to the applicant by the authority under paragraph 1(3) of Schedule 1 to that Act and of any information furnished in response to such a notice;

(c) all particulars of any representations made by persons required to be consulted under regulation 4(1);

(d) all particulars of the authorisation;

(e) details of any variation, enforcement or prohibition notice;

(f) all particulars of any notice issued by an authority withdrawing a prohibition notice;

(g) all particulars of any notification given to the holder of an authorisation by the authority under section 10(5) of the EPA;

(h) all particulars of any application to vary the consent;

(i) all particulars of any revocation of an authorisation;

(j) all particulars of any notice of appeal under section 15 in respect of authorisations or against variation, enforcement and prohibition notices.

The amount of information stored on the register will vary from case to case. An examination of the register will give the history of the consent for up to four years (regulation 17). These time limits are important in the event that the details on the register might be used as evidence in any civil proceedings. Further details are contained in sections 20–22 of the EPA. Under section 20(7) the public have a right to examine and photocopy the information subject to a reasonable charge. In some circumstances, confidential information may not be included on the register, subject to an order by the Secretary of State.

As with the rights of access to other environmental information, there are no restrictions on who may consult the registers or the uses to which the information may be put. At present, registers appear to have been little used by the public with the exception of environmental consultants and rival operators of prescribed processes. This is largely due to the fact that despite being public registers, their availability has received little publicity or promotion.

Aside from challenges in judicial review, a person who can show that his or her legal rights have been infringed, eg the plant is causing a nuisance or has caused an injury, may prosecute or pursue a claim against the polluter at law. Some of the principles on which action can be taken are explained in Chapters 4 and 6.

Other parts of the EPA

Part II of the EPA deals with waste disposal and the appropriate licences, authorisations and other statutory controls (see Chapter 10).

- Sections 35–44 deal with waste disposal licences and offences of making false statements.

- Sections 45–61 deal with the collection, disposal or treatment of controlled waste.

- Sections 64–67 cover public registers for waste regulation.

- Sections 68–72 give powers of supervision and enforcement, powers of entry, and so on, to HMIP.

Part III of the Act covers statutory nuisances and clean air, and proceedings for statutory nuisances in magistrates' courts.
Part IV deals with litter and abandoned shopping and luggage trolleys.
Part V covers radioactivity and amends the Radioactive Substances Act 1960.

Part VI covers genetically modified organisms and related controls. Enforcement powers are provided and a public register kept. Genetically modified organisms are likely to be increasingly important in years to come.

Part VII provides for nature conservation and the establishment of new councils in England and Wales

Part VIII includes a large miscellaneous section covering contaminated land, penalties for polluting controlled waters, pollution at sea, stray dogs, the burning of stubble and straw and abandoned shopping trolleys.

Sixteen Schedules follow giving further details from which the necessary regulations have and may be developed.

Toxic inventory

At the time of writing, the Department of the Environment has issued a consultation paper on a proposed chemical release inventory, similar to the Toxic Release Inventory which operates in the United States. The inventory would record annual releases of chemical substances and place duties to monitor on the operators of prescribed processes. The details would be aggregated and included in a register which would be open to public inspection. This would enable managers to obtain an overall picture of the processes which were being operated and identify particular local blackspots. Information would also be available to the public and environmental groups which could form the basis for public action and involvement which is already available in the authorisation process.[14]

NOTES

[1]   *A Strategy for Justice*, Legal Action Group, 1992.
[2]   Hawkins K., (1984), *Environment and Enforcement - Regulation and the Social Definition of Pollution*, Clarendon Press.
[3]   1991 edition.
[4]   See *NEST*, NCVO, 1992
[5]   DoE guidance and a list of relevant publications are available from HMSO, London.
[6]   Legal Action Group, op. cit.

[7] Royal Commission on Environmental Protection, Tenth Report, (1984).

[8] Legal Aid Act 1989; further changes introduced April 1993.

[9] RCEP Tenth Report, op. cit.

[10] See section 23, Environmental Protection Act 1990, in Chapter 4.

[11] See (1992), *Environment Today*, Brodie Publishing Ltd.

[12] Town and Country Planning Act, 1990.

[13] Planning decisions and procedures may provide a useful guidance.

[14] DoE consultation paper published in January 1993.

Chapter 4

Prosecuting Environmental Crimes

An important case which is still good law but seems to have been largely forgotten is *R* v *Stewart* (1896) 1 QB 300. It is important because it establishes that any citizen may bring a private prosecution for any crime, unless an Act of Parliament restricts the class of persons who may prosecute.

The facts of *R* v *Stewart* were that the local chair of the RSPCA in Liverpool, a Mr Walter Burnham, sought to prosecute the master of a steam ship transporting cattle, sheep and pigs under the Animals (Transit and General) Order 1895, a measure made under the Diseases of Animals Act 1894. This statute gave a Victorian local authority the right to prosecute for breaches of the Act. The local Magistrate refused to issue the summons as both the statute and a set of regulations made under it only envisaged the local authority having a right to prosecute. As Mr Burnham was clearly not a local authority he had, said the Magistrate, no right to invoke the criminal law.

Far from satisfied, Mr Burnham took his case to the High Court for an order of mandamus (see Chapter 6) to compel the Magistrate to try the case. Giving judgement, Lord Lindley and Lord Kaye both stated that unless a statute clearly prohibited the right of a citizen to take action, any person was entitled to prosecute a crime.

The result of *R* v *Stewart* is that no one has to wait for the police, the local environmental health officer or HMIP to prosecute a crime, whether under the EPA or any other Act. The individual may prosecute an offender themselves – providing they have the evidence. The right to bring a private prosecution has been preserved by the Prosecution of Offences Act 1985. Every year there are hundreds of private prosecutions brought by individuals and bodies such as the RSPCA, the RSPB, Customs and more recently HMIP and NRA inspectors and local government officers.

The only restriction on the right to prosecute is that certain offences may need the consent of the Director of Public Prosecutions, such as conspiracy charges or the offence of damaging a site of special scientific interest under the Wildlife and Countryside Act 1981. Subject to such restrictions, the only way a private prosecution may be halted is under section 6(2) of the Prosecution of Offences Act 1985 which provides that the Director of Public Prosecutions can take over a prosecution which has been commenced and decide to discontinue proceedings. Such a power is only likely to be used where proceedings are felt to be an abuse of the court – the taking over of proceedings could easily prove politically controversial.

However, where a statutory nuisance originates from a business with an authorisation under the IPC or APC, proceedings in criminal law by a local authority may only be commenced with the permission of the Secretary of State for the Environment (section 79(10)) (see Chapter 6).

Evidence supplied by citizens

Although not restricted from bringing proceedings, citizens may well be reluctant to do so for a variety of reasons. However, there is nothing to stop citizens supplying evidence for use in criminal proceedings brought by an enforcing authority. The powers of entry, search and seizure available to an 'inspector' or a police officer are much wider than those enjoyed by a private citizen, which may make the collection of evidence easier than for a private individual. However, in many cases, particularly in cases of local authority enforcement, it will have been the public who have alerted the authorities to begin with.

Where a person discovers or witnesses an incident which could amount to an environmental offence she/he will generally be a competent witness for the prosecution. Unless blessed with an extraordinary power of recall, it is advisable that a witness should make a note as a record of what has taken place as soon as practicable.

Commencing proceedings

Nearly all legal proceedings are a gamble – there is nearly always a risk that something may go wrong and a prosecutor may end up paying the costs if she/he loses the case. Most enforcement agencies prefer to use the criminal law as a last resort and achieve their goals through bringing any cause of complaint or breach of the law to the attention of the person responsible for appropriate action. Furthermore, there may be other ways in which the public may exert influence over the behaviour of operators of prescribed processes by way of what could be called the three 'Ps' – persuasion, protest or publicity.

In many cases, those who wish to take out private prosecutions would be best to accumulate evidence and present it to the relevant enforcing authority. Only where an enforcing authority declines to act for no good reason might it be worth embarking upon a private prosecution, and even then if such a course of action is taken, caution should be the watchword. The public registers established by the EPA will contain basic information about operators of prescribed processes which may form a starting point for commencing a prosecution.

JURISDICTION

Magistrates' courts in England and Wales have jurisdiction which is essentially territorial in nature – generally, they can only try offences which have been committed in England and Wales. Courts also have a local jurisdiction. Basically, a summons may be issued by a justice attached to a particular court, if the offence was committed or suspected to have been committed in the area covered by the court.

Under section 1 of the Magistrates' Courts Act 1980 individuals and all types of organisation would appear to be capable of giving information to a justice to obtain the issue of a summons. Groups and organisations such as local authorities and companies can lay information by the means of their members or staff. Local pressure groups, via one of their members, may also start proceedings, although in some cases the justice may request that proceedings are begun in the name of the individual. A range of offences, including those contained in most environmental legislation, are open to prosecution by the individual. In certain instances, an explicit statutory right is given, as with the new nuisance provisions which are open to an 'aggrieved person'.

In most criminal cases, it is not complex aspects of the law which are usually crucial but the evidence which is produced by the prosecutor and this is no different with environmental offences. There must be enough evidence for a prosecutor to satisfy the court beyond reasonable doubt, with the prosecutor being required to prove every element of the case at law. Providing a court applies the correct standard of proof there is no reason in law why it should not convict on the word of a single witness, unless a specific statute requires more than one witness. After all, some crimes – such as many cases of murder – have no witnesses at all, but the court may still convict if evidence is available.

Evidence is often a problem in cases of environmental crimes. Crime, by its nature, tends to be a secretive activity and the emission of pollution may be very hard to detect. Not only may it take place away from the public gaze, but it may even be invisible and its effects may not become apparent immediately, in some cases for years. A further problem is tracing pollution to its actual source; environmental pollution may appear many miles and many months from its point of origin. With the regime laid down by the EPA, where certain emissions may be allowed within authorised limits, proving such limits have been exceeded requires specialist equipment. In some cases there may be a scientific dispute as to whether any environmental harm is being caused at all.

Selection of appropriate charges can be difficult. Should a prosecutor bring proceedings for the release of one substance or several ? Or for breach of conditions ? In the case of irregular leaks occurring from a plant over a 24 hour period, should the incident be treated as one release (and hence one offence) or several? This is a practical as well as legal decision and a would-be prosecutor should consider what offences are the easiest to prove. In many cases there may well be a number of offences committed by the operator of a prescribed process.

Even where evidence is obtained, it has to be admissible and presented in a way accepted at law. If a prosecutor embarks upon a case where there is no evidence and does not act in good faith but purely out of malice or spite, a claim could be brought for malicious prosecution. This is not a book about evidence, particularly forensic evidence, and it should be remembered that some forms of pollution have to be proved with specialist monitoring or sampling equipment used by a qualified person. This may or may not be an obstacle depending on the knowledge and resources of the prosecutor.

Offences triable only in magistrates' courts

Some offences are only triable in magistrates' courts, but most pollution offences are also triable before a jury. Where either court can hear the case, the offence is one which is 'triable either way'. In the early stages of enforcement of the EPA most prosecutions are likely to be through the magistrates' court. For offences triable in magistrates' courts, prosecutors should refer to *Stone's Justices' Manual* which is an essential source of information. If a point of law or procedure arises in a prosecution most courts will accept a statement in *Stone's* as conclusive.[1]

The choice of where a case which is triable either way is heard belongs to the defendant, unless the magistrates believe the case should go before the Crown Court. It is probable that most defendants will seek to have their case heard only in the magistrates' court because of the £20,000 limit on the fine that may be imposed. Juries might be considered to take an even dimmer view of polluters than magistrates and the risk of an unlimited fine is likely to make most defendants stay in the local court.

Range of offences

A range of offences is set out in section 23(1) of the EPA, which provides as follows:

'It is an offence for a person –

(a) to contravene section 6(1) (carrying out a prescribed process without an authorisation or in breach of an authorisation);

(b) to fail to give notice required under section 9(2);

(c) to fail to comply with or to contravene any requirement or prohibition imposed by an enforcement notice or a prohibition notice;

(d) without reasonable excuse, to fail to comply with any requirement imposed under section 17;

(e) to prevent any other person from appearing before court or from answering any question to which an inspector may, under section 17(3), require an answer;

(f) intentionally to obstruct an inspector in the exercise of his performance of his powers or duties;

(g) to fail, without reasonable excuse, to comply with any requirement imposed by a notice imposed under section 19(2);

(h) to make a statement which he knows to be false or misleading in a material particular, or recklessly to make a statement which is false or misleading in a material particular where the statement is made

    (i) in purported compliance with a requirement to furnish any information imposed by or under any provision of this Part; or

    (ii) for the purpose of obtaining the grant of an authorisation to himself or any other person or the variation of an authorisation;

(i) intentionally to make a false entry in any record required to be kept under section 7 above;

(j) with intent to deceive, to forge or use a document issued or authorised to be issued under section 7 above or required for any purpose thereunder or to make or have in his possession a document so closely resembling any such document as to be likely to deceive;

(k) falsely to pretend to be an inspector;

(l) to fail to comply with an order made by a court under section 26 below.

A person guilty of an offence under (a), (c) and (l) will be liable to a fine not exceeding £20,000. On indictment, up to two years imprisonment may be imposed or an unlimited fine.

If the offence involves a matter under (b), (g), (h), (i) or (j) a fine not exceeding £2,000 on summary conviction may be imposed and, on indictment, an unlimited fine or not more than two year's imprisonment.

COMMENCING PROCEEDINGS

Proceedings are instigated through the magistrates' court by laying information before a justice of the peace. This can usually be done at the local magistrates' court during working hours (though some rural courts are only open a few days each week.) Normally, this is a simple matter of going before a justice or a court and requesting the issue of a summons to the person accused. A summons can be issued by a justice from his or her home and the Clerk is empowered to issue summonses in certain cases.

Section 96 of the Magistrates' Courts Act 1980 requires the request to be made orally and sufficient information must be given to identify the offence. The prosecutor must be prepared to answer such questions as may be raised by the justice. The summons must also contain the date of the hearing which must provide a reasonable time for the accused party to prepare their defence. It is filled in by the Clerk to the Court and sent by registered post to the defendant.

In the case of a company the summons has to be addressed to the registered office of the company concerned. Care has to be taken in selecting the company or business which is responsible for the pollution when providing the information for the summons. Information contained in the public registers should be sufficient for this where the pollution involves a prescribed process.

In the case of a summary offence, triable only before justices, the summons must be requested within six months of the cause of the complaint (section 127, MCA 1980). In the case of an offence which is triable either way, there is no time limit, so this will only affect a minority of offences.

More serious matters must be tried on indictment, and only the most serious pollution offences should go before the Crown Courts where more than a £20,000 fine may be imposed. Justices may use their discretion to commit to the Crown Court for sentencing or for a trial of the offence. Alternatively, HMIP, the local authority or the National Rivers Authority would be responsible for instigating proceedings, whereby they are represented by a barrister for a jury trial of a case.

Section 157 of the EPA

Section 157 of the EPA provides that where an offence under any part of the Act is committed by a corporate body and is proved to have been committed with the consent or connivance of, or to be attributable to any neglect on the part of any director, manager, secretary or other similar officer of the corporate body or a person who was purporting to act in any such capacity, he or she as well as the corporate body shall be guilty of that offence and shall be liable to be proceeded against and punished accordingly.

Under section 157(2), where the affairs of a corporate body are managed by its members, subsection (1) applies in relation to the acts or defaults of a member in connection with the functions of management as if she or he were a director of the body corporate. Under section 157(2), in cases involving management by members, subsection (1) applies in relation to the acts or defaults of a member functioning as a manager as though she/he were a director.

The effect of section 157 is to render individuals liable to prosecution in addition to the company with which they are connected. As many environmental offences are strict liability ones, it may be relatively easy to take a case against a named individual. The wording of the sections cover anyone who is a director under the Companies Act 1985, section 741, and anyone who acts in the capacity of a manager (whether their job title is that of a manager or not). Secretary presumably means company secretary (or anyone else who acts in that capacity). The courts are likely to look closely at the job details rather than the job descriptions to determine liability.

It should not be assumed that these provisions necessarily exempt other employees who act in the knowledge that environmental offences are being committed. Members of the work force who knowingly participate in illegal acts may be open to prosecution for aiding and abetting (see below). In such cases of knowledge, the defence of 'The boss told me to do it' or 'I was only obeying orders' will not be available.

The ability of companies and individuals to insure against criminal proceedings is restricted by the Companies Act 1985 to offences where the defendant is ultimately acquitted at trial.[2]

Attendance by the defendant

On receiving the summons, the defendant party must attend the hearing to answer the plea. If the defendant does not attend, the court has a number of options. It may issue an arrest warrant to bring the person before the court. Alternatively, on the non-appearance of the defendant the case may proceed in his or her absence. As it is obviously not practical to arrest a company, the court may proceed, but only if satisfied that the interests of justice require it.[3]

If the defendant does attend, she/he will be asked to plead. Usually, the accused will plead not guilty. The case may not necessarily proceed immediately, but a further date may be set. Either side is entitled to be represented by a barrister or solicitor at the hearing or assisted by a friend.[4]

On the date fixed for the trial, the prosecutor must attend court together with witnesses and other evidence to prove their case. In most cases evidence must be given orally by those who directly witnessed or measured the incidents. It is necessary to prove every element of the offence.

Non-appearance of a party to the case

Occasionally a prosecutor or a defendant will fail to appear at a hearing. In such a case where the prosecutor fails to appear, the case may be dismissed against the defendant. If the defendant fails to appear, the court may proceed to hear the evidence from the prosecutor and try the case. The discretion to proceed in the absence of the defendant must be exercised judicially, including a fair opportunity for the accused to be present and call witnesses. The court may make further inquiries and consider any evidence for the reason for non-appearance before proceeding. Alternatively, another date may be set and the case adjourned.

Magistrates who try the case

The principles of natural justice apply to the hearing and no Magistrate may sit who has an interest in the outcome of the proceedings (for more information see Chapter 5 on judicial review).

In the case of a prosecution by HMIP, the justice of the peace should step down and be replaced by another if she/he has an interest in the company, for example by way of share ownership. If a prosecution is being brought by the local authority, no JP should sit who is a member of that local authority, unless a statutory exception can be found.

However, not every interest should prevent a justice from sitting on a case. For example, in *R v Deal Justices* (1881) 45 LT 439 the fact that a justice was a member of a society for the prevention of cruelty to animals did not stop him sitting in a prosecution brought by the society.

As a matter of law, justices should not unreasonably refuse to give their names to those appearing before them (see *R v Felixstowe Justices ex parte Leigh* (1987) 1 All ER 551).

Where a case is part heard, it should be re-convened before the same bench of justices who originally heard the first part of the case (section 122(6), Magistrates' Courts Act 1980).

Proceedings to be held in public

Proceedings in a magistrates' court must be held in public under section 121(4) of the Magistrates' Courts Act 1980. The press and public should be admitted and all evidence communicated to the court should be raised in open court. The only exceptions are circumstances where there are persons in the public gallery who are likely to disrupt proceedings.

Appearance at the hearing

Environmental Health Officers and HMIP inspectors are entitled to prosecute in proceedings involving environmental matters even though they may not be legally qualified. Local Government officers may appear by virtue of section 223(1) of the Local Government Act 1972 where authorised by the authority and HMIP officials may appear under section 23(6) of the EPA.

Officers from either HMIP or local authorities should always bring a copy of their correct authorisations to court with them. If they fail to do so, it is one of the easiest tricks of the defence to suggest that the person is not authorised and is therefore legally absent! If a party is absent, the case should be dismissed.

In the case of proceedings against a company, a representative of the company may make a plea of guilty or not guilty and make a statement before justices under section 12(2) of the Magistrates' Courts Act 1980.

Conduct of proceedings

Probably the best way to learn how to conduct proceedings is to observe them taking place in the magistrates' courts. The strict rules of procedure are laid down in the Magistrates' Court Rules 1981, although they are not always observed in practice. The best advice that can be given to any prosecutor is to stick by the rule book! If you go outside it, for reasons of expediency, administrative convenience or any other reason you will be open to an appeal.

The prosecution opens the case with a preliminary statement. This may be by an officer, and if she or he has special qualifications in the environmental field which are relevant, these should be stated.

Rule 13 of the Magistrates' Court Rules 1981 sets out the procedure in a criminal offence, and any prosecutor should seek to follow it.

(a) On a summary trial of a complaint, where the accused does not plead guilty, the prosecutor shall call evidence for the prosecution, and before doing so may address the court. The prosecution should seek to put in all the relevant evidence at this stage. Normally, no further evidence may be admitted, except in rebuttal of the defence, subject to a limited discretion in court.

(b) At the conclusion of the evidence for the prosecution, the accused may address the court whether or not he calls evidence afterwards.

(c) At the conclusion of the evidence for the defence, the prosecution may call evidence to rebut that evidence. Rebuttal evidence must be confined to matters which arise unexpectedly in the course of the defence.

(d) At the conclusion of the evidence for the defence and the evidence of rebuttal (if any) the accused may address the court.

(e) Either party can, with permission of the court, make a further statement. If the court grants permission to one, it should not deny it to another.

EVIDENCE

Great care should be taken with evidence used to prove a case at stage (b) above. All too often in the past, local authorities have taken a corner-cutting approach in proceedings, and magistrates' courts have let them get away with it; it is bad practice. The prosecution should have enough evidence to prove matters beyond reasonable doubt to the satisfaction of the court and have every regard for the rules of evidence. If it does not, there is the risk that a represented defendant will pick up on a technicality and have the case dismissed with a submission of 'no case to answer'. A court becomes a lonely place for any prosecutor in this position and even more unpleasant when the matter of costs arises. With higher penalties now available for many environmental offences, more companies are likely to be represented by lawyers and such challenges should be expected.

Evidence is usually presented by producing witnesses who are subjected to questioning by the prosecutor. The purpose of the questioning is to obtain the facts relevant to the offence, a process known as examination-in-chief. When this process is completed, the defence have the right to cross-examination. This consists of the asking of questions to test the statements given and to cast doubt and expose any weaknesses in the evidence. Obviously, a witness who changes his/her story under cross-examination is unlikely to be believed.

If an expert witness is called, she/he should be asked about their relevant qualifications and what experience they have with regard to the matter charged, eg previous inspections.

Securing the attendance of a witness

In some cases a witness may be reluctant to attend or there may be no other way of proving a certain matter than the evidence that such a witness may have. For example, a council officer may refuse to attend over a certain matter or a regulatory body might refuse to produce a document in a particular case. Where a witness will not voluntarily attend or produce a particular document, a person may apply, under section 97 of the Magistrates' Courts Act 1980, for a justice of the peace to issue a witnesses summons to compel attendance, or produce the document at court.

On such an application for a witness summons, the justice may enquire as to the nature of the evidence and whether it is material. This does not allow a prosecutor to go fishing for evidence. If the person is not likely to give material evidence or the evidence may be inadmissible, the witness summons may be quashed by the High Court. It should also be remembered that some documents may be legally privileged from production as evidence.

State of mind of an offender

With most criminal offences it is necessary to prove that a person had criminal intent (known as 'mens rea'), that the person was conscious and aware of the nature of the act she/he was doing. In some cases, this mental element refers to knowingly committing an act or having a reckless state of mind.

With many environmental offences there is no need to prove the state of mind of the polluter – the mere fact that the pollution occurred is sufficient for responsibility for an offence. Such offences are known as 'strict liability' offences, or cases of 'no fault liability'. If the pollution occurred because of the actions of the polluter, the polluter will be guilty in law.

In cases of offences where knowledge of a mental element is necessary, evidence must be available to prove the state of mind, making it more difficult to convict both the company and its officials.

Types of evidence in criminal prosecutions

The following is a summary of certain key principles of evidence which apply in criminal prosecutions. For more information, the reader is referred to *Stone's Justices' Manual* and key text books on the subject.

Oral evidence from witnesses

Most evidence is from witnesses' recollections of what they saw or experienced which is recounted in court. This is known as oral evidence. Oral evidence must relate to what the person saw or experienced individually.

Witnesses giving evidence must either swear an oath on a religious book according to their religion or make an affirmation (a non-religious oath). [5]

Memory-refreshing documents

When giving evidence in court, a witness is permitted to refer to a document that she/he made when the events were clearer. Both witnesses in prosecutions by public bodies and private individuals are entitled to do this, and the rules of evidence set standards which those collecting evidence involving environmental offences should have regard to. This is particularly important for bodies which have an enforcement role whose investigating officers are likely to be faced with a large case load to cover.

In practice, a note of what happened should be made as soon as practicable. In some cases a delay of over two weeks has been held acceptable, but a witness should err on the side of caution and try and record the facts as close to the events as possible.

The document on which a witness relies should be made available to the defence, who may cross examine on the strength of it. Where notes have been taken from a witness and recorded by someone else, the witness should have had the opportunity to verify the accuracy of the notes at the time they were recorded.

In certain exceptions, the court may allow a witness to refresh their memory from a document, whether made contemporaneously or not, providing the court is satisfied that the witness cannot remember the events. The court must also be satisfied that the statement was made near to the events the witness seeks to recall and that she/he wishes to read the notes before giving evidence (*R* v *Da Silva* (1990) 1 All ER 29).

Hearsay evidence

What someone else may have said or told a witness outside the court is known as hearsay and will not generally be admissible as evidence. Such a statement, recalled by the witness second hand, cannot be tested by cross examination. If a person states that someone else told them, or they learned the information from another person via a letter or a document, it will be hearsay and generally cannot be used by either the prosecution or the defence. Witnesses must confine themselves to what they have personally experienced and know to be true. However, as with most aspects of the law, there are a number of important exceptions to this principle, some of which are considered below.

One unfortunate implication of the rule against hearsay is that it probably includes the information contained on the public register, leaving a private prosecutor with the problem of having to produce evidence in a way which is admissible at law to prove any relevant matter.

If a document from the register is certified in accordance with section 3 of the Evidence Act 1851, it *may* be possible to admit the register as evidence; but in the absence of any specific statutory provision to admit hearsay, there may be considerable difficulties in some criminal cases. It is an area which needs clear government intervention to put the matter beyond doubt.

Documentary evidence

Other forms of evidence include documentary and scientific evidence. The law relating to documentary evidence is complex, and if at all possible the maker of document should be available. The evidence of maps, plans and designs is usually acceptable.

With readings of scientific instruments, evidence should be available from witnesses that the device or machine was working correctly and accurately and that it had been tested satisfactorily. This is an area which is likely to yield defence challenges in years to come. In the case of computer evidence, section 69 of the Police and Criminal Evidence Act 1984 applies. Care should be taken to ensure that any scientific points are explained properly to the Magistrates.

Local authority records

Legal proceedings involving documents held by local authorities have the advantage of section 229 of the Local Government Act 1972 which allows photocopies to be produced where the original cannot be used.

Public documents

A document made by a public officer for the purpose of public use is usually admissable as evidence. However, some problems may arise over the use of the registers established by the Control of Pollution Act 1974 (COPA) or the EPA which, as mentioned, may be hearsay evidence. In the case of a private prosecution, obtaining the necessary evidence from HMIP might entail obtaining a witness order for a particular HMIP inspector.

Public documents which may be used in environmental prosecution include: Acts of Parliament, regulations, local bye-laws and EEC documents. Under section 41 of the Local Government (Miscellaneous Provisions) Act 1976, resolutions are proved by means of signed certificates.

Until the case law is settled, care should be taken with the public registers established under the COPA, the EPA or the Water Resources Act 1991. While these registers are designed to give crucial information to the public and form a starting point from which concerned citizens may act, no proper provision has been made for the information contained in them to be used in criminal courts. As a result they may be open to attacks from the defence that the matters contained in them are hearsay. This would not be a problem in civil cases. Some amendment of the law may be necessary. One possible solution may be found for HMIP inspectors in section 24 of the Criminal Justice Act 1988; section 78 of the

Police and Criminal Evidence Act 1984 covering confession evidence may also be admissible. Where a public document is admissible in proceedings, the Evidence Act 1845 could be utilised provided it was supported by an official signature confirming that it was a true copy.

Business records

Section 24 of the Criminal Justice Act 1988 makes a number of important provisions for the admissibility of documents. Under section 24(1) a statement in a document shall be admissible in criminal proceedings as evidence of any fact of which direct oral evidence would be admissible, if the following conditions are satisfied:

- the document was created or received by a person in the course of a trade, business, profession or other occupation, or as the holder of a paid or unpaid office; and

- the information contained in the document was supplied by a person (whether or not the maker of the statement) who had, or may reasonably be supposed to have had, personal knowledge of the matters dealt with.

Under 24(2), where the information has been passed through more than one person, it will only be admissible if each person who passed on the information was acting in the course of a trade, business, profession or other occupation or was the holder of a paid or unpaid office.

Confession evidence

An exception to the rule against hearsay are statements made against interest – confession evidence – under section 76 of the Police and Criminal Evidence Act 1984. The exception covers any statement against interest, the idea being that no person would make any statement whether made verbally, in writing or otherwise which was liable to incriminate them. Thus an admission made by a director of company that they carried on a prescribed process but did not have a licence, would be admissible evidence that the company concerned did not have the correct authorisation.

A statement that is obtained through the threat of violence, inhuman or degrading treatment, or in circumstances that render the confession unreliable will be excluded. (Hopefully such circum-stances will be rare indeed!)

The fact that a confession is wholly or partly excluded does not affect the admissibility of

• any facts discovered as a result of the confession (provided the facts are admissible in themselves);

• the confession if it is to show how the accused expressed himself orally or in writing.

Statements by employees of companies may be used as evidence in proceedings against companies. *Edwards* v *Brookes (Milk) Ltd* (1963) 3 All ER 62.

Photographs and sketches

Photographs are admissible as evidence, provided they are verified on oath by a person able to state their accuracy. This need not necessarily be the person who took the photograph.

Video recordings, in this age of hand-held camcorders, may seem an attractive method of proof in environmental cases. For example, video footage of waste pipes gushing out effluent or smoke billowing from chimneys can be highly dramatic and effective as evidence. However, care must be taken, and the general rule is that such evidence will be treated as the equivalent of documents.

Section 26 of the Criminal Justice Act 1988 provides that documents that appear to have been prepared for purposes in criminal proceedings or investigations shall not be used without the permission of the court. As a consequence, the person who recorded the film should attend court if at all possible to give oral evidence as a witness.

Evidence obtained unlawfully

In some cases evidence may be obtained unlawfully – for example, environmental protesters may trespass in the course of entering a site to obtain video or photographic evidence.

At common law the courts are not so much concerned by how evidence is obtained but its probative value. Whether such evidence is now admissible will depend on the view taken by the judge or the court under section 78 of the Police and Criminal Evidence Act 1984. In any proceedings the court may refuse to allow the prosecution's evidence to be given if it appears to the court that, with regard to all the circumstances, including the circumstances in which the evidence was obtained, the admission of the evidence would have such an adverse effect on the fairness of the proceedings that the court ought not to admit it.

The court should consider the prejudice to the accused and the weight to attach to any evidence. This is usually more likely to be an issue in a Crown Court trial before a jury, but the same matter may be raised in proceedings before justices, who may decide to exclude the evidence during the prosecution case or at the end of the trial. The court will only look at the admissible evidence and whether it affects the fairness of the trial.

Previous convictions and judgements as evidence

It is possible, particularly in the case of large-scale industries, that more than one offence may have been committed. In the case of those operating prescribed processes, any convictions will be recorded in the public register. While this problem only really arises in cases before a jury (justices are expected to ignore any prejudicial information concerning a defendant's record) it is likely to become an increasingly important consideration, should considerable numbers of pollution offences be tried in the Crown Court in years to come. Great care should be taken by a prosecutor before introducing evidence of previous convictions, because of the wording of the Criminal Evidence Act 1898. This puts limits as to when previous charges and convictions can be raised as evidence in proceedings and when an accused person may be questioned about them. In the absence of any authority, it is presumed that this protection extends also to corporations and not only individuals.

Previous convictions can only be introduced when relevant to proving guilt, or where the accused attacks the character of the prosecutor or witnesses for the prosecution, or where an accused asserts good character. For example, if a company began to promote its corporate image in court and sought to portray itself as concerned with protecting the environment, claiming a 'green' image, it might be appropriate to introduce its previous convictions. The ultimate discretion as to where previous convictions may be introduced in a case tried before a jury lies with the judge, but is probably unlikely to occur because HMIP might well act to restrict authorisations where a company was a 'repeat offender'.

However, following the principle in *R* v *Winfield* (1939) an accused may be asked questions about wholly unrelated convictions. Thus, in a case of water pollution, questions could be asked about convictions for pollution of the air – or for that matter tax evasion (care has to be taken that it is the same company and not a subsidiary). The risk of prejudice is potentially very great in this respect, as a jury may not appreciate the scale of the operations or the scale of pollution involved.

Breach of licences

In cases involving the breach of a licence or conditions, the onus is on the defence to prove on the balance of probabilities that the necessary licence was held and the conditions were complied with (Magistrates' Courts Act 1980, section 101).

In *Ashcroft* v *Cambro Wastes Ltd* (1981) it was held that the prosecution did not have to prove knowing breach of conditions of a licence; it was sufficient to establish the breach and allow the defence to show that the conditions to carry out the operation concerned existed.

Onus of proof in cases of best available technique

Section 25(1) of the EPA states that in any proceedings for an offence under section 23(1)(a), consisting of a failure to comply with the general condition implied in every authorisation, it shall be for the accused to prove that there was no better available technique not entailing excessive cost, than was in fact used to satisfy the condition. Where:

(a) an entry is required under section 7 above to be made in any record as to the observance of any condition of an authorisation; and

(b) the entry has not been made

that fact will be admissible as evidence that the condition has not been observed.

Other offences for the prosecution notebook

In some cases the existing provisions of the law may be ineffective. An example is the legislation which is meant to protect sites of special scientific interest (see Chapter 11). It may be more effective for an environmental prosecutor to consider two other possible offences rather than one specific crime. For both offences it is necessary to show a mental element, even though the matter is one of strict liability. For example, if you are able to obtain evidence that a company was deliberately planning to make an unauthorised release of pollution into the environment, in breach of a licence, or that it had a policy of deliberately committing some offence – thinking it could get away with it – other offences could come into play.

The most serious offence for which a company may be convicted – applicable only for major environmental disasters involving loss of life – will be corporate manslaughter.

Another serious offence is that of conspiracy under the Criminal Law Act 1977, although proceedings for a summary offence may only be instigated with the permission of the Director of Public Prosecutions.

Under section 1 of the Criminal Law Act, if a person agrees with any other person or persons that a course of conduct shall be pursued which, if the agreement is carried out in accordance with their intentions, either

• will necessarily amount to or involve the commission of any offence or offences by one or more of the parties to the agreement, or

• would do so but for the existence of facts which render the commission of the offence or any of the offences impossible,

the person will be guilty of conspiracy to commit the offence in question.

This would be wide enough to catch any agreement to commit an offence under the EPA, such as a plan to carry on a process without seeking a licence, or a plan to release substances into a controlled water.

It has been held that in a case for a conspiracy to commit a public nuisance, it is not necessary to prove actual danger to the public but only potential danger (*R* v *Soul* (1980) 70 Cr App Rep 295). This is a particularly useful decision for environmental crimes where a charge might be met with a plea that the process would be harmless.

Following on from conspiracy is the Criminal Attempts Act 1981 which applies to any offence which may be triable on indictment – therefore covering the most serious types of pollution. However, it may be tried in the magistrates' court as an offence in its own right.

Section 1(1) of the Criminal Attempts Act 1981 provides that 'If, with intent to commit an offence to which the section applies, a person does an act which is more than merely preparatory to the commission of an offence, he is guilty of attempting to commit the offence.'

Under section 2, a person may be guilty of attempting to commit an offence to which this section applies, even though the facts are such that the commission of the offence is impossible. The effect of this is that if a person believes himself to be knowingly committing pollution offences, he could be convicted even though the substance turned out not to be a controlled one!

In practice, evidence would have to be particularly strong to ensure a conviction for an attempt. A potential offence might have to be followed almost to completion – with unacceptable accompanying risks. In cases involving HMIP, powers under section 17 and 18 (power to deal with causes of imminent danger or serious harm) or powers under section 24 of the EPA for action through the High Court might be more appropriate. Evidence to satisfy a charge under the Criminal Attempts Act 1981 might well be obtained in the process, though ultimately any proceedings will be at the discretion of the prosecutor.

Aiding and abetting

In addition to section 157, making managers and directors liable, section 158 makes others who, through their own acts or defaults, participate in offences, open to prosecution. This establishes a statutory equivalent to being prosecuted for aiding and abetting.

A person who aids, abets, counsels or procures an offence carried out by another person has the same criminal responsibility as the main party responsible, providing the person acts with knowledge that an offence is being committed (Accessories and Abettors Act 1861, section 8).

The person who acts as the aider or abettor can only be liable if actually present when the offence was committed. This can be done by deliberate neglect of duty by looking on where there is a responsibility to discharge a duty. An example could be aiding and abetting the operation of a prescribed process without an authorisation, or damage to a site of special scientific interest. Proof of knowledge, however, is an essential requirement and could be difficult to obtain. Section 158 would appear to impose an even wider liability, whereby knowledge may not be necessary – an extension of strict liability.

Interestingly, a person is not entitled to be acquitted merely because the offence by the principal has not been proved (*R* v *Humphreys and Turner* (1965) 3 All ER 339; *Morris* v *Tolman* [1923] 1 KB 166).

DEFENCE TACTICS

The defence may adopt various trial tactics. Where a defendant pleads not guilty and is represented, their advocate is likely to demand strict proof of the offence. As often as not the possible tactics adopted at trial will be determined by the likely financial implications, in court or out.

Companies are faced with large penalties – but the cost of legal proceedings may be exceeded in terms of adverse publicity and the damage done to the reputation of the company in the eyes of consumers. If the case against a company is overwhelming, the defendant may plead guilty hoping to attract a more lenient sentence. If convicted, the company will probably issue its own press releases and indulge in a public relations exercise to try and minimise damage.

At the end of the day the only way a company can win a trial is to avoid being charged in the first place.

Sentencing

The court may pass sentence immediately or defer sentence until a later date. The magistrates' court may also refer a case to the Crown Court for sentencing under section 38 of the Magistrates' Courts

Act 1980. Where the defendant is convicted, the court will consider information from both the prosecutor and the defence as to the penalty to be imposed. The rules of evidence do not generally apply in connection with this information, so any relevant matters contained in the registers could be introduced here. A plea of guilty generally attracts credit.

Speeches of mitigation

A speech of mitigation is likely to be delivered if the defendant is a company. The sensible company will probably seek legal representation to do this. Any false information could lead to prosecutions for perjury.

Powers of criminal courts

Fines or imprisonment may be awarded within the statutory maximum. Where a person is convicted under section 23 (1)(a) or section 23(1)(c) of the EPA, a court may order that the guilty person shall take such steps as to remedy such matters which appear to be within the power of the person. This power should be brought to the attention of the court. This could mean the clean up of a site, the installation of new equipment to prevent the repetition of the release or any other action to ensure that 'the cause of offence is remedied'. This can be in addition to or instead of any other punishment imposed by the court. In severe cases, the cost of remedial action to the accused could exceed the cost of the fine. It is also an extremely useful environmental remedy to try to ameliorate the damage.

Power to order offence to be remedied

Section 26 of the EPA gives what at first instance appears to be considerable power to a court to order remedial action following a pollution incident. This is in addition to or instead of imposing a punishment order. The order for remedial action is confined to 'any matters which appear to the court to be matters which it is in his power to remedy.'

Under section 26(2) the time fixed by order under subsection (1) above may be extended or further extended by order of the court on an application made before the end of the original fixed time or as extended under this subsection. Where a person is acting in accordance with such an order, they are not liable to further proceedings for an offence under section 23. This gives the convicted person or company an opportunity to remedy the state of affairs which led to the conviction in the first place.

The scope of an order is potentially wide although the number of orders may be limited. Firstly, once a pollution incident has occurred, remedial action may be impossible. Secondly, the court is confined to making orders over matters which appear to be within the power of the convicted person to remedy. This opens up the possibility that a financially pressed individual or company could plead poverty as a way of avoiding a potentially expensive operation. A further reason is that in some prosecutions, particularly private ones, the prosecutor may lack the scientific knowledge to recommend remedial steps that could be taken. Since it would be open for the convicted person to challenge such an order on scientific grounds, the court may be faced with considerable difficulties. Ultimately, few courts will be qualified to make decisions in isolation on what may require detailed scientific and ecological consideration. In future years these areas are likely to be fruitful sources of appeal.

Costs

The general rule is that costs will be paid by the loser at a trial. Magistrates also have the power under section 64 of the Magistrates' Courts Act 1980, to award costs. Guidance is contained in Practice Note (Criminal law: costs) [1989] 2 All ER 604. In certain circumstances the justices may refuse to award costs. For example, where there is ample evidence to support a conviction but the defendant is acquitted of a charge on a mere technicality, the court may exercise its discretion against awarding defence costs.

APPEALS

There is a right of appeal by the convicted person from the magistrates' court to the Crown Court on the basis of a conviction or sentence. If the person has pleaded guilty, the only basis of an appeal will be against the sentence.

Appeals on points of law are open to both the prosecutor and the defendant under section 111 of the Magistrates' Courts Act 1980. The proceedings may be questioned on the basis that they were (i) wrong in law or (ii) in excess of jurisdiction. The appeal moves to the Queen's Bench Division of the High Court and must be commenced within 21 days. This is done by writing to the justices concerned and asking them to 'state a case' on questions of law which are to be raised on the appeal. The appellant has to identify the areas of law which are to be challenged and the justices set out their reasons. Originally this was a right which could be exercised free of charge (although the justices could exercise a discretion not to state a case) but since 1992 a cost of £300 has been imposed by most courts, with the exception of defendants who are eligible for legal aid.

A third route of appeal is judicial review, where justices have failed to observe the rules of natural justice or have been in breach of principles of administrative law. This is considered in Chapter 5.

Fines and enforcement against companies

A company which fails to pay any fine or costs order whether on summary conviction or on indictment will face various sanctions. Distress may be levied against the company to seize goods and vehicles (persons levying distress against companies have greater powers of entry than against individuals). Where distress is unsuccessful, section 87A of the Magistrates' Courts Act 1980 enables a Clerk to the Court to take civil proceedings against a company in respect of any sum which remains unpaid.

An administration order may be sought against the company under the Insolvency Act 1986 or steps may even be taken under section 124 to petition the winding up of the company. [6]

NOTES

[1] For information on practice and procedure, the reader should refer to the Magistrates' Courts Act 1980, the Magistrates' Court Rules 1981 and *Stone's Justices' Manual.*
[2] For detailed consideration see Warren, M., 'Personal liability for environmental mistakes', *Environmental Information Bulletin,* 4 February 1992.

3 *R* v *Swansea Justices ex parte DPP* (1990); each case will depend on its facts.
4 Previously known as a 'McKenzie friend' after *McKenzie* v *McKenzie* (1971) but frowned upon later. See *R* v *Leicester Justices ex parte Barrow* (1991) for the latest exposition of this principle.
5 Oaths Act 1978.
6 See Lomax, Ian S. and Reynolds, S., (1988), *Enforcing in the Magistrates' Courts: A guide to enforcing money payments*, Fourmat Publishing.

Chapter 5

Judicial Review – Challenging the Decisions of Public Bodies

Potentially the most powerful legal weapon that an aggrieved citizen can use to tackle breaches of the law and administrative failure by public bodies is the remedy of judicial review. It is the great leveller which (in theory at least) puts individual citizens on the same footing as those in positions of power. It provides the method by which public bodies are made answerable at law to those over whom they exercise power.[1]

Many decisions made by public bodies which have environmental consequences, including public hearings and planning decisions, are open to challenge through the High Court by judicial review. A number of control and enforcement systems relating to preventing harm to the environment have a basic format under which there is a right of appeal to the Secretary of State, and often a right to a public hearing usually carried out under a system of rules.[2] For those dissatisfied with the outcome of a public inquiry or a decision by the Secretary of State a judicial review may be a route of legal challenge if the decision making body has acted unlawfully.

THE REASON FOR ADMINISTRATIVE LAW

Administrative law is used to make public servants and public bodies accountable, and there is a good reason for its existence. Behind such sterile and faceless terms and identities as 'local authority', 'planning authority', 'court' and 'Inspector', contrary to popular belief there are not some wise, elite members of humanity who have never been known to err, but instead ordinary human beings. Human beings are known to make mistakes and act in error and some are known to be biased, prejudiced, corrupt, sometimes power-crazed, immoral and careless. Wherever power is given, there is the possibility that it may be abused.

This is not to suggest that all errors in administration are based on ill-will or incompetence. Sometimes legal powers may be misinterpreted or innocently misconstrued, perhaps by a public body acting with what it sees as the best of intentions. Honest mistakes as to jurisdiction are probably more likely than dishonest ones, given the complexity of the law.

All these factors may result in those who are given powers under public law failing to perform their legal duties. Administrative law acts to remedy any such abuse of power. Indeed, English law goes further in requiring that not only is justice to be done but that it is *seen to be done* [3] since (with a few exceptions) courts are required to hold proceedings in public.

The second reason for having a body of administrative law is that errors made by governments and bureaucracies can have very significant effects, not least in the area of environmental protection. Once the system is set in motion on the basis of error, the results can be disastrous and a person's rights can be completely overridden. There is considerable scope for personal, social and environmental damage. Certainly many citizens who have been given an opportunity to express their views at some kind of public inquiry feel dissatisfied with the procedures and the outcome. They have no idea where to turn next. Judicial review is the next procedure.

JUDICIAL REVIEW DEFINED

Judicial review is the method by which the High Court controls and regulates decision making by what are called 'inferior tribunals'. Where the law gives power to a body or, in some instances, a public figure such as a Minister, to make decisions, judicial review allows the High Court to ensure that such decisions are made lawfully.

It is a complex area and its limits are far from clear.[4] Judicial reviews have been held to cover decisions by magistrates' courts, planning authorities, local authorities, ministers who have judicial functions in judging a particular matter such as a licence or a planning permission, and will cover a number of other public bodies whose decisions affect the public or are given certain duties at law.

There are a number of important provisos - not least that the remedy is discretionary. If the High Court doesn't believe an applicant genuinely deserves justice it will not grant a remedy. Obviously, this can be a subjective matter as to what amounts to justice! A successful judicial review gives rise to a number of important remedies (which the applicant has to select in advance). These include:

Certiorari – an order which effectively cancels a decision made by a tribunal (known as 'quashing' the decision). It is used where a decision is invalid in itself or has been made improperly. The High Court may, in certain cases, order that the matter is sent back to the tribunal to make the decision properly, according to the law.

Mandamus – this is an order to the public body or individual to carry out certain actions, in accordance with duties at law. If the public bodies fail to carry out their duties at law an order of mandamus compels them to do so. An example would be the duties placed on local authorities to collect waste and rubbish and to enforce clean air legislation.

Prohibition - this is an order to restrain tribunals or bodies acting in a certain way. For example, if an authorisation to discharge pollution was given which was contrary to law, an order of prohibition could be sought to stop the body repeating such an action in future.

In addition a High Court may also grant an injunction – an order to do or cease to do something until the judicial review is heard. This is not necessarily the same as mandamus, which also awards costs.

If a tribunal or body ignores an order from the High Court, such as an order of mandamus to carry out its functions, they will be guilty of contempt of court and may be committed to prison.

The uses of judicial review

In planning and environmental law, judicial review has largely been monopolised by developers and industrialists, particularly to challenge refusals by local authorities and government bodies to grant licences or planning permissions. In terms of its impact on the environment, judicial review must, thus, be understood to be a double-edged sword.

Judicial review has generally been little used by environmentalists, and often then with little success because of irregularities in the application or through the exercise of discretion by the courts.[5] Some academic commentators occasionally appear scornful of challenges made by the public (sometimes with justification), yet accept without reservation the right of industry and developers to challenge decisions, perhaps because these interests are in a better position to pay for the exercise of their rights. In fact, judicial review is available to every citizen, putting them on an almost equal footing with the most powerful public bodies or ministers of State.

However, it must be said that any person or group will be largely on their own in taking action to the High Court. Unlike breaches of criminal law there is not currently any State body or public defender that will take up actions on the part of the citizen. There does exist the office of Ombudsman in the form of Parliamentary Commissioners overseeing the civil service [6] and the local government Ombudsman discussed earlier. Both undertake thorough investigations, but any remedy or compensation they may consider should be paid is not enforceable.

In some cases the maladministration will be more suitable for action by the Ombudsman; in others it may be suggested that judicial review is sought by the person adversely affected. To make matters worse, where the government does occasionally intervene in judicial review cases, it is through a barrister appointed by the Treasury.[7] In doing so, it will be seeking to protect its interests and obtain a judgement favourable to its decision or view of matters, its policies or immediate concerns which will rarely coincide with the interests of the person or group seeking the review.

Where judicial review lies

Determining whether a matter is capable of being judicially reviewed by the High Court can be difficult. It is important to distinguish between private and public law, which may in some circumstances overlap. Judicial review will only be available if a public law interest can be identified. For example, if a local authority breaks a contract or commits a tort against one person, that person will have a right of private action against the authority for compensation. No one else may be involved and the rights of the parties are determined according to the contract which is made or the duty of care which is owed under the law of torts. Where such private cases go to another court on appeal, the appeal concerns whether the right or wrong decision has been made in the case.

In a judicial review case, the issue is not whether the decision is necessarily right or wrong but whether the public body which made the decision has been acting lawfully when making it. For example, if a public body makes contracts it has no right in law to make, this will be a matter for judicial review. If it could be shown that the public body had a policy of breaking all contracts, the policy itself could be open to judicial review by any person who had an interest.

In a case where a public body exercises a power or is under a duty which affects everybody – such as a duty to enforce clean air legislation – the way in which the authority exercises its power can be open to legal challenge. Where public bodies are exercising powers given to them by law or are given discretionary powers, these have to be used properly according to administrative law principles. Generally, judicial review can only be obtained where there is no other remedy available.

Is there a right to bring judicial review?

The courts operate to establish the rights of individuals at law in resolving real disputes, not to prove moral or political points.

Where public bodies exercise their powers correctly, behave fairly and observe the principles of administrative law outlined below, they will have acted lawfully under English law. The courts will not interfere with the decisions of those public bodies. So no matter how much a citizen dislikes a decision, providing it has been properly made there will be no right of challenge.

Types of decisions which cannot be challenged at all are Acts of Parliament (*British Railways Board* v *Pickin* (1974) AC 765). The courts refuse to question the validity and circumstances in which Acts of Parliament are made. Acts of Parliament can only be revoked or amended by other Parliaments and not by the courts. However, statutory instruments can sometimes be challenged where a minister has acted outside powers given by Parliament, on the basis that they are *ultra vires* (see below).

The individual's right to bring an action

In order to have a right to judicial review, a person must have '*locus standi*' – a right to bring the action. An underlying theme in judicial review decisions is the need to protect public authorities from what Lord Diplock referred to as 'groundless and unmeritous claims' in *O' Reilly* v *Mackman* (1982) and what Warner J called actions by 'cranks and busybodies' (*Barrs* v *Bethell* (1982) Ch 294).

To prevent falling into the 'crank' or 'busybody' category, a person must have some kind of right or interest in the proceedings which requires protection. When challenging a decision of a local authority, it is arguably open to any local taxpayer, and certainly any local councillor would have a right to commence an action. Anyone who has genuinely had his or her personal rights infringed by a public body acting in a public capacity may have *locus standi*.

Nature and conservation groups have found it more difficult than individuals to persuade the courts that they have the necessary *locus standi*. For example in *R* v *Poole BC ex parte Beebee* [1991] JPL 643, Schiemann J considered whether various environmental groups could challenge a decision to grant planning permission on a site of special scientific interest.[8] The World Wildlife Fund for Nature failed to have the necessary interest but the British Herpetological Society, who had been involved with the preservation of rare reptiles on the site, were held to have sufficient standing and could proceed by way of judicial review. Eventually the planning application was called in by the Secretary of State for the Environment and quashed so the development did not go ahead.

In *Turner* v *Secretary of State for the Environment* (1973) 72 LGR 380, an amenity society which was permitted by an inspector in a planning inquiry to make representations was held to have sufficient interest as a 'person aggrieved' to bring a challenge through the High Court. This case underlines the importance of becoming involved with inquiry procedures at the initial stages.

GROUNDS FOR JUDICIAL REVIEW

Over the years various concepts of English law have been refined to produce a body of rules and principles that are termed 'administrative law'. These principles establish whether a public body has acted lawfully and thus whether the right to a judicial review may arise. The principles may be outlined as follows.

Failure to comply with the rules of natural justice

In addition to providing legal rules, English law has a concept of fairness surrounding and underlying the decision making process – known as 'natural justice'.

In *General Medical Council* v *Spackman* (1943) AC 627, Lord Wright stated:

> 'If the principles of natural justice are violated in respect of any decision, it is indeed immaterial whether the same decision would have been arrived at in the absence of the departure from the essential principles of justice. The decision must be declared to be no decision.'

Where the rules of natural justice apply, judicial review will be available if the rules have not been observed. All the public hearings and proceedings involving environmental law issues must comply with natural justice. The rules can be broken down into basic categories:

(a) *The right to a fair hearing*

The right to a fair hearing provides that nobody is penalised by a decision affecting their rights or legitimate expectation unless they have been given notice of the case which is to be met or answered and a fair opportunity to put forward their case.

Where a person enjoys a right or benefit at law, it cannot normally be lost arbitrarily without an opportunity to put forward a case. For example, this rule applies in cases of compulsory purchase for new roads and development schemes.

In cases where a hearing takes place, the proceedings must be fair. A person is entitled to a fair hearing to make his/her case, to call witnesses and make submissions. A person should also have an opportunity to see and examine the evidence raised. If necessary, an adjournment of the hearing should be granted to prevent a party being taken by surprise. (*R* v *Thames Magistrates ex parte Polemis* (1974) 1 WLR 1371). All evidence must be put before the decision maker, such as an Inspector, whether on the initiative of the Inspector or as a result of personal expertise or consideration to the case. All letters and information must be made available – as is required by the regulations on applications.

Decision makers should take care not to give the appearance that they have given any special favour to one side or another. For example where a decision maker or decision making body is seen to be discussing a matter in private with one party but not the other before the decision is given, an appearance of bias or favour may arise. The presence of a non-member of a tribunal when a decision is being made will usually be sufficient to invalidate the decision at law.

Other cases which have been held in breach of the right to a fair hearing have been cases where the right to cross-examine a person at the hearing has been denied (although cross-examination may be disallowed if irrelevant).

There is a general right to legal representation (see *R* v *Assessment Committee of St Mary's Abbots, Kensington* (1891) 1. QB 378) or a friend to give assistance. The right to have a person, whether a lawyer or not, assisting a litigant was affirmed by the Court of Appeal in *R* v *Leicester Justices ex parte Barrow* (1991). Such an assistant may make notes, suggestions and give quiet assistance to the litigant in presenting his/her case. If a court of tribunal denies a litigant the help of an assistant, judicial review will be available for an order of *certiorari* to quash any decision that the court or tribunal has reached.

(b) *The rule against bias*

This falls into two categories of financial bias/pecuniary interest and other types of bias. Administrative law includes cases where there is both an actual bias, and situations where there is an appearance, risk or suspicion of bias – whether of not there actually was. That justice is being seen to be done is of vital importance in administrative law.

A person given the power to make a decision must not have any financial interest, no matter how small, in the outcome of the decision. No matter how unlikely it may be that financial interest could affect any decision, no person should act unless the interest is made clear to those affected and they waive their right to object, or the law empowers the person to adjudicate in any case regardless of the interest. Perhaps the clearest example of where the rule against bias will not apply is in cases in which it is the Secretary of State for Environment who may determine an appeal. The Secretary of State is, of course, a politician and may have all kinds of political, social and economic views and be suspected of all manner of biases. However, because the law empowers the minister to determine the matter, these considerations will be irrelevant and judicial review will not be available on the reasonable suspicion of the bias test. However, the Secretary of State will still be under a duty to observe the rules of natural justice on other grounds and to exercise any discretion correctly, so judicial review may be available on another basis.

If an adjudicator is likely to be biased she/he will be disqualified from acting. This covers family relationships, personal animosity and political bias. The test may be considered to be: 'Would a reasonable person think there was a real likelihood or real possibility of bias?' For example, members of local authorities are not allowed to sit as justices where the local authority is a party before the case.

For proceedings in magistrates' courts, the test has been taken to be 'Would a fair minded person sitting at the back of the court and knowing all the relevant facts suspect that a fair trial was not possible?' (*R v Liverpool Justices ex parte Topping* (1983) 1 All ER 490).

Ultra vires as a ground for judicial review

Public bodies have to operate within their legal powers and observe the limits which law places upon them in carrying out their functions. They are not allowed to exceed their powers. If a minister or a local authority exceeds its powers as given by statute, the action will be regarded as *ultra vires*, going beyond what it is legally entitled to do.

This can cover actions by a public body doing things it is not entitled to do such as granting a planning permission where an environmental impact assessment is required, and also failures to act. For example, if a body fails to maintain a register required by the EPA it will be failing in its legal duty. An order of mandamus may be sought to compel it to carry out its functions.

As with natural justice, *ultra vires* can be broken down into a number of areas:

(a) *Powers must be exercised in good faith*

Persons exercising statutory powers must act in good faith. They must not seek to achieve improper purposes or make decisions in bad faith or act corruptly. Where planning permissions or licences have been obtained by bribery or fraud, the decision will be open to judicial review. Statutory powers must be exercised fairly and with no ulterior or malicious motive.[9]

(b) *Failure to follow statutory requirements*

Certain procedural steps are often laid out in regulations before decisions can be made. Public bodies must follow the steps that they are required to at law before making the decision. Where the regulations state that a party 'shall' do certain acts, what is known as a 'mandatory requirement' – a compulsory step or requirement – arises. These steps must be followed. Any decision made without following the correct procedure is likely to be *ultra vires*.

Where time limits or publicity requirements are imposed, or an environmental impact assessment must be carried out, such steps must be observed. For example, if a decision granting development permission goes ahead without the steps being followed, the decision may be quashed. Similarly, failure to give an address where an appeal may be lodged will lead to a decision being quashed. See, for example, *Agricultural etc Training Board* v *Kent* (1970) 2 QB 18.

(c) *The use of discretionary powers*

Where an action set out by statute is preceded by the word 'may', the authority or decision-maker need not necessarily carry out the action it is empowered to take. The public body is given a discretion whether or not to act, but at law such discretion must be exercised reasonably.

One of the most important cases in administrative law is *Associated Provincial Picture Houses Ltd* v *Wednesbury Corporation* (1948) 1 KB 223 which gave rise to the famous 'Wednesbury principles'. In practice, this is one of the cases most frequently relied upon by individuals seeking to challenge administrative decisions.

If the court, on an application for judicial review, concludes that no person or body directing itself properly on the relevant law and acting reasonably could have reached the conclusion, it may grant the review and a remedy.

The implications of the *Wednesbury principles* are that any decision making body must consider only relevant matters and not consider irrelevant ones. A decision-making body must keep an open mind and have regard to any guidance and any codes of practice. It must not fetter its discretion by considering irrelevant matters and must not reach a decision which is absurd and which would lead a person to believe it could only have been reached in bad faith. Where a body is given a discretionary power it must exercise it – not delegate it to another person or body to make the decision instead. [10]

Providing that bodies act reasonably, observe the rights of natural justice and operate their policies within the law, they have nothing to fear from judicial review. It is only the abuse of power, not its lawful exercise, which is challengeable in the courts. As a result, actions for review commenced upon political or moral grounds or merely from a difference of opinion will have no standing in law.

ENVIRONMENTAL LAW DECISIONS AND JUDICIAL REVIEW

It is impossible to produce a complete list of decisions by ministers, public bodies and public officials which are amenable to judicial review, not least because it is a developing area of the law and because the area of environmental law itself grows wider each year. However, some of the following matters are likely to arise in practice over the next few years

Decisions suitable for review are likely to include those made in relation to the release of environmental information, the granting of licences and the decisions made by the Secretary of State and inspectors at public hearings and inquiries. In cases concerning the grant or refusal of licences for the IPC or APC, appeals are likely to be brought, in the early stages at least, by industrial interests. Decisions involving environmental matters are likely to become increasingly common as the courts set the legal parameters which apply to authorisations. The attitude of the courts is likely to play a major part in both the attitude of enforcing authorities and the applications made by the operators of prescribed processes.

The decision to adjourn a hearing or inquiry is one which will apply generally to all types of proceedings amenable to judicial review if exercised unreasonably.

Public inquiries over planning matters are likely to remain a fertile area for legal challenges but it should be noted that in a number of areas the time limit to appeal is likely to be limited to six weeks and by a separate procedure under RSC Order 94 (see Chapter 7).

Decisions by public bodies to exclude certain evidence from consideration may become fruitful grounds for review on the *Wednesbury principles*. With more environmental data becoming available to the citizen (see Chapter 2), the public are in a better position to scrutinise decisions by public bodies on environmental matters and examine if relevant facts have been considered. At public inquiries all relevant information put forward by citizens should be considered, and the question of 'what is relevant environmental information?' is likely to be one which faces the courts in the next few years.

Problems have already arisen as to what extent government policy in different areas may legitimately be introduced. In *Bushell* v *Secretary of State* (1981) AC 75, the House of Lords held that objectors at a public inquiry had no right to cross-examine witnesses from the government on the methods of traffic forecasting. Guidance as to when aspects of government policy could be considered may be drawn from *R v Secretary of State for Transport ex parte Gwent County Council* (1986) 2 All ER 18 (an inquiry of road tolls). An inspector acting on behalf of the Secretary of State for Transport rejected objections based upon the principle of tolls.

Giving judgement, Mr Justice Webster stated that a Secretary of State could reject certain matters being raised at an inquiry, but not merely because it was stated on his behalf to be policy. A minister (or an inspector acting on his or her behalf) could reject a matter where investigation would not be of assistance in exercising a particular power without considerable disruption or inconvenience amounting to a reversal of the existing policy or a major difficulty in investigating the matters. However, where a policy was directly relevant to an issue before an inquiry and there was not a risk of considerable disruption the inquiry could be opened up to policy matters.

Attempts to coerce or prevent witnesses giving evidence at public inquiries which materially affect proceedings may lead to a decision being quashed (although a party can legitimately trade the right to make objections). Witnesses at inquiries also have a wider protection granted by the Witnesses (Public Inquiries) Protection Act 1892, which protects witnesses appearing before any Royal Commission, Parliamentary Committee or other public inquiry. The term 'public inquiry' is wide enough to cover any inquiry for planning or a hearing concerning an authorisation for IPC or APC. Any person who threatens, or in any way punishes, damnifies or injures a witness is liable to a fine of up to £400 or three months in prison. Prosecution is through the magistrates' court. Examples might be a case where a developer or a government department tried to apply improper pressure on a witness from giving evidence, or a threat of job loss or disciplinary proceedings by an employer against an employee who gives evidence at an inquiry.

Initial considerations to judicial review

Before embarking on judicial review, serious consideration should be given to whether the case is worth pursuing. It should be remembered that at all times the decision is discretionary and the High Court may refrain from giving a remedy where the matter is a trivial one or the applicant is not pursuing a serious claim. While authorities may bend the law, it is possible for an applicant to also distort an issue and try and imagine that the law should be in his or her favour. It is not perhaps a question of what seems reasonable only to an applicant but what also seems reasonable to an outside observer, such as a court, as the principles of judicial review will be applied to what is considered reasonable in law. Legal opinion and advice is recommended before pursuing a claim. Serious consideration should also be given to *locus standi*.

Secondly, before embarking on judicial review, the applicant must be clear as to the exact nature of the remedy which would be most appropriate and the precise administrative failure complained of. In some cases, these principles will overlap – bad decisions may contain a number of grounds for review.

HOW TO COMMENCE JUDICIAL REVIEW

The decision to commence judicial review will depend on an initial decision: does it involve a matter at law which is suitable for judicial review? If there is some other right of appeal or some other legal remedy which could be pursued, then the matter will be unsuitable for judicial review.

Legal aid is available for some judicial review proceedings, but relatively few people will currently be eligible without some kind of contribution. The rules of legal aid may also have the curious effect of reducing the numbers of people who have *locus standi*. As assets are taken into consideration, anyone who owns property may be unable to obtain legal aid. Since in many cases *locus standi* will depend on rights and interests arising from property, many people will simply be unable to sustain a claim unless directly affected or where rules of natural justice have been breached.

It should be noted that the Crown Office does not deal with inquiries over legal aid; these have to be dealt with locally. In any matter involving judicial review, the applicant should consult the current Order 53 of the Rules of the Supreme Court, contained in the current edition of the *White Book*.

Time limits

Applications for judicial review must be made speedily and, in any event, within three months of the decision or action involved. The time limits can be extended in certain circumstances, but this is rare. In certain planning cases, the time limit is limited to six weeks (see Chapter 7 on Planning).

Even if the applicant has a good case, the application for judicial review will be dismissed if there has been a delay of more than three months. Many would-be litigants acting without legal advice or assistance pursue cases for years in ignorance of this rule. So if the events you might wish to take action over occurred more than three months ago from reading this, don't bother applying !

Even where a person does apply in the three month period, the court may still dismiss the application for not having been brought quickly enough, as the remedy is always discretionary. In *R* v *Swale BC ex parte RSPB* [1991] JPL 39, the Royal Society for the Protection of

Birds sought to judicially review a planning decision. In the decision the court held that the short delay had been unacceptable and that the application could not proceed. The court may also consider administrative inconvenience. If a case is likely to cause a great amount of trouble for administrative bodies, the remedy may be restricted in part, or completely.

The two-stage process

Applying for judicial review is a two-stage process. The first stage is to obtain leave for judicial review which is a clearing system – a way of weeding out the unmeritorious or 'flakey' cases.

If the court thinks that a serious matter is revealed by an initial examination of the claim it will then be listed for a judicial review. It is this application for leave which must be commenced within three months.

Applying for leave

An application for leave is made on Form 86A obtainable from the Crown Office of the High Court. The Crown Office usually supplies some helpful guidance notes to applicants and some queries may be answered over the telephone. Regard should also be had to the directions and guidance contained for Order 53 in the current edition of the *White Book*. The applicant fills in the name and address and details of the case. The applicant must give the details of the decision or order concerned, eg 'the decision by the Secretary of State for the Environment to grant of an authorisation to carry out a prescribed process, pursuant to Applications, Appeals, and Registers Regulations S.I. 507 on (date)' or 'Refusal to supply environmental information on (date) in accordance with the regulations S.I. requested on (date)' or 'Decision to deny cross-examination by an inspector' etc .

The remedy sought also has to be set out in the section 'relief sought'. Depending on the nature of the case, one or more remedies may be appropriate. If there is a risk of harm or damage arising before the appeal is determined (it could take some time) the applicant should seek 'an order to restrain [insert the potential source of the harm]'.

It is worth noting that where similar proceedings may be going on, perhaps in different parts of the country, it is permissible to ask for an adjournment pending the decision of the High Court. It is possible to apply for more than one prerogative remedy. For example, suppose a person seeks some environmental information from a public body which holds it. In reply, the public body refuses to supply the information and informs the applicant that it will neither supply that nor any similar information to the applicant in the future.

Aggrieved by the decision, the applicant might seek judicial review of the refusal to supply the information. The applicant would seek an order for mandamus to supply the information requested. This would obtain the information specifically requested, but what if the applicant wants to obtain information in the future? If the public body has a policy of unlawfully refusing to supply requested environmental information, the one-off remedy of *certiorari* will obviously be inadequate if the applicant has to start fresh proceedings each time at the High Court. In such a case an order of prohibition may also be sought to prevent any future repetition. Where there is more than one remedy sought, the following phrase should be added: 'To join with the motion for *certiorari* an order for prohibition'.

In the section covering 'grounds of the appeal' on the form, one may state the general principle involved and any authorities at law which support the argument. This is done by citing the point of law and the name and reference number of the cases illustrating the point, eg 'No reasonable authority properly instructing itself and given all the circumstances could have reached such a decision at law. See *Associated Provincial Picture Houses* v *Wednesbury Corporation* (1948) 1 KB 223'. Having a number of authorities cited will generally weigh in favour of leave being granted as it will reveal a serious case.

EVIDENCE

There is no evidence in the general sense as in a prosecution in a criminal case or a claim in civil law. The main argument is an argument at law, eg did the authority have the power in law to make a particular order or was this an acceptable use of discretion?

Instead, such evidence as there is comes in two forms: affidavit evidence giving an account of the circumstances which led to the decision and on what basis the decision was made or appears to have been made; and copies of relevant documents known as 'exhibits'.

Affidavits are little 'books' setting out the statement of witnesses on oath. The affidavits must give sufficient information as to the identity of the applicant and their background and the events which have led to the application. The applicant must truthfully give the facts. If the applicant does not act in good faith or gives false information, the remedy may be denied. Affidavits must comply with the rules set out in Order 41 of the rules of the Supreme Court.

All documents have to be written in the form prescribed in the examples at the back of the *White Book*. They should carry on the front page wording which identifies the nature of the proceeding, the traditional formula being 'In the matter of...', eg 'In the matter of an application for judicial review of the decision of... etc'.

Because of the limited evidence available on a judicial review, affidavits should be as comprehensive and detailed as possible – providing the information is relevant! The court will not be interested in extraneous issues, just the substantive legal issues. Where complexity demands it, a *dramatis personae* should be added listing all the persons named in the affidavit.

The respondents will also be given an opportunity to submit their own affidavits, although on occasions they may omit to supply any at all.

A specimen affidavit is produced at Appendix 1. All other papers must have the correct heading and be correctly numbered at the top. Where an order of *certiorari* is sought, the applicant must lodge with the Crown Office a copy of any order, record or other relevant document.

PROCEDURE

Once the form has been drawn up and the affidavits completed, the affidavits must be sworn. This can be done at a solicitor's office or at a commissioner for oaths or in the High Court itself. A fee of £3.50 is currently charged. The papers should be taken to the fees office at the Court and a £10.00 fee paid. The document is then stamped and lodged in court. There are then two possible routes.

In a paper application, the papers are placed before a single judge for consideration. Since the application will depend on consideration of the documents, it is necessary to ensure the papers are clear and readily understandable.

If the judge takes the view that leave should be granted, the papers are endorsed with any comments and a copy of the direction is sent to the applicant. An oral hearing will only be granted if it is requested with the preliminary application. These are normally done by barristers, although an applicant can appear in person. The hearing is normally held in private, although in certain cases it may take place in open court.

It should be remembered that the condition of leave acts as a filter. If the judge considers that a serious issue is revealed, leave will be granted and the application may proceed. However, if the judge considers that the case is without merit, the application will be refused. As with most situations in English law, a right of appeal lies to a single judge or a divisional court. The refusal of leave may be overturned, sometimes with a comment from the court that the parties should try and settle their dispute without taking proceedings further. If the appeal is lost there is a further right to take the matter to the Court of Appeal within seven days. If this does not succeed there is no further right of appeal.

The applicant is then required to serve 'notice of motion' – that is, notice that the application for judicial review is being made. This is done by simply providing a copy of the papers. This has to be done within 14 days of receiving notice of the grant of leave by the judge and is a very strict requirement. A copy should be sent or delivered to the person or body against whom the appeal is being lodged, and any other party who may have been involved in the decision.

For example, in an appeal arising from a public inquiry over a planning matter, judicial review may be made of the Secretary of State (acting through the Inspector), and a copy of the papers should also be served on the developer. In an appeal arising from a hearing over an IPC consent, papers should be served upon the Secretary of State, the enforcing authority and the operator of the prescribed process.

An affidavit of service then has to be drawn up to verify that the papers have been delivered to the respondent and any other party which may be affected by the judicial review. The affidavit, stating the relevant name and address, is then handed in with a copy of the completed application. A sum of £60.00 has to be paid at the High Court fees office and the completed papers are lodged at the Crown Office.

A period then follows in which affidavits may be put forward by the respondent and any other party involved. In some cases there will be no representations – in others the respondent may use a separate procedure to dismiss the judicial review. If the respondent simply supplies affidavits, as happens in most cases, these must be lodged in the High Court within 56 days of service. Occasionally an application may be made to submit an affidavit outside this period.

Listing

The documents then go onto what is known as the 'B' list as cases ready to be heard. The Crown Office will contact the applicant or his/her solicitors when the case is due to be placed on the list. When the case has moved to the top of List B, the Crown Office will contact the applicant or his/her solicitor to confirm whether the case is still going ahead or not. The Crown Office will also request an estimate of how long the hearing is likely to take. Naturally, this depends on the complexity of the legal issue involved.

There can sometimes be a considerable wait before the case actually goes to a hearing. This is due to the growth in judicial review applications. Once listed, an approximate date set for the hearing can usually be obtained from the Crown Office Listing Department. In practice, the effect of delay may have a major impact on the issues raised in the case, particularly with planning cases.

As a date comes nearer, the application goes on to the warned list. An applicant should also be aware that the High Court may vary the time and date set for the hearing with little notice.

Lodging of bundles

Preferably at least 14 days before the set date, but a minimum of one working day before the hearing, a bundle of papers should be compiled for the consideration of the court. This must contain:

• a paginated and indexed bundle of documents – basically the judicial review papers;

- a list of issues to be considered – sometimes called the skeleton argument;
- a list of authorities at law, with page references;
- a chronology, cross-referenced to the bundle.

The list of cases should cover reported cases which illustrate the legal principle or point of law involved. Bundles must comply with Practice Direction (Evidence: Documents) [1983] 3 All ER 33.

Fresh evidence

Fresh evidence may sometimes be admitted in order that the Court can consider the material before the minister or tribunal. Other evidence that may be received includes that relating to the jurisdiction of the body or where fraud or misconduct are suspected. Where evidence may have been suppressed, the Court may consider further evidence (*R* v *Secretary of State for the Environment ex parte Powis* [1981] 1 WLR 581 1 All ER 788 CA).

The hearing

A litigant in person or their barrister may appear at the hearing, as may the respondent, whether represented or not. The hearing will take place in open court, before one or more judges. Providing an applicant is reasonable and polite, the court will usually seek to be as fair as possible to an unrepresented litigant. The applicant is entitled to have a person to assist him/her and the judge may put questions to the applicant and the respondent to clarify the issues.

Persons who have not been served with papers may appear at the discretion of the Court, but only if the Court considers that the application comes from a 'a proper person'. In some cases, a lawyer appointed by the Treasury Solicitor may appear.

Depending on the complexity of the issue, the court may give judgement on the day of the hearing, or reserve judgement to be given on another date. Where an order of *certiorari* is sought to quash the decision, the court has the additional power to remit the matter back to the public body, Court or minister concerned with a direction of what should be done.

Costs

Costs are at the discretion of the Court. The loser in a contested case could expect to pay several thousand pounds at least. Even if a citizen succeeds, it may be difficult to obtain costs against the public body, even if they are the applicant, since the decision to award costs is discretionary. Much will depend on the view the High Court or the single judge takes of the conduct of the parties. For example, costs will only be awarded against Magistrates only where they have acted perversely, oppressively or in bad faith. (R v *York Justices ex parte Famery* (1988) 153 JP 257). However, if an alternative respondent is available, such as a local authority, the court may award costs against one respondent but not another.

Further appeals

If a person loses at judicial review it is possible to appeal to the Court of Appeal. If the applicant fails here, an appeal can only go to the House of Lords with the leave of the Court of Appeal if a major point of law is involved.

NOTES

[1] See Craig, P. P., (1989), *Administrative Law*, Sweet & Maxwell; also Wade, J., (1988), *Administrative Law*, Butterworths.
[2] For example Town and Country Planning Act 1990; Part I Environmental Protection Act 1990.
[3] R v *Sussex Justices ex parte McCarthy* (1924) 1 KB 256 at 259 per Lord Hewart C J, who said that it was 'of fundamental importance that justice should not only be done, but should manifestly and undoubtedly be seen to be done'.
[4] Wade, op. cit.
[5] Hough, B., (1992), 'Standing in Planning Permission Appeals' in *Journal of Planning Law*.
[6] Parliamentary Commission Act 1967; Part II Local Government Act 1984.
[7] Or in some cases the Attorney General. See *Stone's Justices' Manual*, vol. 1.
[8] See Chapter 11.
[9] *Asher* v *Secretary of State for the Environment* (1974) Ch 208.
[10] Known as the *Delegatus non potest delegare* principle.

Chapter 6

Civil and Private Law

Apart from the punitive and preventative sanctions of criminal law, civil legal rights may also be available to a citizen concerned with protecting the environment. These rights attach to a particular person, whether human or 'legal' persons such as companies, and will vary considerably from person to person. In order to take action under the civil law, a person must show that his or her private rights *as they stand at law* have been harmed or prejudicially affected.

While individual citizens may instigate private prosecutions for general breaches of the criminal law and challenge public bodies by way of judicial review, a private citizen can only use the civil law if their own personal and private rights are infringed. Essentially a citizen must show that a legal right particular to him or herself has been affected (the right to bring civil actions is narrower than the right to bring judicial review proceedings described in Chapter 5). With few exceptions, other citizens are in the position of bystanders who cannot become involved – hence the 'private' character of civil actions.

The civil law applies to both the physical person of a citizen and any property owned by the citizen. Where a person's health or property are threatened or harmed, the civil law gives various means of redress, based upon the right to bring an action in the courts. This puts major limitations on the scope of the civil law as a means of protecting the environment. This is because the environment or the life forms which fill it are not recognised categories that are entitled to legal protection under civil law, unless they happen to be owned by an individual or land-owning organisation (whether statutory agencies such as the Countryside Councils or conservation groups). Since no one actually owns the atmosphere or the oceans and many other features of the natural environment, no one can commence legal action, so it has been left to the State to create protection.

Historically, many matters which are now covered by the criminal law would once only have been actionable as civil wrongs. While certain common rights were accepted in the Middle Ages, it was the Industrial Revolution which provoked these developments in the criminal law to restrain harm caused by industrial pollution which civil law could not effectively deal with, either conceptually or in practice. [1]

WAYS IN WHICH THE CIVIL LAW CAN BE USED

There are a number of ways in which the individual citizen can use law and private remedies. The aim of a civil case is not to punish the party responsible (though costs can be punitive) but to provide compensation for any loss or injury. In addition, certain civil orders may be obtained to prevent injury.

- Claims for compensation for personal injury or other harm caused by pollution under the law of torts (see below).

- To bring injunctions to prevent or abate harm.

- To restrain statutory nuisances (now largely covered by criminal law).

- Rights which can be used in negotiation with planning authorities, developers or as a basis for *locus standi* for judicial review proceedings.

Civil law – problems with claims

Civil actions are limited by the problems that beset any individual litigant – costs, complexity and delay. To find oneself becoming involved in a civil case for compensation is likely to mean that other methods of legal regulation through authorisation in the planning system and administrative law will all have failed.

Tortious claims

The great majority of civil claims over environmental action brought by ordinary citizens will be claims arising in tort. Torts are harms which one person may cause to another and which are not caught by the provisions of the criminal law (usually because of lack of intention). Civil law gives rights to citizens to seek redress for actual harm to themselves or their property, and comes down to proving that a party has been at fault. Actions in tort may range from claims for death caused by exposure to radiation, such as those commenced in November 1992 against the Nuclear Industry in Britain,[2] to actions for noise pollution caused by neighbours. Most claims in tort are for financial compensation in the form of damages. The purpose of damages awarded in tort is to put the injured person or party back into the position which would have been enjoyed had the harm never been suffered (so far as money is able to).

Types of tort

Most tortious claims arise in negligence. In law negligence arises from breach of a duty of care imposed on persons to avoid harming others through carelessness. Deliberate attempts to cause harm can also be a breach of this duty. If any injury or harm can be shown to be the result of negligence by a party, an action in tort will lie against the party responsible. [3]

Other torts include trespass and nuisance. Trespass is the unlawful interference with a person or their property such as a deposit of waste without permission on private land. Nuisance covers activities which repeatedly disturb an individual and the quiet enjoyment or exercise of their legal rights. Examples of nuisance include persistent noise or frequent releases of unpleasant fumes from an industrial plant which cause discomfort to the residents of nearby dwellings. For most nuisances the criminal law may now provide a more satisfactory remedy for a private individual in proceedings for statutory nuisances (see below).

In a claim for tort, the person bringing the case (known as the plaintiff) may seek compensation for all loss and damage which has arisen from the tort. The defendant responsible for the tort must 'take the plaintiff as he finds him' – special features which make a plaintiff more susceptible to harm than the average person are not relevant and cannot provide a defence. [4]

The rule in Rylands v Fletcher

In examining possible tortious claims, some mention must be made of *Rylands* v *Fletcher* (1865) 3 H&C 774, which could potentially cover many pollution cases had it not been limited by a series of court judgements over the years. In *Rylands* v *Fletcher,* Lord Cairns (referring to a person 'whose habitation is made unhealthy by the fumes of his neighbour's alkali works' as an example) laid down the rule that:

> 'Where a neighbour has brought something on to his own property which was not naturally there, harmless to others so long as it remains confined to his own property but which he knows will be mischievous if it gets on to his neighbour's, he should be obliged to make good the damage.'

Where the principle in *Rylands* v *Fletcher* applies, the matter is one of strict liability and the defendant will be liable simply because there has been an escape of a pollutant.

Over the years this strict liability principle in *Rylands* v *Fletcher* has been severely curtailed by a series of judgements which distinguished what was a non-natural use of the land, to such an extent that it could be called the 'non-natural user defence'. Effectively the rule was hedged with so many restrictions that it was no longer worth attempting. Instead, a plaintiff had to show that the actions of a defendant had been negligent in some way and the mere fact a substance had been released was not sufficient to pursue a claim.

However, a recent decision of the Court of Appeal in November 1992 has re-opened the thorny issue of liability. In *Cambridge Water Company* v *Eastern Counties Leather,* (1992) *(The Times,* 29 December), the defendant company were held liable for pollution of ground water which occurred years earlier. This reversed the decision of the judge at the initial trial who held that the non-natural user defence was applicable. But on appeal, the Court of Appeal held that liability could be established on the basis of a claim of nuisance on the principle of *Ballard* v *Tomlinson* (1866) 29 ChD which established strict liability for pollution percolating ground waters. So the principle of *Rylands* v *Fletcher* may yet have new life in it – the issue has yet to be finally settled. Certainly, the judgement, if not altered on a future appeal, will have serious implications for insurers and future litigation and claims brought against polluters.

In a number of cases, Acts of Parliament have imposed civil liability on the oil, nuclear and waste industries.[5]

COMMENCING A CIVIL ACTION

Time limits

If a right to bring an action can be established, the person or party bringing the case has certain time limits in which to commence action. Most actions will be subject to the Statute of Limitations 1980. This places a three year limit on a claim for personal injury, trespass and nuisance from the date the harm occurs or is discovered.

In the *Cambridge Water* case, the limitation periods will not have applied – they will start to run from the point when the damage became apparent and there was a risk of harm and injury to other persons.

Burden of proof

As with criminal cases, the question of evidence is likely to be the determining factor in the success or otherwise of any court case and whether it is worth commencing proceedings in the first place. In a civil case the standard of proof is lower than with a criminal one, being on the balance of probabilities (ie it is more likely than not that the defendant is liable). As a result far more relaxed – but nonetheless complicated – rules of evidence operate, allowing the admission of evidence which would be excluded as hearsay in a criminal case.[6] However, in many environmental cases a tremendous amount of evidence will have to be examined. Proving liability – that a party has been responsible for causing harm – can still be difficult in an environment containing a wide range of potentially harmful substances, from a variety of diverse sources. In many environmental cases a tremendous amount of evidence will have to be examined. Cases involving the releases of radioactivity or toxic substances may be linked with birth defects or cancer appearing many months or years later. To show a causative link to a potentially harmful process and the resultant harm may be particularly difficult and require a great deal of expert scientific and medical evidence. For a plaintiff this can be difficult, not least because of the paucity of independent forensic laboratories. However, records opened up for inspection by the Access to Environmental Information Regulations may be of assistance in future.

Tactical matters

The complexities of civil litigation give rise to tactical considerations in bringing a case, which will not be appreciated by non-lawyers or by other lawyers who do not specialise in the subject. Proceedings can drag on for years. Finally, there is nearly always an element of risk in any civil claim – all proceedings are to an extent a gamble. Tactics adopted by companies will be affected by many matters, not least publicity.

CIVIL AND CRIMINAL PROCEEDINGS

Often rights to bring actions in tort will overlap with criminal law – many environmental 'torts' are likely to include a breach of the criminal law either in terms of the IPC or offences in connection with waste. With regard to the latter, in section 73 of the EPA liability is specifically imposed in civil law for harm arising from offences concerning waste.

There is no right to silence in civil proceedings except where to answer a question would expose a person to the risk of a criminal penalty (see *AT & T Istel Ltd* v *Tully* (1992) NLJ 13 July). This could be an extremely important tactical consideration as to when to launch a civil case, especially for those with obligations under the EPA which, as we have seen, may impose substantial criminal liability, not only for companies but also for managers and employees. This could pose some problems unless the company or individual concerned has already been convicted or acquitted (although an acquittal does not prevent a civil action) or is no longer at risk of criminal proceedings. As a convicted or acquitted person will no longer be at a risk it may be worth delaying a civil claim until the completion of criminal proceedings. Where a conviction is subject to an appeal, any civil proceedings should be adjourned if the conviction is relevant evidence (*Re Raphael, Raphael* v *d'Antin* (1973) 3 All ER 19).

Procedure for civil claims

Detailed guides for civil procedure in environmental cases are likely to emerge in the next few years. The following is no more than the barest skeleton outline to proceedings in civil law, and interested readers are referred to standard text books on civil procedure (see Appendix). Proceedings take place within the framework of the Orders and Rules set down in the *White Book* and the *Green Book*.[7]

Negotiations and out of court settlements

All kinds of factors can bring a civil action to a halt, such as a death or disappearance of one of the parties or bankruptcy of the defendant. It is not worth suing a party who has no money, although emerging EC proposals for lender liability covering banks and lending institutions mean that an alternative defendant may be available where this occurs. Because of such factors many civil actions are settled out of court. Indeed, the long drawn out nature of civil proceedings often encourages the settlement of private disputes.

Where a civil claim arises, most people affected will consult solicitors and there will be an attempt to negotiate with insurers. This is done by way of 'without prejudice' correspondence, so that the letters cannot be referred to in any subsequent litigation. Attempts will be to try and achieve a settlement to the claim without court proceedings. Frequently negotiations will continue while a case goes through the courts; it is possible to settle a claim at almost any point up until the judgement in the case. How a large company reacts to a claim and decides whether to settle may be influenced by all kinds of factors.

Generally, English law is against group actions involving multiple plaintiffs, although both the county court and High Court will allow a claimant to join an action in certain cases, where the same matters arise from the same circumstances or event (see RSC Order 15 and County Court Rule 5).

At this early stage, even before proceedings are commenced, certain orders such as RSC Order 24 etc may be used to obtain evidence such as medical records, a process that is known as 'pre-trial discovery'. Not all forms of evidence may be obtained by these orders; some are subject to public policy and legal privilege. Where there is a danger that evidence may be concealed or destroyed, other orders may be granted to enable a plaintiff to ensure this does not happen. These rights may only be exercised for the purposes of a civil case by or on behalf of the person bringing the action. The

Access to Medical Reports Act 1968 may be of assistance (allowing a person to see their own medical records). Other information may be acquired from any inquest which may have been held in the case of fatal accidents.

In cases involving personal injury or physical harm, a medical report is an essential prerequisite to bringing any claim. The right to bring an action may not be confined to persons who were born at the time of the pollution incident – actions may be sustained on behalf of those who have suffered genetic damage or who have been harmed while in the womb. Thus civil liability can be owed to a child born disabled (under the Congenital Disabilities (Civil Liability) Act 1976).

Size of the claim

Legal proceedings will be commenced through the county court where the claim is £50,000 or below; where the claim exceeds £50,000 the case will be heard in the High Court. Proceedings in both courts bear certain similarities and in the event that county court practice proves insufficient, the High Court practice will be adopted. For example, the practice under Order 38 of the RSC for expert evidence is adopted in the county court.

A recent case, brought for pollution to water supplies, suggests that claims for punitive damages or exemplary damages (where the court exercises the opportunity to show its dislike of the defendant's behaviour) are unlikely to succeed. This may change, however, as the damage to the environment becomes increasingly unacceptable.

However, in a recent decision in *Gibbons* v *South West Water Services Ltd* (1992) (*The Independent*, 18 November), it was held that punitive damages and exemplary damages may not be awarded. Such damages might be awarded where a court concludes that an example should be made of the person who caused the harm or where profit was made from causing the harm. Effectively, the current position is that the court will only award such damages if the grounds of the claim existed in law before 1964, the year in which this point of law was settled in a case called *Rookes* v *Barnard*.

However, as this is currently a decision on a point of law before final judgement, a future Court of Appeal may not consider itself bound to follow this decision in the future.

Form of proceedings

In the county court most types of cases are covered by a standard form which must be completed by the party starting the action. In the High Court most proceedings will be initiated by a document known as a writ. These documents are endorsed by the court and will be sent to the defendant to give notice that the case has been commenced. The defendant is required to acknowledge service – a process of contacting the court if there is an intention to defend the action. Usually included with the writ or form will be a statement of claim setting out details of the claims being brought by the plaintiff. In the county court, a similar document known as 'particulars of claim' must be served at the same time as proceedings are started.

Where a defendant fails to acknowledge service within 14 days, the plaintiff may claim judgement in default for simply failing to respond. It is possible to obtain judgement without the need to prove the case. Where damages are to be assessed, a date will be fixed to work out the size of the damages. However, it would be very rare for this to happen in a pollution case, and any default judgement is likely to be set aside on application by the defendant.

If the defendant gives notice of an intention to defend and/or submits a defence (which most alleged polluters are likely to do) a further claim for a quick judgement may be made. This procedure relies on there being no basis to the defence. However, the chances of this succeeding are unlikely as the defendant merely has to show a triable issue. In most cases involving environmental liability this will be easy to show, so applications for a summary judgement will be rare.

Following through, the parties may then exchange detailed lists of allegations, and defences. These documents are known as pleadings and each side may seek further information from the other – known as obtaining further and better particulars. Given the complexities and scientific aspects of some environmental cases this stage could take some time. Pleadings may also be amended.

Where a defendant maintains that a third party is responsible for the harm and seeks to attribute liability to that party – for example a waste carrier who is being sued for an unlawful deposit may seek to sue a waste producer in turn – what are termed 'third party proceedings' may be issued, with an indemnity or a contribution being sought from the third party.

Discovery of documents and expert evidence

The parties may then exchange documents with which they seek to prove certain matters – a stage known as discovery of documents. This saves time at the actual trial. Discovery may sometimes be ordered by the Court against non-parties, for use at trial, through subpoenas. Expert evidence is likely to be of great importance in many claims related to environmental law. Expert reports are among the documents which must be produced at this stage in an action, unless special reasons apply. Expert reports include both medical and other reports which either party seeks to produce at trial. Under RSC Order 38 no such evidence may be admitted at trial unless the documents are released at this stage or an order is made concerning the production of evidence by the Court. Under Order 38 r 38, the Court may direct that there be a meeting 'without prejudice' of such experts within such periods after the disclosure of their reports as the Court may specify. The purpose of such a meeting is to identify those parts of evidence which are at issue. If such a meeting is ordered, the experts may produce a joint statement indicating those parts of their evidence on which they agree and those on which they do not.

Expert evidence must normally be released within ten weeks of the close of pleadings unless the court directs otherwise. In some cases the court may admit the report rather than have the expert witness attend the trial.

Evidence in civil cases

Section 4 of the Civil Evidence Act 1968 provides that a statement contained in a record compiled by an official acting under a duty to collect information from persons who had or may reasonably be supposed to have had personal knowledge of the relevant facts, may be used as evidence. This would include information contained in the public registers held by HMIP, the National Rivers Authority, Waste Regulation and Hazardous Substances Authorities (see Chapter 10). The concept of a person acting under a duty is taken by section 4(3) to include any person acting in the course of any trade, business, profession or other occupation in which he is engaged or employed or for the purposes of any paid or unpaid office held by him. This widens the definition to include any environmental information held in a record by a public body which has been supplied in accordance with section 4 and could also extend to records of statements collected by voluntary organisations and environmental groups.

Any party wishing to submit such a statement is expected to comply with the notice requirements of RSC Order 38 and supply a copy of the statement to the other party at least 21 days before the trial date, if not already made available. Ultimately, the final discretion whether the statement may be admitted or not lies with the judge at trial.

Continued negotiations and payment into court before trial

During these procedures, 'without prejudice' negotiations may continue between the parties. There may also be payment into court by the defendant, a process which involves paying a sum of money for which the defendant is prepared to settle the case. If the plaintiff does not immediately accept the payment into court, but does so at a later stage, the plaintiff may have to pay some of the defendant's costs. Payments into court are a tactical matter which may induce a claimant to settle early.

Eventually the case will move up the court lists to trial unless settled beforehand or coming to an end. Cases will normally be before a single judge. Documentary evidence is produced and witnesses called to give oral evidence.

Questions on EC law

Where a question arises in a case before either the High Court or the county court as to the validity or interpretation of any acts of the Institutions of the EC regarding the interpretation of the Treaty of Rome, and a ruling on the question is necessary to determine that case, the court may refer that question to the European Court for a preliminary ruling.

The basis of a ruling must be that, on a point of law, it is necessary to enable the English court to give judgement. It would only be necessary if the facts of the case had been judged and the point of law was not already covered by clear authority or so straightforward that an English court could readily decide the matter itself.

The court may, however, consider whether in order to save time and cost it ought to exercise its discretion to rule on the matter itself. Only points of major difficulty should be referred to the European Court.

Costs

Even if a party wins the case, they are only entitled to their 'taxed' costs – the essential parts of litigation which will not include all the work of a solicitor. The loser pays the winner's costs, if the case goes as far as trial. This could mean financial ruin in the scope of environmental liability.

Injunctions

Injunctions are orders obtained from a court to prevent a defendant from doing acts that infringe the rights of another, and in some cases to ensure a person carries out certain required acts. Injunctions may be obtained before trial or sometimes as a final remedy, with or without damages, and may be granted by both the High Court and the county court (in exceptional cases outside of court hours). In addition to their other powers HMIP inspectors may obtain injunctions under section 24 of the EPA: local authorities have a general power to apply for injunctions under section 222 of the Local Government Act 1972. If a person disobeys an injunction they may be punished by imprisonment for contempt of court. Injunctions are a powerful remedy but are used at the discretion of the court. An important principle was established in the case of *American Cyanamid* v *Ethicon* (1975) 1 All ER 504; the court weighs up the seriousness of the harm and whether parties may be compensated adequately by money if the injunction is granted or refused. The need to seek an injunction by a private citizen is likely to mean that other systems of environmental protection and regulation will have failed. However, they may be of use where a person or company exceeds the limits of any right or authorisation which they have been granted at law and which infringes upon the property or comfort of a private citizen beyond the terms of any planning permission or agreement, or where a person is contravening the IPC or APC to the detriment of the plaintiff.

Statutory nuisances

As an alternative to civil claims for nuisance, a quicker and speedier remedy may be to use the statutory nuisance powers contained in the EPA. Although this is under the criminal law, it is essentially a private remedy being limited to a person 'aggrieved'. In some cases a civil injunction may be sought instead (see below) if there is an urgent need to restrain the nuisance (eg a risk to someone with a severe medical condition).

Claims in nuisance have a long history in Britain. One of the earliest recorded was *Aldred's* case (1610) 9 Co Tep 57 in which an action was held to lie from the operation of a lime kiln near the house of a plaintiff so that he could not live there. The case looked to an earlier common law principle which was applied to air corrupted by the presence of a pig sty.

Over the years successful actions have been brought against such trades as bone boiling, soap manufacture, smelting works, brick burning, fat melting and chemical works, although the smell from fish frying did not qualify in *Braintree Local Board of Health* v *Boyton* (1884) 52 LT.

Actions for statutory nuisance are contained in sections 79-82 of the EPA. An important limitation for local authorities is that they are not entitled to bring a claim for statutory nuisance against a process which is allocated for the IPC under section 79(10).

Under section 79 a statutory nuisance arises with regard to:

(a) any premises in such a state as to be prejudicial to health or a nuisance;

(b) smoke emitted from premises so as to be prejudicial to health or a nuisance;

(c) fumes or gases emitted from premises so as to be prejudicial to health or a nuisance;

(d) any dust, steam, smell or other effluvia arising on industrial, trade or business premises and being prejudicial to health or a nuisance;

(e) any accumulation or deposit which is prejudicial to health or a nuisance;

(f)   any animal kept in such a place or manner as to be prejudicial to health or a nuisance;

(g)   noise emitted from premises so as to be prejudicial to health or a nuisance;

(h)   any other matter declared by any enactment to be a statutory nuisance.

Under section 80, where a local authority is satisfied that a statutory nuisance exists, or is likely to occur or recur, the authority is under a duty to serve an abatement notice requiring either

(a)   the abatement of the nuisance or prohibiting or restricting its occurrence or re-occurrence;

(b)   execution of such works and the taking of such steps as may be necessary for those purposes,

and the notice shall specify the time or times within which the requirements of the notice are to be complied with.

Under section 80(2) the abatement notice shall be served on the person responsible for the nuisance. This can be done by personal service, hand delivery or by the post in accordance with the Interpretation Act 1978

(a)   on the owner of the premises where the nuisance arises from any structural defect in the premises ; or

(b)   where the person responsible for the nuisance cannot be found or the nuisance has not yet occurred, on the owner or the occupier of the premises.

Anyone served has a right of appeal to the magistrates' court against the notice within 21 days of the date of service (see below). In practice, the notice provision gives the opportunity to environmental health officers to negotiate with the person causing or responsible for the nuisance.

Once the 21 days have elapsed and there has been no appeal, an offence will be committed if the person acts in contravention of the notice. A fine of up to £20,000 may be imposed. A person who commits an offence in the course of private activities, such as a noisy neighbour, in contravention of the notice may suffer a fine of up to £2,000. In the case of an offence committed by a trade or business the penalty leaps ten-fold with a maximum penalty of £20,000. In addition the local authority may also take steps to reduce or abate the nuisance and recover costs from the person responsible.

Apart from highly technical defences, the only other defence available is that the best practicable means were used to prevent or counteract the effects of the nuisance. This will only apply to nuisances arising from trade premises. Other possible defences include a notice under the Control of Pollution Act 1974 (construction sites). In cases where more than one person was liable under section 80 above, the measures will apply to both, regardless of whether one or the other was responsible.

Proceedings by an aggrieved person

Procedure exists under section 82 of the EPA for an aggrieved person to make a complaint to the magistrates' court. Some commentators viewing the EPA have expressed doubts about the provisions for private prosecutions (overcome as explained by *R* v *Stewart)* but have hailed section 82 as establishing the clear right of a private citizen to take action. If anything, the range of persons who may prosecute is actually a limitation on the range of persons who may take action, the wording of section 82 being limited to or envisaging someone who is 'aggrieved'. This is wide enough to include a person directly affected and perhaps a relative or helper acting on behalf of a disabled person who is directly affected. In *Att-Gen (Gambia)* v *N'Jie* [1961] 3 All ER 385 a person aggrieved was defined by Lord Denning as follows:

> 'The words "person aggrieved" are of wide import and should not be subjected to a restricted interpretation. They do not include, of course, a mere busybody who is interfering in things that do not concern him; but they do include, of course, a person who has a genuine grievance because an order has been made which prejudicially affects his interest.'

The first step to be taken is to serve a notice on the person or premises concerned. In the case of a noise nuisance this should be done with three days' notice and 21 days' notice in the case of any other nuisance. The notice must specify the intention to bring proceedings and shall specify the matter which is the source of the complaint.

The complaint is then laid by visiting, in person, the magistrates' court and making the complaint. Such evidence must be given on oath and a summons should be issued. Despite the use of the word 'complaint' the proceedings are criminal and will follow the procedures set out in Chapter 4. *Herbert* v *Lambeth LBC* (1991) *(The Times,* 21 November), held that a statutory nuisance had been committed and ranks as a conviction.

If the court is satisfied that the alleged nuisance exists it may make an order either:

*   requiring the defendant to abate the nuisance, within the time specified in the order;

*   prohibiting a recurrence of the nuisance, and requiring the defendant, within a time specified in the order, to execute any works necessary to prevent the recurrence.

The court may impose a fine and a compensation order in addition to the orders above. Where a person contravenes any requirement or prohibition imposed by an order, a fine of up to £2,000 may be imposed, together with a fine at a rate of £200 a day for each day on which the offence continues after conviction.

Under section 82(13) if it appears to a magistrates' court that neither the person responsible for the nuisance nor the owner or the occupier of the premises can be found, it may order the local authority, in whose area the nuisance occurs, to undertake work that the person responsible would have been ordered to undertake.

A right of appeal exists for a person who has been served with an abatement notice. The relevant provisions are included in the Statutory Nuisance (Appeals) Regulations 1990 (S.I. 1990 No. 2276 as amended by S.I. 1990 No. 2483). Grounds of appeal include defect in the abatement notice, a claim that the notice is not justified, that the best practical means have been used to prevent or counteract the nuisance and that the notice should have been served on some other person responsible for the nuisance.

Actions can only be brought on an individual basis for harm which is caused to the plaintiff or to interferences with personal property.

CIVIL LAW – A NEW RELEVANCE IN ENVIRONMENTAL PROTECTION ?

Inquiries and tribunals

The right to quiet enjoyment and not to fall victim of civil wrongs is one that can be used in other related proceedings. The right to quiet enjoyment may be used as a negotiating 'chip' which may be raised in any public inquiry or hearing such as a planning appeal. These rights are material factors to be considered by the tribunal and will also be taken seriously by developers or persons seeking authorisations under Part I of the EPA.

The last thing that operators of prescribed processes and the holders of discharge consents want is to run the risk of having to meet civil claims, or even the increased insurance premiums that are likely to be payable. Representations will be taken all the more seriously if those affected are likely, or considered likely, to be able to enforce those rights. In some cases, developers or industry may offer various inducements or seek to enter into agreements with persons holding private interests.

Such agreements may become more common in years to come because of forthcoming EC regulations on waste (see below). It should be noted that any exclusion clause contained in any agreement which purports to restrict liability for death or personal injury will be invalid at law (section 2 of the Unfair Contract Terms Act 1977).

Civil rights – judicial review

A second area where civil rights may have an important effect is providing individuals or organisations with *locus standi* for judicial review proceedings. As explained elsewhere in this book, the High Court is usually loathe to allow a person lacking a perceived legal interest in an administrative law matter to apply to the High Court. Rights and concepts of civil law such as rights over land and property may provide a ground for obtaining leave for judicial review. However, only what are perceived to be legitimate and *bona fide* rights will be upheld, as shown by the failure of various opponents to road and motorway schemes. One tactic of recent years has been to divide up packages of land scheduled for compulsory purchase and sell them off in miniature plots to objectors in an attempt to obstruct the land selling process. In such cases, the courts are to look with suspicion on the rights asserted by the parties and the motive behind them and refuse leave. Just such cases were involved in the fate of the site of the Battle of Naseby.[7]

Corporate liability – the wider implications

These rights become all the more important when set in the context of likely developments in liability. For companies and business services the possibility of civil actions in environmental law are an increasing cause of concern. Among legal developments are EC proposals for new legislation, in particular the draft Directive on Civil Liability for Damages caused by waste (Com 91 219 Final) which imposes a wide civil liability for damage, including environmental damage. Liability for contaminated sites and ground water pollution could result in claims against industry and business running into millions.

Lender liability

Liability for environmental damage imposed upon lenders already exists in the United States and is of growing importance for Europe. The important development will be the definition to be adopted for a 'producer' of waste or harm. This could include not only the actual business which produces the waste but also the deemed producer – the person or body who falls to be in control of the site which produces the harm. This could arise where a bank or financial institution lends money to a company which generates waste or toxic substances, with the land and assets providing the security for the loan. Where the bank or financial institution enforces its security, it will find itself in control of the security and also its accompanying waste. The threat is, of course, that the bank will then be asked to pay the clean-up costs which it will be in a better position to pay than the (probably insolvent) business whose assets have been seized.

While there will not be a retrospective element in many proposals, liability for waste could extend up to 30 years after the date of an incident.

Implications of civil liability

At first sight an environmentally minded citizen might take these measures for greater corporate liability to be a good thing. Since the civil law applies only to those directly involved and bearing direct responsibilities, the feeling may develop that industries which have hitherto produced pollution without scruples are at long last about to get their just and well deserved legal denouement. The reaction of some may be to sit back and let the law take its course, amid a chorus of 'about time too'. However, nothing could be further from the truth since the increased liability is likely to have some serious implications.

In one sense it is a welcome development that the 'polluter pays' principle is becoming more widely accepted. However, such costs – like corporation tax - will be passed on to the rest of the community by way of increased charges for goods and services.

What has perhaps not been fully recognised is that if, in future, the polluter is made to pay, the polluter will accordingly seek to avoid liability. In many instances, in relation to ground water or contaminated sites, the issue of concern will not be what developers and industry may do or fail to do but *where they will go*. Contaminated land sites are likely to have all the attraction of a medieval plague pit to businesses who take the trouble to think ahead. They will seek to avoid such sites, particularly when more stringent EC legislation is anticipated.

If liability is imposed for the clean up of contaminated sites and the contaminated land registers come into play, it is likely only to push developers and industry into non-polluted sites – that is the unspoiled areas of the country, the so-called 'green field sites'. With neighbours already potentially liable for clean-up costs for sites on which waste has been deposited (see Chapter 10) by merely owning land adjacent to a contaminated site, businesses will move as far as economically possible from such sites. This will make involvement by the public in the planning and development processes (outlined in Chapter 7) all the more important.

NOTES

[1] See Chapter 1.
[2] *Legal Action*, November 1992 (monthly update).

[3] *Donoghue* v *Stevenson* (1932).
[4] Known as the 'egg shell skull rule'.
[5] See Merchant Shipping Act (Oil Pollution) 1971; Nuclear Installations Act 1965; EPA 1990.
[6] Civil Evidence Act 1968 and 1972. RSC Order 38.
[7] *R* v *Secretary of State for Transport ex parte Blackett* JPL 1041.

Chapter 7

Planning and the Built Environment

The control of development and land use under Britain's complex planning legislation is one of the most important ways in which the law affects the environment. When it comes to new development, the law may determine not just how a piece of the natural environment may be affected but whether it will continue to exist at all.

Planning law was born out of an early attempt to protect the environment – the human environment – of the early nineteenth century. The impact of the Industrial Revolution was disastrous on communities, creating far more unpleasant conditions than in today's 'inner city' area. The memory of the legacy of the 'dark satanic mills' is still with us. Indeed, the worst aspects of nineteenth century industrialism have sometimes been thrown back at environmentalists to refute suggestions that modern activities are particularly damaging in comparison.[1]

Planning laws are laid down by Central Government and put into practice by local government, acting as local planning authorities. Prior to 1990, planning law did not attach any particular importance to the need to protect the natural environment, with the exception of certain special types of development such as major roads or power stations, for which special studies were needed before development could go ahead (see below). However, under new legislation contained in the Town and Country Planning Act 1990, extensively amended by the Planning and Compensation Act 1991, environmental considerations rank higher than ever before. Under these two Acts, the need to protect the natural environment has become an integral feature of the planning system. Local planning authorities must now take environmental factors into account as a key part of the planning process. Environmental considerations will now, directly or indirectly, affect every piece of new development which takes place.

Coupled with this, a new significance is given to the environment in planning legislation. Central Government has stated its intention for the law to give greater power to local people to influence the planning policies which affect their areas and the planning decisions which are made. The Town and Country Planning Act 1990 and the Planning and Compensation Act 1991 both provide wider opportunities to the public to participate at a local level in the planning process than ever before. Details are set out in a series of *Planning Policy Guidance Notes* issued by the Department of the Environment.[2]

The citizen can:

- affect the overall policies affecting an area;

- affect decisions in individual planning cases;

- participate in public inquiries over certain planning decisions;

- scrutinise applications where environmental considerations may be taken into account.

Potentially the most important part the citizen can play is the first of these – help in the drawing up of development plans which set out the general policies which will affect an area. It is at this stage that environmental factors are given most attention and the contents of development plans are also of major importance in the fate of conservation areas (see Chapter 11).

Other ways in which the citizen can influence planning and development include participation in public inquiries which may be called in respect of particular development decisions and in reporting cases of breaches of planning control to the local authority.

Encyclopedias of planning law and specialist texts should be referred to for up to date information, a list being provided in the Appendix.

Finally, a major feature of planning law is rights of appeal against administrative decisions to the High Court. Reference should be made to the details in Chapter 5 and the *White Book*.

What is development?

Development is defined by section 55(2) of the Town and Country Planning Act 1990 as

'the carrying out of building, engineering, mining or other operations in, on, over or under land, or the making of any material change in use of any buildings or other land.'

Effectively, the law recognises two kinds of activity which require planning control: 'development' and 'material change of use'. The first occurs where a building or structure is built or erected (or occasionally demolished). The latter takes place where the use of a building changes, eg an office is turned into a shop. Certain types of development are automatically to be given deemed planning permission, such as internal works in a house, granted by General Development Orders made by the Secretary of State for the Environment. Such development is permissible without the approval or scrutiny of the local planning authority. However, if a developer goes outside the terms of a General Development Order the development may be controlled. Anything else must go before the local planning authority for consideration.

Local planning authorities

District councils and county councils act as local planning authorities and play a major part in controlling development. Among their functions are: the approval of development and structure plans for their areas (controlling overall policies for development of a county or borough); the consideration of applications for planning permission as to what may be built or how land use may alter in individual cases; and setting conditions on such developments which can be very important in terms of environmental preservation and protection.

Planning authorities can stop development that has not received planning permission through the magistrates' court. Local planning authorities may also regulate development by way of agreements with developers, outside the normal scope of planning control with a concept of 'planning obligations' imposed on developers. These may prove increasingly important in the future. In the past a great deal of planning of such things as petrol stations took place by means of agreement.[3]

STRUCTURE AND DEVELOPMENT PLANS

Development plans outline the main general considerations on which planning applications by developers will be decided by the local planning authority. Section 54(A) of the Town and Country Planning Act 1990, as inserted by the 1991 Act, makes an important change as to how decisions to grant planning permission are to be determined. Under the old system, there was a presumption in favour of development – basically a developer should be allowed to go ahead with the proposed scheme in the absence of any important reasons or factors to the contrary.

Under the new section 54(A), local planning authorities must now look at what the local development plan says when considering whether a development should go ahead. There is significant change in that any decision to grant planning permission must be in keeping with the relevant development plan. The contents of the development plan will provide the basic framework for reference. Fortunately for environmentally concerned citizens, the development plan process is intended to be open to public involvement – to take into consideration environmental matters.

Ultimately, the development plan may determine whether potential polluting industries develop in the first place. As a consequence, citizens concerned about the future of their local environment should make every effort to involve themselves in the drawing up of development plans.

Development plans are covered by the Town and Country Planning (Development Plan) Regulations 1991 S.I. 2794 which came into force on 10 February 1992. These apply to the different categories of plan which may make up a development – structure, local waste disposal and mineral extraction.

Development plans may be broken down into smaller parts, depending on the area covered. In a metropolitan area the development plan will consist of a document or set of documents comprising a 'unitary development plan'. In a non-metropolitan area, the development plan will consist of the area structure plan (covering strategic objectives and large scale policies such as roads) and a local plan which will have more specific policies and objectives. Public consultation for structure plans and local plans are separate but involve broadly similar procedures. In addition, plans for waste disposal and mineral workings may be included in the development plan.

The development plan will contain the details of these individual plans and must contain diagrams, maps and a reasoned justification of the policies. Under regulation 9(1)(b), development plans must contain environmental considerations, in addition to social and economic matters. This does not go as far as the environmental impact assessments required for major projects, but guidance issued by the DoE suggests that reference should be made to national policies contained in *This Common Inheritance*, on global warming and energy conservation. The Department of Environment also cites its own guide for Central Government, *Policy Appraisal and the Environment*, as containing useful guidance to local authorities.

Just how far planning authorities will be able to go into putting these good intentions into practice remains to be seen. Much will depend on the quality of the information which is supplied to them concerning the local environment.

THE MAKING OF DEVELOPMENT PLANS

The local planning authority is required to consult with the Secretary of State for the Environment, other local planning authorities, the Countryside Councils and the National Rivers Authority when drawing up a development plan.

Plan proposals must be deposited at the principal office of the authority and also advertised in a local paper so that residents may be aware of their existence. Details on the procedure for objections should be included with the deposited plan. There is likely to be a form for each area of objection. The *Planning Policy Guidance* notes state that objections should be as specific as possible, with reference to a particular policy or proposal number (it is advisable to include any reference to paragraph numbers and pages). The local planning authority will also seek to discover, at the earliest stage, whether objectors (or supporters) are prepared to appear at inquiries, whether they wish to call witnesses and be legally represented (if a person wishes legal assistance from a non-lawyer this should be included at this stage). If a person is not in a position to give any information at this stage, they should supply it as soon as possible.

Under regulation 12, objections and representations concerning the plan must be made within six weeks beginning with the date on which the plan is advertised in a local newspaper. Under regulations 14 and 15, the local planning authority may call for a hearing or inquiry to be held (unless all objectors wish merely to make written representations), following which the local planning authority must prepare a report for the Secretary of State for the Environment.

With a local plan or urban development plan, an inquiry is held to enable the plan to be examined. Hearings are presided over by an Inspector appointed by the Secretary of State. With a structure plan, an examination in public (EIP) must be held unless the Secretary of State dispenses with the need for one. The aim of an EIP is to provide more information to a planning authority and an open discussion of the issues. With an EIP, proceedings take place before a panel whose chairperson has been appointed by the Secretary of State. As befits a more general type of consultation exercise, proceedings will be more informal so that the local planning authority has the opportunity to hear the views of local people.

Obviously, greater access to environmental information (see Chapter 2) will enable citizens to be in a better position than ever before to make well-informed and effective representations.

The rules of natural justice will apply to both types of proceeding, so objectors should be given a fair opportunity to present their case for consideration by the Inspector or the panel involved.

After the plans have been considered and a decision made, the documents must be available for up to six weeks after adoption, approval or rejection to allow for legal challenges by persons who may still have objections to the contents of the plan (see below). Under regulation 27 the authority must keep a copy of the altered plan available at the principal office for consultation and arrange copies for purchase by the public at a reasonable charge.

When it comes to considering waste policies, the planning authority must have regard to any waste disposal plan for their area made under section 50 of the EPA. If local waste plans conflict, regulation 27 provides that the more recently adopted plan will apply.

To an extent, planning law since the 1940s has recognised certain environmental matters such as the green belts, tree preservation and conservation. The new approach is to take into consideration such matters as global warming, in terms of re-active changes and preventative measures.[4]

PLANNING PERMISSION

The decision to allow development to go ahead is decided with reference to the planning and policy considerations of the development plan, which are themselves based in part upon environmental considerations. If the planned development is in keeping with the contents of the development plan there will be a presumption in favour of it going ahead.

If a development is likely to have effects that go beyond what is permitted or required by the development plan, the developer has to show that there are 'material considerations' which apply – particular or special factors which override the considerations of the development plan. The impact that a development has on environment and pollution control will be a material factor. Whether an authorisation is needed from HMIP, the NRA or under APC may also be a factor.

Applying for planning permission

Planning permission may be sought by anyone; a person does not need to be the owner or have an interest in the land to be developed. Making the application has been used as a publicity stunt in the past, such as proposals to build huge underground shelters to house the population in the event of a nuclear attack. However, section 70A of the 1990 Act, as amended by the Planning and Compensation Act 1991, states that a local authority may decline to determine an application if, within two years of the date on which the application is received, the Secretary of State had turned down such an application and, in the opinion of the local planning authority there has been no change in the development plan or in a material consideration relevant to the application.

Planning permission may be sought under section 78 of the Town and Country Planning Act 1990. A register of applications must be kept by the local planning authority on a planning register. The register is required to keep:

• particulars of the application, including name and address of the applicant and details of the proposal,

• any decision made by the authority concerning the application,

- the reference number, the date and effect of any decision of the Secretary of State in respect of the application, whether on appeal or on a reference under section 77 of the Act.

Each entry must be made within 14 days of the local planning authority receiving the application.

With certain exceptions there is no requirement to advertise every application for planning permission through a local newspaper or notify neighbours, so inclusion in the register may be the only public notice available (see *R* v *Secretary of State ex parte Kent* (1990) JPL 124). However, sections 65-68 of the 1990 Act (as amended by section 16 of the Planning and Compensation Act 1991) give a new power to impose special publicity requirements in future General Development Orders with which all applicants will be expected to comply. If applicants do not follow any prescribed publicity, a planning authority may decide not to consider the application (section 65(5)). In future, this may prove a fruitful ground for legal challenge by parties who have been affected by a lack of appropriate publicity for an application.

Representations may be made to the planning authority, giving an opportunity for neighbours and the public to express their views. The local authority will also consult with any other bodies over the matter, such as the National Rivers Authority. The authority is required to consider representations and must not dismiss them out of hand.

A local authority has four options when considering an application for planning permission. It may:

(a) grant planning permission;

(b) grant permission subject to conditions;

(c) refuse permission; or

(d) grant part permission.

Reasons must be given in writing for whatever decision is made.

There is no right of appeal from a refusal of planning permission except by the applicant to the Secretary of State for the Environment. Similarly, there is no right of appeal against a grant of planning permission by someone objecting to it unless:

- it would clearly infringe the legal rights of others; or

- the decision has in some way been made contrary to the rules of procedure or is *ultra vires* and is thus subject to judicial review.

It is very difficult for a third party to interfere with a consent to planning permission or a positive development decision but judicial review is available in certain cases. Examples where such challenges have been attempted include: *R* v *Hillingdon BC ex parte Royco Homes* (1974) QB 720; *Covent Garden Community Association* v *GLC* (1981) JPL 183; *R* v *Secretary of State for the Environment ex parte Rose Theatre Co.* (1990) 1 QB 504.

Permission subject to conditions

A developer can appeal to the Secretary of State for the Environment against conditions which the planning authorities impose. Any conditions imposed are subject to a test of reasonableness and must be imposed for a valid planning purpose, and not for some ulterior motive. These can have an important role, such as in waste management cases.

PUBLIC INQUIRIES

Where a developer fails with an application for planning permission, an appeal may be made to the Secretary of State. In some instances the development is a controversial one, in which case a public inquiry is ordered by the Secretary of State. At present approximately 10 per cent of appeals go to a public inquiry. Usually, the inquiry will be determined by an inspector, who will provide a report to the Secretary of State who makes the final decision.

It is often felt by those attending a controversial inquiry that such inquiries operate as a sop to public opinion, as a cover for decisions which have already been made. Many people all too readily assume that inquiries are rigged, not least because of the lack of information available on the process. Non-lawyers may also find the court-like atmosphere intimidating and, to make matters worse, developers and the more powerful interests may be represented by barristers who carry out cross-examinations. These lawyers are likely to have been drawn from specialist 'sets' of chambers who deal specifically with planning and local government matters. However, the inspector may order limits on cross-examinations if she/he feels certain lines of inquiry are inappropriate.

If any pattern can be identified as determining the outcome of an appeal it is considerations arising from the development plan which will prevail.[5]

The law is not concerned with supplying remedies to those who merely wish to delay proceedings. Occasionally, objectors may succeed in a legal challenge on wholly unrelated grounds, such as an inquiry into the M11 in London in 1989 where an adjournment was forced because of a breach of fire regulations caused by the presence of large numbers of people at the meeting.

Rules of the inquiry

Inquiries into a grant or refusal of planning permission are covered by the Town and Country Planning (Inquiries Procedure) Rules 1992 S.I. 2038 and the Town and Country Planning Appeals (Determination by Inspectors) (Inquiries Procedure) Rules 1992 S.I. 2039. These replace and make amendments to the last set of rules published in 1988. Both came into force on 30 September 1992.

The Inquiries Procedure rules provide that where a planning authority receives notice of an inquiry from the Secretary of State, it shall inform the applicant and any party who has made representations. After receipt of such notice the parties may make written representations if they have not already done so.

The Secretary of State may require a pre-inquiry meeting to be held, publicised in a local newspaper. The inspector may also call for a pre-inquiry meeting where it is felt necessary. The planning authority and the applicant are required to serve copies of their outline submissions to each other and under regulation 5(5)(b) serve a copy of their statement on, among others, any person who has made representations.

A person may notify the Secretary of State if they wish to appear at the hearing. Not less than three weeks written notice will be given to the applicant, the local planning authority and any other person entitled to appear or whose presence at the meeting seems desirable.

At the meeting the inspector will preside, deciding the matters to be discussed and the procedure to be followed. The inspector is given the power under regulation 5(9) which may require 'any person present at the meeting who, in his opinion, is behaving in a disruptive manner, to leave and may refuse to permit that person to return or attend any further meeting, or may permit him to return or attend only on such conditions as he may specify.'

Regulation 6(11) provides that a local planning authority shall afford to any person who so requests, a reasonable opportunity to inspect and, where practicable, take copies of any statement of case or other document which has been served on the authority.

People entitled to appear at the hearing

The following bodies have a right to appear at an inquiry if they own land in the area:

- the applicant,
- the local planning authority,
- a county or district council,
- a National Park Committee,
- a joint planning authority under the TCPA 1990,
- an urban development authority or an enterprise zone authority,
- a housing action trust,
- a statutory party,
- any other person who has served a notice in accordance with rule 6(6) or rule 5(6).

Any other person may also appear at the discretion of the inspector. Permission to appear under regulation 11(2) 'shall not be unreasonably withheld'. This includes another local authority under the Local Government Act 1972. Government departments and Ministers of the Crown may also be represented. Inquiries may be reopened under regulation 16.

PROCEDURE

Procedure is governed by the rules which apply to any inquiry held in England or Wales by an inspector regarding planning permission under The Town and Country Planning Act 1990 section 78,

Listed Building Act or in relation to conservation areas, but no other inquiry, such as to highways. However, principles regarding natural justice will apply to other inquiries.

The procedure adopted by the inquiry is subject to the discretion of the inspector, except as provided by the rules. The inspector may arrange for witnesses who have work commitments to be able to give their evidence at the opening of the inquiry, subject to the agreement of all the parties represented. This is common practice as it is convenient to all parties and ensures that no one is unfairly denied a chance to put forward their views.

The local planning authority is required to supply the names and addresses of statutory parties; the Secretary of State makes a similar exchange with the planning authority. The name of the Inspector is circulated to everyone who has made representations (regulation 5 Determination by Inspectors Rules).

An inspector may at any time arrange a timetable for the proceedings – or for part of an inquiry – which is open to variation.

Any party intending to call witnesses to give evidence must put a summary of the written proof of evidence to the inspector. The summary must be limited to 1,500 words and sent to the inspector not less than three weeks before the fixing of the inquiry. The summary can be read at the inquiry. The inspector also has a discretion over what evidence can be used at the inquiry. The inspector may refuse to permit:

- the giving or production of evidence,
- the cross-examination of persons giving evidence,
- the presentation of any other matter,

but only if the inspector considers it to be 'irrelevant or repetitious'. However, where oral evidence is refused by the inspector, the person may submit the evidence in writing before the close of the inquiry. At the inquiry the appellant has the right to make any opening statement and to make any closing submission.

Persons may also be excluded, but may submit their evidence or other information in writing. The inspector may also take into account any written representation or evidence, provided he discloses it at the inquiry. This conforms with the right to a fair hearing and that matters should not be decided in secret.

Cross-examination

Witnesses who attend may be subject to cross-examination. Under regulation 12(4) a representative of a minister or a government department is not required to answer any question which, in the opinion of the inspector, is directed to the merits of government policy. Thus, ministers or their representatives may claim to have a protection from any cross-examination about Government policy contained in the rules, but inspectors must act reasonably so that the matter is not beyond legal challenge (see Chapter 5). Subject to this restriction, a person acting as a representative of a government department or minister may be subject to cross-examination like any other witness.

Natural justice

Proceedings before inspectors are subject to natural justice. The person applying for judicial review faces a heavy burden. In *Hambledon & Chiddingford Parish Councils* v *Secretary of State for the Environment* [1976] JPL 502 it was stated that although the inspector complied with the rules this did not mean that the rules of natural justice had been observed as well. However, any complainant would have to produce cogent evidence of a breach. As a consequence, it is vital that any aggrieved parties keep as detailed a note of the proceedings as is possible.

It is possible that where a breach of natural justice is revealed to the Secretary of State before the close of the inquiry, the inspector may be removed and replaced by another. In *Granada Theatres Ltd* v *Secretary of State for the Environment* [1976] 96 it was held that taking into account petitions not disclosed to the applicant was a breach of natural justice. In *DE Hudson* v *Secretary of State for the Environment* [1984] JPL 258 an inspector was held to have erred in not giving the parties an opportunity to deal with a matter of substance which had influenced his decision.

A good example of where there was an appearance of bias, although there was no actual evidence, was in *Simmons* v *Secretary of State for the Environment* [1985] JPL 253 where the inspector was seen by the appellant in discussion with the chairman of the planning committee after the close of the inquiry. The decision was quashed.

A decision may be quashed where the rules of natural justice are breached (see page 90). If the inspector appears to be asleep or draws on experience of the parties in other proceedings or departs from the rules, grounds for challenge will lie through the High Court.

Procedure following inquiry

Regulation 17(2) states that if, after the close of an inquiry, an inspector proposes to consider any new evidence or any new matter of fact (except a matter of government policy) to be material to the decision, no decision may be made without taking certain steps. An important opportunity exists for persons affected to demand a re-opening of the inquiry.
The inspector is not entitled to come to a decision without first:

• notifying the persons entitled to appear at the inquiry of the matter in question; and

• affording them an opportunity to make written representations to the Inspector within three weeks of the date of notification on the issue, or asking for a re-opening of the inquiry.

Where an inspector re-opens the inquiry (which *must* be done where the request comes from a planning authority or the appellant), a statement must be sent to all persons who appeared at the inquiry covering the matters on which further evidence is invited. The notice requirements for a re-convened inquiry are the same as for the original inquiry itself.

Notification of decision

Regulation 18 provides that an inspector must notify all persons who appeared at the inquiry of the decision on the appeal. In addition any person entitled to be notified may apply in writing within six weeks of the decision to examine any documents listed in the notification. This gives an opportunity for a person to consider whether a legal challenge should be commenced.
After the inquiry, the inspector makes his report to the Secretary of State, who then upholds or rejects the application. A further right of appeal only then exists to an aggrieved party on a point of law.

LARGE SCALE DEVELOPMENT AND THE NEED FOR AN ENVIRONMENTAL IMPACT ASSESSMENT

Under EC Directive 85/337, certain major projects must have an assessment in environmental terms before permission is granted. This has entered into UK law in the form of a statutory instrument – the Town and Country Planning (Assessment of Environmental Effects) Regulations 1988 (S.I. No. 1199). These have undergone some recent amendments under the Town and Country Planning (Assessment of Environmental Effects) (Amendment) Regulations 1992. Among developments covered by these regulations are oil refineries, aerodromes with runways over 2,100 metres and storage facilities for radioactive waste.

A general power to make regulations covering any planning matter has been given to the Secretary of State with a new section 71A in the Town and Country Planning Act 1990, inserted by section 15 of the Planning and Compensation Act 1991. Other legislation also requires assessments with projects which are included below and in Appendix 1.

- Trunk roads and motorways – after consultation under the Highways Act 1980, with route consultation and a public inquiry. The Secretary of State must publish an environmental assessment where draft orders involve roads over 10 km long, or 1 km in the case of a national park. See Highways (Assessment of Environmental Effects) Regulations 1988 (S.I. No 1241).

- Power stations proposed by the Central Electricity Generating Board and Area Electricity Boards require an environmental impact assessment and the approval of the Secretary of State for Industry. The regulations cover any application involving the building of a nuclear power station, a non-nuclear power station producing 300 megawatts or more, or where it is considered significant environmental effects may arise. Assessments are also required for power lines on land, on overhead lines or for the construction or diversion of oil and gas pipelines 16 km or more in length.

- Cases involving afforestation on land, likely to have significant effects on the natural environment or which may cause adverse ecological changes in the locality, require an environment assessment if funded by the Forestry Commission.

- Other projects and developments for which an assessment is necessary include enterprise zones, land drainage operations and salmon farming.

- Where a local authority grants itself planning permission, an environmental assessment must be carried out. This will cover such things as waste disposal arrangements.

There is no doubt that Brussels had good intentions with these requirements but in practice they can prove something of a developer's charter where loopholes and various devices can be used to escape the legislation. For example, to evade the necessity of environmental impact assessment in the case of a road, a developer merely has to make the length of the highway shorter than the specified length, or to make a runway 2,000 metres. Accordingly, the fine print of a planning proposal may need close examination to see if a developer is seeking to avoid the requirement for an assessment. Conversely some developers have undertaken assessments where none is strictly required, on a voluntary basis, although it is possible – if not likely – that this is an exercise in public relations and winning acceptance rather than a concern for the affected environment.

There has also been increasing concern as to the adequacy of some assessments. While proving a lucrative business for many environmental consultancies, doubts have been expressed about the quality of some assessments produced with suggestions that they fail to cover relevant facts or fulfil the requirements of the legislation. A study conducted by Manchester University assessed 83 statements submitted between 1988 and 1991. Of these only 60 per cent could be considered satisfactory, and although quality has improved in recent years some 25 per cent were submitted in 1990–91.[6]

Challenging an environmental impact assessment purely on scientific grounds may be difficult; corresponding scientific evidence would have to be provided in rebuttal. Where an assessment has been obtained in bad faith, through bribery or underhand dealing, or does not meet the requirements of the legislation, it could be challenged by judicial review.

Drawing up an environmental assessment under the Town and Country Planning Act

The process requires:

(a) the developer to submit an environmental statement to a

'competent authority' conforming with the requirements of Schedule 3 to the regulations. The information to be specified includes:

(i) a description of the proposed development containing information about the site and the design or scale of the development;

(ii) the data necessary to identify and assess the main effects which that development is likely to have on the environment;

(iii) a description of the likely significant effects, direct and indirect, of the development on the environment, explained by reference to its possible impact on:

human beings; flora; fauna; soil; water; air; climate; the landscape; the interaction between any of the foregoing; material assets; and cultural heritage. As can be seen, these are particularly wide categories; for example, there is no reason why, under the heading of 'climate', regard should not be made to the impact on global warming by carbon dioxide emissions, an area on which the law has precious little protection to offer (see Chapter 8 on atmosphere).

(iv) where significant adverse effects are identified, a description must be given of the measures envisaged to avoid or reduce the harm caused;

(v) a summary in non-technical language of the information contained in the assessment.

Further information may be included covering land use, materials involved, processes, the use of natural resources and other issues.

(b) the local planning authority may consult with any county council, the Countryside Commission, and the Nature Conservancy Council and Her Majesty's Inspectorate of Pollution and other relevant bodies. An oversight appears to be the omission of the National Rivers Authority, though some scrutiny may be achieved through the provisions of the General Development Order. The public is also entitled to make representations with the environmental statement being made publicly available. Rights under the Access to Information (Local Government) Act 1985 may be used.

(c) the competent authority must prepare an environmental assessment before deciding whether it should go ahead.

Public information and publicity

Under regulation 13, the applicant must publish a notice giving the name and address of the applicant, the address, location and nature of the proposed development and details of where the plan can be inspected. This must be done in a local newspaper circulating in the locality where the land is situated. The advertisement should also give details of the proposal.

The applicant is also required to post on the land the same details unless they do not have a legal right to do so (for example, ownership of the land has not yet been transferred). Such a notice must be displayed not less than seven days in the month before the application and not less than 20 days before the last day for inspecting the document.

When submitting the environmental assessment, the developer must supply a certificate stating that the application was publicised by way of notice on the site (so far as was possible). If a false certificate is issued, the applicant will be committing a criminal offence and may be fined up to £400.

Under regulation 18, an applicant for planning permission or an appellant who submits an environmental statement in connection with his application or appeal shall ensure that a reasonable number of copies of the statement are available at the address named in notices under regulations 12 or 13. These provide the basis for representations by the public to either the local planning authority, the Secretary of State or an inspector appointed by the Secretary of State.

As with other aspects, this decision-making must be carried out reasonably and is open to judicial review, particularly by those who have a legal right which may be infringed.

Other projects may require an environmental impact assessment to be carried out where they are 'likely to have significant effects on the environment by virtue of their nature, size or location'.

Small scale projects could be included and it is open to members of the public to put forward this suggestion to the local planning authority.

Failure to conduct an environmental impact assessment may not necessarily render a planning application invalid, providing an authority considers all the relevant facts (see *R* v *Swale BC, ex parte Royal Society for the Protection of Birds* [1991] JPL 39). Cases where this principle may be applied will depend on the facts, and much will depend on the quality and variety of representations made to the planning authority. There could potentially be challenges where environmental impact assessments are *prima facie* insufficient or do not correspond to the requirements of the legislation. Such cases will certainly have to be approached carefully by applicants for judicial review. Certainly, the task of those determining planning applications is likely to become more complex in years to come.

Environmental impact assessment and highways

There is a separate procedure for highways to have environmental assessments under section 105A of the Highways Act 1980 as inserted by the Highways (Assessment of Environmental Effects) Regulations 1988 S.I. 1241.

In any case where the Secretary of State for Transport has under consideration the construction of a new road or the improvement of an existing one, a duty to consider if an environmental assessment is necessary is imposed.

If the Secretary of State considers an assessment is required, an environmental assessment must be undertaken and published at the same time as the road proposal. The assessment must cover details relevant to the proposal and include as a minimum:

• a description of the project including its site, design and size,

• a description of measures envisaged in order to avoid, reduce and, if possible, remedy significant adverse effects,

• the data required to identify and assess the main effects which the project is likely to have on the environment,

• a non-technical summary of the information.

Appeals from the Town and Country Planning Act

There are two types of legal challenge available to persons aggrieved by planning decisions affecting their legal rights and the development of their neighbourhood.

One is the route of judicial review under RSC Order 53 as outlined in Chapter 5. The other is the restricted right of challenge under section 288 of the Town and Country Planning Act 1990. Matters challengeable under section 288 are largely those relating to development plans and decisions of the Secretary of State. The mode of challenge is by motion under RSC Order 94 rather than judicial review by way of RSC Order 53, although there may be similar grounds such as natural justice. Another major difference is that the restricted right of challenge must be commenced within six weeks of the decision concerned. Anyone seeking to challenge matters covered by section 288 should refer to RSC Order 94 and RSC Order 8 in the *White Book* and the standard forms set out in the book.

To use the section 288 procedure an appellant must have a case to bring an action and be able to show substantial prejudice, unless the complaint is that the decision is outside the powers of the Act. From decisions over the years it is not precisely clear who may claim a right to instigate section 288 proceedings, but rights will probably extend to any individual or pressure group that appeared at the inquiry or was denied an opportunity of submitting evidence.

On *PG Vallance Ltd v Secretary of State for the Environment* (1992) *(The Independent,* 19 November), it was held that where an Inspector had erred in law but there was no substantial wrong or miscarriage of justice as a result, the court on an application for leave to appeal against a decision did not automatically have to remit the case to the Secretary of State for a re-hearing and could refuse relief.

Section 284 precludes decisions challenging the validity of structure plans, local plans, unitary development plans and a number of decisions of the Secretary of State. Decisions of the Secretary of State concerning planning appeal applications under section 78 are included among these decisions.

Section 287 provides that any person aggrieved by a unitary development plan or a local plan may lodge an appeal to the High Court. An application can also be made over the repeal or replacement of any such plan. A person may question the validity of the plan or 'the alteration, repeal or replacement' of the plan on the ground that:

- it is not within the powers of Part II of the Act; or

- that a requirement of this part, or any regulations made under it, has not been complied with in relation to the approval or adoption of the plan, or, as the case may be, its alteration, replacement or adoption.

These two considerations give rise to a plan which is beyond what the law allows under the Town and Country Planning Act or which is in breach of the Town and Country Planning (Development Plan) Regulations. For example, if the local planning authority appears to have failed to give consideration to environmental matters, as it now must under regulation 9(1)(b), the plan should be challenged through this procedure.

Section 287(2) provides that on an application being made, the High Court may, by interim order, wholly or partially suspend the operation of the plan, or its alteration. The application must be made within six weeks from the relevant date, that is,

- in the case of an application in respect of such a plan as is mentioned in subsection (1), the date of the publication of the first notice of the approval or adoption of the plan, alteration, repeal or replacement required by regulations under sections 26 or 53;

- in a planning zone scheme, the date of publication of the first notice of the approval or adoption;

- the date of publication.

If a person misses the date, even through no personal fault of their own, no challenge can be commenced. In *Stainer* v *Secretary of State for the Environment* (1992) EGCS 130, six weeks in section 288 was taken to include bank holidays over the Christmas period.

A request for an order suspending the plan would be added in the list of points as interim relief before the substantial hearing to prevent any harmful development going ahead, based upon the operation of the plan. This is naturally an important matter and any person seeking to challenge a plan should include it in the 'relief sought' section of the form. The power to do this is contained in section 287(2).

In most cases the applicant will be seeking an order of *certiorari* to quash the whole plan or any part of it. Under section 287(2) the High Court may quash the plan if it finds the plan is 'to any extent' outside the powers of the Act or regulations.

The plan may also be quashed if the High Court finds that,

> 'the interests of the applicant have been substantially prejudiced by the failure to comply with any requirement of that Part or of any regulations made under it, may wholly or in a part quash the plan or as the case may be, the alteration, repeal or replacement either generally or in so far as it affects any property of the applicant.'

Not every decision need be challenged through the procedure based on section 288; some fall outside its provisions, including a grant of planning permission by the local planning authority; interlocutory decisions of the Secretary State prior to the final decisions, eg the decision to grant an adjournment or denial of cross-examination of the witness; and probably the refusal by the Secretary of State to consider an appeal at all. In such cases, judicial review will be available as a route of challenge on grounds of unreasonableness (such as failure to follow *Wednesbury principles* or other principles of administrative law).

Procedure

The application is made under RSC Order 94 which must be read in conjunction with Order 8, for a motion to challenge the order of the Secretary of State. Evidence is by affidavit and an important limitation is that, even where the order is successful, the matter is merely remitted to the Secretary of State for further consideration.

NOTES

[1] See for example Beckman, W., (1974), *In Defence of Growth*, Oxford University Press.
[2] HMSO, 1991-1992
[3] See TCPA (1971) section 52; TCPA (1990) section 106 as amended by the Planning and Compensation Act 1991.
[4] At present the exact approach to be taken remains somewhat vague.
[5] See Chapter 11 in relation to SSSIs.
[6] Brown, D., (1992), report from Manchester University.

Chapter 8

The Atmosphere

Global warming and the depletion of the ozone layer are two of the most serious environmental problems of the late twentieth century. Either problem occurring alone would have been bad enough, but together they pose a serious threat, the consequences of which cannot be adequately predicted. Yet in tackling these two threats, the law is currently at its most inadequate. There is, presently, more provision for the control of unpleasant smells than for reducing carbon dioxide emissions, although the prospect of climate change was mentioned in a Government White Paper on the Environment as long ago as 1970.[1] (This was, of course, a mere 74 years after the idea had been first postulated by the Swedish chemist Arrhenius in 1896). Ozone depletion was the subject of a report issued by the DoE in 1979 (suggesting that we wait for international action) which stated that there is little that can be done within the existing legislative framework.[2] Although there are an increasing number of reports (one which actually suggested that the climate change may in fact be beneficial, causing less damage in winter, for instance)[3], legal measures and concepts have failed to keep up with the situation. But at least the issues are slowly coming on to the political and legislative agenda.

There are three distinct ways in which the law controls air pollution. These can be classified as follows:

(1) The Clean Air Act legislation.

(2) Controls under the EPA.

(3) Miscellaneous controls.

At present, the control of pollution of the air is largely administered by local government. Many emissions in the air fall under the pollution control process allocated to local control under the EPA. However, it is possible to find indications in the law[4] that these powers may be replaced by increasing control exercised by Central Government.

With the control regime being in the hands of elected authorities, there is a limit to the amount that an individual citizen may be able to do to curb atmospheric pollution. Major difficulties also exist with collecting evidence – many emissions being invisible. To uncover a number of offences under the Clean Air Acts requires both a relevant knowledge of engineering and a power of entry to obtain access to the premises concerned. Nonetheless, much could be done to encourage existing bodies to exercise their statutory powers and influence policy. The new right to information in the Access to Information Regulations opens up data obtained from national monitoring of air quality to public scrutiny.[5]

In November 1992 a new Clean Air Bill received its first reading in the House of Lords and will probably, if it enters into force, consolidate the existing Clean Air Acts. Air Quality Regulations are due to come into force in 1993 under an EC Directive. These impose fixed emission standards for sulphur dioxide and suspended particulates, lead and nitrogen dioxide. Among pollution effects which will be reduced will be acid rain.[6]

In the 1990s, atmospheric pollution is no longer the acute visible problem of London smog; instead it is an insidious chronic problem which manifests itself in respiratory problems and higher cancer rates.

THE CLEAN AIR ACTS OF 1956 AND 1968

Various attempts to curb air pollution in Britain have been made over the years in different forms. Smoke nuisances were included in a number of Victorian statutes such as the Sanitary Act 1866 and the Public Health Act 1875.[7] Later legislation such as the Public Health Act 1936 provided further sanctions enforceable at criminal law and section 104 of the Act also empowered authorities to make bye-laws regulating smoke emission. However, it took a series of tragedies in the 1950s, in particular December 1952, which killed 4,000 people (it is worth considering that similar numbers died at Bhopal) to alter things. The increased use of natural gas and the Clean Air Act 1956 reduced many of the problems of smoke, particulates and sulphur emissions, although sulphur dioxide pollution increased over the following decade.[8]

Section 29 of the Clean Air Act 1956 places local authorities under a legal duty to enforce the provisions of the Act. The Clean

Air Act 1956 establishes a number of strict liability offences covering emissions of smoke, grit and dust. Amendments under the EPA have added to the power of the Secretary of State to make regulations extending the controls to cover prescribed gases from furnaces in the same way that smoke, grit and dust are covered. The Clean Air (Units of Measurement) Regulations 1992 S.I. No. 36 inserts metric measurements into the imperial units of measure contained in the two Acts.

Section 1 of the 1956 Act prohibits the emission of dark smoke from a chimney of any building. Dark smoke is defined as dark or darker than shade 2 on a Ringelmann Chart (section 34). A Ringelmann Chart is a method of measurement originally devised by a Professor of the same name in the nineteenth century. The method of observation is to set up the chart in daylight, facing the observer at a distance at which the lines on the chart are seen to form a uniform shade. The shades of the chart are then compared with the shade of the smoke as it appears at its point of emission from the chimney. Observation should be for a period laid down in the Dark Smoke (Permitted Periods) Regulations 1958 S.I. 498 which lays down permitted periods in which smoke may be emitted. Any continuous emission of dark smoke, caused otherwise than by soot blowing, that exceeds more than four minutes, will amount to an offence. In any eight hour period, no more than ten minutes is permitted (14 minutes if soot is blowing out) in the case of a chimney serving one furnace.

Section 1 of the Clean Air Act 1968 extends the prohibition on dark smoke to trade and industrial premises. Trade and industrial premises are defined by section 1(5) as any premises used for any trade or business, or where any burning for trade purposes takes place. At law the term 'premises' is wider than building, covering vessels and open sites. Bonfires and fires in scrapyards etc do not fall within this definition, and may be actionable as statutory nuisances.

In addition to dark smoke, the regulations cover cases of chimneys emitting black smoke (level 4 on the Ringelmann Chart); any emission exceeding two minutes constitutes an offence. The person guilty of an offence will be the occupier of the building from which dark or black smoke is detected and any person who causes or permits the emission (section 1(1) of Control of Smoke Pollution Act 1989). Where there is more than one occupier, the occupier responsible for the offence will be the person controlling the fireplace from which the smoke originates. Again the offences are of strict liability. A fine of up to £1,000 may be imposed.

Information-gathering powers

In order for the local authority to properly perform its functions under the Clean Air Acts, it may serve notice on the occupier demanding information it may reasonably require concerning the furnace, its fuel and processes, to be supplied within 14 days.

Any person who, having been duly served with a notice under subsection (1) of this section, fails to comply with the requirements thereof within the time limited or furnishes any information in reply thereto which he knows to be false will be guilty of an offence, and risks a fine not exceeding £2,000.

Rules for furnaces

Section 3(1) of the 1956 Act prohibits the installation in a building, boiler or industrial plant, of any furnace which, so far as is practicable, cannot operate continuously without producing smoke. Any person who instals a furnace in contravention of this section will be guilty of an offence. Notice must be given in writing to the local authority by a person installing such a furnace or boiler under section 3(1). It should be noted that the local authority cannot prevent the installation of the furnace – it must merely be notified. Only if a furnace is capable of being operated, so far as is practicable, without the emission of smoke – not necessarily dark smoke – will it be legal.

Section 3(4) provides that this section does not apply to furnaces solely or mainly for domestic use.

Grit and dust from furnaces

Subject to the provisions of section 6(1) of the 1956 Act, no furnace in any building is to burn pulverised fuel or solid fuel or solid waste at the rate of more than 1.02 tonnes (as inserted by S.I. 1992 No. 36) unless the furnace is provided with a plant for arresting grit and dust, approved by the local authority. The plant must be properly maintained. If it is used in contravention of the section, a fine of up to £400 may be imposed.

Under section 7(2) (as amended by section 5) the Secretary of State may make regulations requiring an occupier to monitor grit, dust and fumes emitted from a furnace and make the results available to a local authority. The Clean Air (Measurement of Grit and Dust) Regulations 1971 currently apply to a small number of furnaces.

Under the 1968 Act, section 4 provides for certain exemptions to fit an arrestment plant. In order for an exemption to be granted, the local authority must first be satisfied that the emission of grit and dust from any chimney serving a furnace in the building will not be prejudicial to health or a nuisance. Application must be made by the occupier.

Where an authority does not grant an exemption, a reasoned statement for the decision must be given. An applicant has a 28 day right of an appeal. The local authority has eight weeks in which to consider an application. If it fails to consider the application in that period, it is deemed granted.

Smoke control areas

Section 11 of the 1956 Act establishes smoke control areas. Any local authority may, by order, declare the whole of a district or any part of a district, as such an area. Under section 31(3), two or more local authorities may combine for the purposes of declaring an area a smoke control area. While the scheme operates jointly between authorities, the individual authorities will remain responsible for enforcement of the Act in their own particular districts. Some 6,000 such orders have been made since the system was introduced.[9]

After making such an order, its existence must be advertised in the *London Gazette* and for at least two successive weeks in a local newspaper, stating that those who wish to object may make representations to the Secretary of State for the Environment. If anyone makes any objections within six weeks (during which the terms of the order must be available for inspection) there are provisions for a public inquiry – but few environmentalists would be likely to object to the making of such an order unless it was felt to be inadequate. When a smoke control area is confirmed, Schedule

1 to the Act provides that it will not come into force for at least six months to allow adaptation by any businesses or trades which have been affected.

Where such an order is in force it is an offence if smoke is emitted from *any* building or chimney. Breach of a smoke control order can lead to a fine of £400 (domestic dwellings) and £200 (trade premises). Under section 30, if a local authority is of the opinion that an offence is being committed, a notification must be given as soon as practicable to the occupiers. A possible defence exists if the smoke was caused by fuel authorised by the authority. Section 9 of the 1968 Act makes the acquisition and sale of an unauthorised fuel for use in a building in a smoke control area an offence.

Section 8 of the Clean Air Act 1968 gives further power to the Secretary of State with regard to smoke abatement. If, after consulting with the authority, the minister is satisfied that the authority have not exercised their powers under section 11 of the Act of 1956, an order may be made for the authority to draw up a plan. This may be considered and varied by the minister. If the authority fails to comply, an order of mandamus will lie against the authority; such an order might also be available to an aggrieved citizen.

Height of chimneys

Under section 6(1), an occupier of a building shall not knowingly cause or permit a furnace to operate unless the height of the chimney is above the approved limit. If the chimney is too short, an offence will be committed. (A similar provision applies to boilers and industrial plants). Ultimately, increasing the height of the chimney does not reduce the pollution caused by a furnace but merely disperses it over a wider area, although reducing pollution in a limited area is a questionable practice, amounting to the export of pollution.

Applications for the approval of chimney heights must be made to local authorities on a prescribed form or in writing where a sufficient amount of information is provided. Authorities must determine the applications within four weeks of receiving them otherwise the approval will be deemed to have been granted (section 6(6)).

Section 6(4) states that a local authority shall not approve an application unless it is satisfied that its height will be sufficient to prevent, so far as practicable, the smoke, grit, dust, gases or fumes emitted from the chimney from becoming prejudicial to health or a nuisance having regard to:

(a) the purpose of the chimney;

(b) the position and descriptions of buildings near it;

(c) the levels of the neighbouring ground;

(d) any other matters requiring consideration in the circumstances.

The local authority may approve the height of a chimney with conditions as to the rate and quality of the emissions. Where a local authority does not approve the height of the chimney they are required to give the applicant notification of their decision. The notification must state the reasons and specify the lowest height which they are prepared to approve with or without conditions.

A right of appeal to the Secretary of State, within 28 days, is available. The Secretary of State may confirm the decision or approve the chimney. The minister may alter, substitute or revoke any conditions imposed.

Section 7 requires measurement of prescribed gases. Section 18(2), exempting emissions of prescribed gases from colliery spoilbanks, imposes controls on emissions into the atmosphere. A fine of up to £2,000 may be imposed where an offence is committed contrary to this section.

Government premises

Where dark smoke is emitted from government premises or in which the Crown has an interest as an occupier, they are exempt from proceedings. Instead local authorities are under a duty to report any such emissions to the Secretary of State (section 22 of the 1956 Act). On receiving such a report, the minister is under a duty to make an inquiry into the circumstances and, if cause of complaint is revealed, employ all practicable means for preventing or minimising the emission of smoke, grit or dust. Steps may also be taken for curbing any nuisance and preventing its re-occurrence. Privatisation and the loss of Crown immunity in a number of sectors, such as the Health Service, will have increased the number of premises which will be liable to prosecution under the Act if an offence is committed.

Prosecuting smoke offences

Before proceedings are instigated, section 30(1) requires that the authority must notify the occupier of the premises or the person responsible for the furnace or plant 'as soon as may be'. Such notice has to be confirmed in writing within two days, as amended by para. 16 of Schedule 3 of the Control of Pollution Act 1974, replacing the original requirement of four days. In any proceedings for an offence under section 1 (or section 11 where a smoke control order is in force – see below), a defence will be available where the notice requirement has not been followed up. The wording of section 30(2) might cause some problems for a private prosecutor as no proceedings may be sustained unless a statutory notice has been served.

One potential way around this legislative obstacle is that the wording of section 30 is wide enough to encompass an officer acting on the strength of emission reported and recorded by a member of the public. There is no requirement that the officer who serves the notice is the same person who has actually witnessed the emission concerned (though the actual witness must attend court). It would be possible for a private prosecutor to observe the emission and collect the necessary evidence and inform the authorised officer, leaving the local authority to serve the necessary notice. Since an officer is under a duty to serve the notice where an offence has been established, the necessary requirements of section 30(1) will be fulfilled. Provided that the information is given to a Magistrate within six months of the reported pollution incident, it would appear that a private citizen could thus instigate a prosecution. Alternatively, the local authority could take up the case itself, under its duty to enforce the provisions of the Act under section 27. Judicial review could be available where a local authority refuses to enforce the Act, but this may be hard to prove and *locus standi* might prove a further problem.

It is not clear how the time limits relate to the dates to be specified in any complaint; probably one summons for each day, listing the emissions according to the time periods, would be appropriate where a chimney is operating for more than eight hours. In a Victorian case, *R* v *Waterhouse* (1872) LR7 QB 19, a decision to issue 19 different summonses in respect of 19 different days on which black smoke had been emitted, was upheld. In *Barnes* v *Norris* (1876) 41 JP 150 an argument that a summons was defective for not specifying which of five different chimneys was responsible, failed.

In the case of black smoke, it is essential that observation and reference is made to the Ringelmann Chart; no other method is approved. The term 'black smoke' was originally contained in the Public Health Act 1936 but is probably now included within the term 'dark smoke'. Since it is not clear that the offence of emitting 'black smoke' is an offence in its own right, accordingly any summons should be worded with reference to dark smoke under section 1, even though the evidence goes to establish that emission of black smoke is involved.

It will be important for an observer to note the time and duration of emissions with accuracy and notes must be made subject to the rules on contemporaneous records.

Obviously, the court is more likely to accept an account by an environmental health officer who has experience in using the chart than of a non-qualified witness. However, the legislation goes on to provide that under section 34(2) 'For the avoidance of doubt... the court may be satisfied that smoke is or is not dark smoke as herein before defined notwithstanding that there has been no actual comparison thereof with a chart of the said type.' This allows an emission of dark smoke to be proved by other scientific methods or by photography, video, the use of a telesmoke device or any other competent method. Whatever the method used, some explanation should be made to the court of the technique of measurement.

'Chimney' includes structures and openings of any kind from which smoke, grit, dust, fumes may be emitted. Certain statutory defences exist to a charge of producing dark smoke, with the onus on the defendant to prove them. With one exception, the defences which are recognised by section 1(3) of the 1956 Act are that the smoke was solely due to one of the following:

(a) a cold furnace,

(b) a breakdown of the furnace,

(c) unsuitable fuel.

Section 1(4) of the Clean Air Act 1968 provides that in proceedings under this section, it will be a defence to show that the contravention complained of was inadvertent and all practical steps had been taken to prevent or minimise the emission.

Under the Clean Air (Emission of Dark Smoke) (Emissions) Regulations 1969 S.I. No. 1269 certain exemptions are made including the burning of timber, the supervised burning of explosives where no other method of disposal is possible, and for matter burnt in connection with fire research or fire fighting. Supervised burning of tar, pitch or asphalt in connection with the preparation and laying of any surface or burnt from any surface in connection with re-surfacing is also permitted. Other exceptions are provided for the burning of diseased animal and poultry carcasses and containers which have been contaminated with pesticides or other toxic substances.

Under section 29(2) a local authority in England and Wales may institute proceedings for an offence under section 1 of the Act in the case of any smoke which affects any part of their district, notwithstanding that the smoke is emitted from a chimney outside their district. Similar provision is made under section 1 of the 1968 Act regarding smoke from premises

Smoke abatement

Section 16 provided for smoke abatement and proceedings against smoky chimneys as a statutory nuisance. This is now replaced by section 79(1)(b) of the EPA which defines it as a statutory nuisance where smoke is emitted from premises so as to be prejudicial to health or a nuisance.

Under section 79(3) of the EPA, proceedings for a statutory nuisance may not be brought where the smoke is:

(a) smoke emitted from a chimney of a private dwelling within a smoke control area;

(b) dark smoke emitted from a chimney of a building or a chimney serving the furnace of a boiler or industrial plant attached to a building or for the time being fixed or installed on any land;

(c) smoke emitted from a railway locomotive steam engine (steam enthusiasts may be relieved!);

(d) dark smoke emitted from otherwise than as mentioned from trade or industrial premises.

The basis for these exceptions lies in the fact that such emissions fall into the Clean Air Act duties which local authorities are expected to enforce. If properly enforced none of these should arise.

CONTROL OF AIR POLLUTION UNDER THE EPA

The EPA extends the scope of the Clean Air Acts and introduces local control for prescribed processes. Section 85 of the EPA inserts a new section 7 into the Clean Air Act 1968 to enable the Secretary of State to make the Act apply to all prescribed gases as they do to smoke and apply the provisions of section 3 to prescribed gases as though they were smoke. Regulations which appear may make different provisions for different gases.

Section 4(3) designates control for substances which are released into the air to the local authority. Under section 4(4) the Secretary of State may direct functions carried out by a local authority to be carried out by HMIP while such a direction remains in force or during a period specified by the direction.

The local authority is left with the role of controlling air pollution where the emission first goes into the air and is a prescribed process falling into Part B of Schedule 1 of the Environmental Protection (Prescribed Processes and Substances) Regulations 1991. Not all emissions will necessarily be subject to local control and an authorisation: under regulation 4(2) an exception is made where a Part B process, (a) cannot result in a release into the air of a prescribed substance or (b) any release is so trivial that it is incapable of causing harm or its capacity to cause harm is insignificant.

However, no exemption from the need for an authorisation under local control is made where the process may give rise to an offensive smell 'noticeable outside the premises where the process is carried on' (regulation 4(6)).

APC control

Under the EPA the local authority has control over noxious substances. These are similar to IPC, and substances controlled are contained in Part B including:

• low grade combustion processes,

• smaller iron and steel furnaces,

• low grade incineration of waste and various coating processes,

• animal and vegetable treatment processes.

For processes requiring authorisation this must be granted by the local authority. Applications are to be in a form specified under regulations and generally the requirements are similar to those for an IPC application. The IPC regime for statutory consultation applies and the application must be advertised in a local newspaper as well as consultation with the NRA etc.

The time permitted for considering an application for a licence is four months under the Environment Protection (Authorisation of Processes) (Determination Periods) Order 1991 (S.I. 1991 No. 513), though such a period can be extended to one year when deciding applications for existing processes.

Under section 7(5) the conditions relating to IPC authorisations in section 7(1)-(4) are taken as applying to air pollution authorisations. For example, in a case of combustion, the local authority may set conditions as to the type of fuel to be burned or to the rate of emissions. Care will have to be taken as to the setting of conditions to ensure that the emissions which the conditions seek to control do not result in a discharge into another environmental medium on first release. For example, processes necessary to reduce an airborne emission to a certain standard may in themselves produce a discharge, for example of effluent, which would exceed an NRA standard. The authority must also ensure that no conditions imposed are *ultra vires* and the issue of such a licence could be judicially reviewed. Similarly, the conditions can only relate to emissions covered by the regulations. The effects of carbon dioxide emissions, for example, cannot be covered by authorisations.

Public scrutiny of applications by larger corporations and multinationals will be important since less well funded companies may seek to appeal decisions over authorisations by local authorities. The risk of costs on appeal may make hard-pressed local authorities veer on the side of caution when determining an authorisation (such an approach would be unreasonable as a fetter on discretion in itself) and a licence may be granted with particularly generous conditions. Obviously, large companies and organisations will be in a better position to appeal than small companies. The impact of public opinion may deter such a course.

In considering whether to grant an application, the local authority must have regard to section 7 requirements to BATNEEC. Guidance notes have been issued.

If an HMIP authorisation is required for a process which also generates emissions into the atmosphere, the overall process will be placed under the control of HMIP.

Amendment of the Alkali Works Act by the EPA

The original Alkali Act was passed in 1863 as a temporary measure. It was intended to control the 'classic' alkali process, the first stage of which was to treat common salt with sulphuric acid to produce saltcake. This process for the manufacture of soda discharged clouds of hydrogen chloride into the atmosphere. The Act was further extended in 1906, which established Central Government inspectors whose powers have now devolved to HMIP. Parts of the Act have now been repealed by Health and Safety legislation. The Act required that four distinct classes of works – alkali works, cement works, smelting works and scheduled works – are required to be registered. The Act required under section 27 that the best practical means were applied. Scheduled works were covered by the Alkali etc Works Orders 1966 and 1971, including sulphuric acid works, chemical plants, nitrate works and a great many others. (Prosecutions were in any event rare – there were only eight between 1967–71 with the average fine imposed being £3.00). Between 1920 and 1967 there were only three such prosecutions. Further amendments, including penalties, were made by COPA, but the Alkali Inspectorate itself was eventually merged with HMIP. These processes have now been taken under the control of the EPA.

Schedule 15 of the EPA amends and substitutes the Alkali & Works Regulation Act 1906 and inserts a new section 2A. This provides that the preceding Part of the Act shall not apply to any process which is a prescribed process as from the date which is the determination date for that process.

The 'determination date' for a prescribed process is:

(a) in the case of a process for which an authorisation is granted, the date on which the enforcing authority grants it, whether in pursuance of the application, or on appeal, of a direction to grant it;

(b) in the case of a process for which an authorisation is refused, the date of the refusal or, on an appeal, of the affirmation of the refusal.

In this section 'authorisation', 'enforcing authority' and 'prescribed process' have the meaning given in section 1 of the EPA and reference to an appeal is an appeal under section 15.

(Immediately before section 25 a new section 24A is inserted to the same effect.)

Other atmospheric controls: health and safety at work

The EPA amends section 5 of the Health and Safety at Work etc Act 1974 to provide that HSA legislation will no longer apply to any process which is a prescribed process as from the date which is the determination date for that process. A determination date is the date on which the enforcing authority grants an authorisation, whether on application, appeal or direction. Where there is a refusal, the determination date is the date of the refusal, or in an appeal case on the confirmation of the refusal.

Asbestos

The Control of Asbestos in the Air Regulations 1990 S.I. 556 regulates the release of asbestos, as a health and safety matter. As may be recalled, where health and safety are the only considerations, no authorisation can be issued under the EPA.

Asbestos is defined as the following fibrous silicates – actinolite, amosite, anthophyllite, chrysolite, crocidolite, or tremolite. The regulations apply to any production involving asbestos cement, asbestos cement products, fillers, floor coverings, joints, packaging and textiles.

Any person who controls premises to which section 5 of the Health and Safety at Work Act 1974 applies and from which asbestos is emitted through discharge outlets during the use of asbestos must ensure that:

- the concentration of asbestos so discharged...does not exceed 0.1 milligrams of asbestos per cubic metre of air;

- the amount of asbestos is measured at least once every six months.

Regulation 4(1) places a duty on any person undertaking activities involving the work of products containing asbestos and the removal of asbestos, and 'shall ensure that significant pollution is not caused thereby'. Any person who causes significant pollution commits an offence and shall be liable on conviction to a fine in the magistrates' court not exceeding a level 4 penalty.

Exceptions from authorisation

The regulations covering prescribed process under Schedule 1 make certain exceptions from the need for authorisation. No authorisation is needed from HMIP or a local authority if the process involves one carried out as a domestic activity in connection with a private dwelling. This does not, however, amount to a generalised right to do anything as a domestic activity – the exception will not prevent proceedings for a statutory nuisance or civil proceedings where a neighbour is adversely affected.

Regulation 4(3) also exempts processes carried out in a museum to demonstrate an industrial process of historic interest or for educational purposes.

Perhaps the most important exception from authorisation is made for 'the running on or within an aircraft, hovercraft, mechanically propelled road vehicle, railway locomotive or ship or other vessel of an engine which propels it'. Accordingly, for the control of emissions arising from road and other transport, other legislative measures must be invoked.

Other controls on air pollution

Problems on a global scale require global remedies and action on the international level and a number of the measures contained in this chapter have only an indirect affect on global warming. As these powers are derived from statute, they should not be exercised with the aim of reducing carbon dioxide emissions but only for their proper purpose. At present the EC is formulating measures on reducing carbon dioxide which are likely to overtake any legislation introduced by a UK Government. In the UK, carbon emission reduction schemes, like those operating in Toronto, might be difficult to initiate, although it is possible to list statutory measures which, if applied, will have the incidental effect of reducing carbon dioxide emissions. While statutory powers always have to be exercised for their proper purpose and not for achieving some indirect goal or benefit, they do illustrate much that could be achieved where there is the political will to put appropriate policies into action.

Vehicle emissions and carbon dioxide

In December 1992, the Government issued a consultation paper on possible methods of reducing carbon dioxide emissions. International obligations have committed the UK to a reduction of carbon emissions to 1990 levels by the year 2000. Among ideas postulated have been a carbon tax. At present other policies, particularly on roads and railway privatisation involving the closure of certain lines, contradict this.

Motor fuel

The Control of Pollution Act 1974, section 75 gives a power to the Secretary of State for the Environment to produce regulations controlling the composition of motor fuel for the purpose of reducing air pollution. For example, these have been exercised to control the amount of lead in petrol under S.I. 1981 /1523 and the sulphur content of oil under S.I. 1976/1988 and 1989.

All cars are required to be capable of running on unleaded petrol and new models had to comply from 1 October 1989; existing models are controlled from 1 October 1990. Regulations affecting the situation are the Road Vehicles (Construction and Use) (Amendment No. 6) Regulations 1988 S.I. 1524. The Road Vehicles (Construction and Use) (Amendment No. 2) Regulations 1990 (S.I. 1990 No. 1131) refer to vehicle exhausts.

Local authorities which feel moved to enforce these provisions may do so through their trading standards departments. The trading standards offices are empowered to make test purchases under the Trades Description Act 1968, section 27. Powers of search, entry and seizure are provided by section 28 and tests can be undertaken by section 30. There is, in theory, no reason why such powers should not be exercised for other areas; it is likely that EC legislation will supersede any developments.

Smoking vehicles are also included in the construction use regulation. At least one London Borough (Westminster) has publicised a scheme whereby members of the public may report the registration numbers of smoking vehicles to the authority. The information is then passed on to the police, who may investigate.

Catalytic converters

From 1993 cars must be fitted with catalytic converters to remove carbon monoxide, hydrocarbons such as benzene and nitric oxide.

The contribution that motor vehicles make towards various types of atmospheric pollution is increasingly being recognised, particularly in urban areas. Current traffic forecasts for the UK predict a doubling of traffic by the year 2025. This doubling in volume, assuming it occurs, will overwhelm the effect of many improvements and reductions in pollution problems.

LOCAL AUTHORITY POLICIES

As the measures to control air pollution lie with local authorities at first instance, it may be worth considering some of the other options and secondary measures which an environmentally minded authority might take.

Much could be done by local authorities by way of encouraging less dependence on motor vehicles, encouraging cycle paths and reducing power consumption. However, with capital expenditure limits placed upon much activity by local government this will prove impossible until these limits are relaxed by Central Government.

The role of the police

A large number of rules and regulations exist to curb and control the use and abuse of motor vehicles. The police play a number of important roles in controlling traffic, not least speeding. The faster that vehicles go, the more fuel is burned.

Policing priorities for those who pose a danger with car use vary widely from area to area. As to whether the police choose traffic control as an area for enforcement is at their discretion, but representations may be made to them under section 106 of the

Police and Criminal Evidence Act 1984, which requires that a Chief Constable must have regard to the opinions of those living in the neighbourhood.

Traffic Calming Act 1992

This short act, introduced curiously enough by a former roads minister, Christopher Chope, shortly before he lost his seat in Parliament, lays the basis for traffic calming. It amends the Highways Act 1980 to enable a local authority to take steps to introduce traffic calming measures into operation, such as road bumps.

A decrease in the speed of traffic leads to less fuel being burned and hence less road pollution. A direct challenge to motorists' right to speed and pollute can achieve much, although it is only a small measure.

Power generation by the local authority

Sections 11–12 of the Local Government (Miscellaneous Provisions) Act 1976 gives a power to local authorities to generate their own electricity, subject to a proviso that they do not sell it without permission from the Secretary of State. There seems no reason why, providing planning and other legal requirements are fulfilled, that this should not form the basis of a means of generating power by way of renewable energy through wind or wave power.

Stubble and straw burning

Section 152 of the Environmental Protection Act 1990 gives a power to the Secretary of State to prohibit or restrict the burning of crop residue – defined as straw, stubble or any crop residue.

Section 152 replaces the power of local authorities to create bye-laws as to offences of burning straw and stubble under section 43 of the Criminal Justice Act 1982. Under section 152(4) the Minister is also given the power by order to repeal or amend any bye-laws of local authorities dealing with the burning of crop residues on agricultural land. Such regulations, if they emerge, may apply only to specific areas or to specific crops and only to certain circumstances. Fines of up to £2,000 may be imposed in the magistrates' court.

Such fires have long been criticised because of the pollution that smoke causes and damage to habitats. Stubble burning has certainly had some curious opponents, including the late Sir Arthur Harris of Bomber Command who instigated massive destruction by fire in the bombing of Dresden during World War II. Calls to ban stubble burning were made in Parliament in 1983.

Section 161A of the Highways Act 1980, as inserted by the Highways (Amendment) Act 1986, created an offence of causing danger or annoyance by fires. Under subsection (1) a person will be guilty of an offence if they light, direct or permit a fire causing the user of a highway to be injured, interrupted or endangered.

Defences are provided such as, if the accused can prove that at any time the fire was lit, he was satisfied on reasonable grounds that users of the highway would not be affected as stated in section 1 and that the accused did all that could reasonably be done to prevent such harm.

EC draft directive on a carbon tax and energy emissions

A proposal was made by the EC Commission on 13 May 1992 to introduce a carbon dioxide and energy tax (Com (92) 226 Final). The purpose of the Directive is to provide for a harmonised introduction of a tax levied on coal, lignite, peat and their derivatives, natural gas oil and other substances including heating and motor fuels. The Directive intends to establish a Committee consisting of representatives from Member States to assist the Commission with the implementation of the carbon tax aimed at reducing the emission of carbon dioxide. The tax will be levied and collected by Member States and will be applied to both national products and those from other Member States.

Under Article 8, the tax will be based upon the energy content of the products and volume of carbon dioxide emitted on combustion, depending on the substance involved.

Partly as a response to this Directive, the British Government produced a consultation paper on various approaches to reduce emissions of carbon dioxide in December 1992. The shape of any legislation which may emerge is likely to depend very much upon the responses and pressure from the public.

NOTES

[1] Government White Paper 1970.
[2] DoE Report 1979, *Chlorofluorocarbons and their effect on stratospheric ozone.*
[3] See Chapter 7, pages 127–8.
[4] DoE, *The Potential Effects of Climate Change in the UK*, 1991, HMSO, London.
[5] See Chapter 1
[6] Stuart Maclanaghan, personal communication.
[7] See Garner J.F. and Crow, R.K., (1976), *Clean Air – Law and Practice*, Shaw & Sons Ltd.
[8] Stuart Maclanaghan, personal communication.
[9] Haigh, N., (1991), *Manual of Environment Policy, the EC and Britain*, Longman, London.

Chapter 9

Water Pollution

Despite attempts having been made for over a century to control the discharges into Britain's rivers, water pollution remains a major problem, brought into focus with the privatisation of the water industry in 1989.[1] Legislation protecting water has grown extremely complex with the privatisation of the water industry which has been consolidated in the Water Resources Act 1991, the Water Industry Act 1991, the Water Companies Act 1991, the Land Drainage Act 1991 and the Water (Consequential and Amendments) Act 1991.

Complex though this legislation may be, there is a potentially wide scope under English law for citizens to take action over water pollution, using both the civil and criminal law. Indeed, because of certain in-built procedural requirements, a private prosecutor armed with the right information may actually find it *easier* to prosecute water pollution offences than an official from the National Rivers Authority.

In the past, detecting water pollution was a relatively simple matter – much of it was clearly visible, such as soot floating on the surface of a river. Today, it may be very much harder to discover pollution arising from chemical compounds and heavy metals produced by industry, unless a person has sophisticated scientific equipment available.

Industry is not the only offender. Modern farming methods generate large amounts of water pollution from fertilisers and millions of litres of excrement and urine produced by intensively-farmed livestock.

Among those who have been convicted of water pollution offences are multinational companies, local authorities and electricity companies. The British Government itself has been held in breach of EC standards by the European Court. In November 1992 the European Court made a finding against the UK for failure to introduce a directive originally issued in 1980 on nitrates content of water in East Anglia.[2]

DUTIES OF THE NATIONAL RIVERS AUTHORITY

The task of controlling pollution in inland waterways today primarily falls to the National Rivers Authority. The NRA has powers to prosecute for a wide range of water offences and it is to the NRA that the public should report instances of water pollution. The burdens placed on the NRA are heavy ones and even an organisation with much greater funding and resources would find it difficult to undertake effectively all its responsibilities.[3]

The NRA is under a number of duties which may be open to judicial review in the event that the NRA ever fails to exercise its powers correctly (see Chapter 5). Under section 16 of the Water Resources Act 1991 the NRA must (rather whimsically):

(a) further the conservation and enhancement of natural beauty and the conservation of flora, fauna, geological and physiographical features of special interest; and

(b) take into account any effect which the proposals would have on the beauty or amenity of any urban or rural area, of any such flora, fauna, features, buildings, sites or objects.

Thus everything from fish to features in Constable's paintings must be considered by the NRA in the exercise of its functions.

Section 17 provides specific duties in relation to sites of special scientific interest. Section 39 makes provision that the grant of a licence does not derogate from the rights of existing licence holders. In addition, the NRA also enjoys certain bye-law making powers under section 210 of the Water Resources Act 1991. Copies of these may be obtained from the NRA and will relate to certain stretches of water.

The Act designates certain waters as 'controlled waters' which it is an offence for any person to pollute. Controlled waters are defined in section 104 as:

(a) relevant territorial waters, ie waters which extend three miles seaward from the coast of England and Wales;

(b) coastal waters, that is to say any waters which are within the area which extends landward from those baselines as far as the limit of high tide or, in the case of the waters of any relevant river or water course, as far as the fresh water limit of the river or water course, together with waters of any enclosed dock;

(c) inland waters – any relevant lake, pond or any relevant river or water course as is above the fresh-water limit;

(d) ground waters – contained in strata including wells and boreholes.

Proceedings for offences in magistrates' courts should be brought in the court having jurisdiction over the controlled water into which an illegal discharge takes place. The same principle should apply for civil actions for damages of up to £50,000 brought through the relevant county court.

In bringing a criminal prosecution for polluting any controlled waters, the prosecutor should prove that the water concerned is a controlled water by reference to the legislation and any relevant documents.

Certain waters fall outside the definition of 'controlled water' including lakes, ponds, reservoirs (other than for public supply), pools of water that do not drain into others and water supply mains. The Secretary of State has issued the Controlled Waters (Lakes and Ponds) Order 1989 S.I. No. 1149 which defines such waters. Although not under the guardianship of the NRA, anyone who pollutes non-controlled waters may be open to a civil claim from a landowner or, where appropriate, a criminal prosecution for a deposit of waste, contrary to Part II of the EPA.

Integrated pollution control and water pollution

One nineteenth century measure, the Public Health Act 1875, is still on the statute book, making it an offence to corrupt water by 'gas washing', though cases of this must now be exceedingly rare and will be illegal unless covered by the IPC provisions of the EPA and the Water Resources Act 1991.

Discharges of prescribed substances into water fall within the IPC system imposed by the EPA. This puts the responsibility for granting a consent on HMIP, and the existence of a consent will act as a defence to a charge of polluting water, unless the terms of the consent are breached. The public will, of course, be able to discover whether a consent exists from the public registers. Although responsibility for authorisations lies with HMIP, the NRA has a watchdog status with wide powers to set conditions or even prevent the authorisation being granted.

Before granting such an authorisation HMIP must consult with the National Rivers Authority under section 28 of the EPA. The NRA can grant conditions which HMIP must include in the authorisation to the person operating a prescribed process. HMIP may also add its own conditions which the NRA can seek to vary. If the NRA considers that an emission will breach water quality objectives (see below) HMIP is under a legal duty to put the wishes of the NRA into practice. However, the NRA does not enjoy the wide powers of prohibition notices and enforcement methods available to HMIP.

It remains to be seen how effective this dual-agency approach will be in controlling water pollution arising from prescribed processes, and whether conflicts will be generated between the two enforcement bodies. It is unclear how far the powers conferred by section 161 of the Water Resources Act may enable the NRA to step in and interfere with the operation of a prescribed process under HMIP control.

Water quality objectives

In addition to the category of controlled waters, section 82 of the Water Resources Act 1991, the Secretary of State may by regulations prescribe a system of classifying the quality of waters as to:

(a) general requirements as to the purposes for which the waters to which the classification is applied are to be suitable;

(b) specific requirements as to the substances that are to be present in or absent from the water and as to the concentrations of substances which are present in the water; and

(c) specific requirements relating to other characteristics.

For instance, under the Surface Waters (Dangerous Substances) (Classification) Regulations 1992 (No. 337) concentrations are to be set for dichloroethane, trichloroethylene, perchloroethylene and trichlorobenzene to achieve water quality objectives for complying with EC requirements in Council Directive 90/415/EEC.

These regulations set out a system of classifying relevant inland, territorial and coastal waters' sampling requirements and list methods of measurement. Samples must be taken at a point sufficiently close to any discharge to be representative.

THE NRA CONSENTS SYSTEM – PUBLIC PARTICIPATION

The NRA is responsible for granting consents under the Control of Pollution Act 1974 and the Water Resources Act 1991 to allow discharges of polluting substances into controlled waters. As with other authorisations, there is an opportunity for the public to participate in the process. The details are contained in Schedule 12 of the Act. Fees are to be paid for each consent, which represents an attempt to make the polluter pay.

Each individual source of discharge must have a separate consent. For example, if a factory has three different discharge pipes, a separate consent must be available for each one. Applications to the NRA for discharge consents are prescribed in Schedule 10 of the 1991 Act.

Unless there is likely to be little effect from the discharge, the application for a consent must be advertised at least twice by the NRA in local newspapers circulating in the area where the discharges are made and in the locality of any controlled waters into which the discharges may enter. The application must also be advertised in the *London Gazette*. The NRA is then under a duty to consider any written representations received within six weeks of the advertisement. Anyone making representations should seek to make them as clear as possible and specific to the controlled water concerned. Supporting or verifying documentation of any rights or interests should also be included.

If the NRA agrees to the consent, it must notify anyone who has made representations. The authority may either grant the application with or without conditions or refuse it. A delay of more than four months is treated as the equivalent of a refusal.

Anyone making representations may do so with reference to the powers to impose conditions and to any civil rights which may be affected (see below). Conditions which may be set are listed in para. 2(5) of Schedule 10 and may cover the following:

(a) places where discharges may be made and the type of outlet;

(b) the nature, origin, composition, temperature, volume, rates of discharge and periods when discharges may be made;

(c) steps to be taken as to treatment or any process for minimising pollution;

(d) sampling requirements;

(e) metering and monitoring volume, rate, temperature, nature and composition of any discharge;

(f) record keeping by the holder of the consent.

The NRA is under an obligation to all persons who have made representations or objections, informing such persons that they have 21 days to make representations to the Secretary of State. During this 21 day period the NRA may not grant the consent, unless the Secretary of State directs that one is given. Alternatively, the Secretary of State may call in the application to be determined and cause a public inquiry to be held. Proceedings must be fair and conform to natural justice – judicial review will be available.

A consent may be granted outright, subject to certain conditions, or refused. The Secretary of State must give an opportunity to all who made representations to be heard.[4]

Any consent granted by the NRA will last for as long a period as specified in it, but in any event cannot be revoked or varied within two years by the authority. The only power to intervene is available to the Secretary of State where the discharge has become a pollution threat or breaches a new legal measure, for example a new water quality standard.

In addition to public consultation over consents, the Secretary of State may cause a public inquiry to be held under section 213 (1)(b) in connection with any of 'the authority's functions'. This might be an alternative to be given to aggrieved persons instead of judicial review of any duties of the authority. An inquiry held under this section may cover water quality objectives, preventing or dealing with pollution. It is to this residual power that citizens should look, where a consent has become hazardous or unlawful within the first two years following its grant.

Registers

Section 190 of the Water Resources Act 1991 contains provisions relating to registers and their contents which cover controlled waters. The contents may be examined by the public to check which waterways have been reviewed and tested by the NRA and what the results were. The registers go back up to five years.

The contents of the registers are set out in the Control of Pollution (Registers) Regulations 1989 including the date of any authorisation for consent, the maximum quantities that may be released into the controlled water and tables of samples which have been taken. There are two types of sample – ordinary and legal. Ordinary samples are for monitoring purposes. Legal samples are those taken prior to a prosecution.

The register will also detail conditions which may have been placed on the consent, including the types of substance which may be lawfully released into the water. Where a sample reveals traces of a substance which is not included in the consent, an offence may have been committed under the WRA section 85. It is worth checking whether the consent contains a clause to the effect that no other substances other than those stated in the consent may be discharged into the water. If other substances are detected outside the terms of consent, there will be no defence to any prosecution in connection with the discharge.

Not every application may be included on the registers; a power is available to the Secretary of State to issue a certificate to withhold an application from any mention in the register, together with the details of any consent, effluent or sample. This power is available to the Secretary of State when satisfied that, to make the information available would either be contrary to the public interest, or would prejudice to an unreasonable degree some private interest by disclosing information about a trade secret. It is arguable how far that public interest can be used as justification for the imposition of this power considering the greater rights of access to environmental information which have entered into the law. Given such considerations, exclusion from a register can only really be justified on the basis of a trade secret. Any claims submitted to the Secretary of State to be entitled by a certificate will have to be scrutinised by the Department of the Environment with care, for it poses the question of how the public will ever find out if a certificate is erroneously granted. Hopefully, the access to information regulations may assist the public in obtaining more information in this area.

Preventative steps

Rather than wait for water pollution to happen, the NRA has powers to take preventative action to forestall pollution under section 161. Where pollution has already occurred, the NRA can take action to clean up the site and recover the cost from the person who caused, or knowingly permitted, the pollution.

POLLUTION OFFENCES AND WATER

There are a number of offences relating to the pollution of water, now contained in sections 85–89 of the Water Resources Act 1991, replacing equivalent provisions under the Water Act 1989. Under section 85 of the Water Resources Act 1991, a person commits an offence if he causes or knowingly permits–

(a) any poisonous, noxious or polluting matter or any solid waste matter to enter any controlled waters; or

(b) any matter, other than trade effluent or sewage effluent, to enter controlled waters by being discharged from a drain or sewer.

These are strict liability offences as the person is guilty of pollution whether she/he knows of the pollution or not. An example under the old legislation was *Rothwell Limited* v *Yorkshire Water Authority* (1984) where a manager disposed of chemicals into a public drain. The effluent escaped into a river where fish were killed. Even though the manager had no idea that the river could become polluted, the company was convicted of the offence.

In spite of this strict liability element, care should still be taken with commencing proceedings, as the section creates two offences, one of simply causing pollution and one of knowingly doing so. The information on the summons should be carefully worded so as to allege only one offence. If the word 'knowingly' is added, some element of the state of mind will have to be proved.

The need to take care with the wording of information and relating them to the events for which complaint is made was shown in the case of *Wychavon District Council* v *NRA* (1992) *(The Times,* 17 September), which interpreted the equivalent provisions in section 107 (c) of the Water Act 1989. Wychavon District Council was charged with causing polluting matter to enter a river following the breaking of a sewerage pipe near a river and their failure to promptly repair it. Convicted in the magistrates' court, the council then applied to the High Court on a case stated (ie a point of law) that the council had not actually caused the pollution by an act – they had simply been inactive. The court accepted this argument and held that the offence of causing polluting matter to enter a river required 'a positive act by an accused and not merely a passive looking on' (per Watkins LJ). What the council should have been charged with was knowingly permitting sewerage to enter a controlled water.

It would thus appear that polluters could have defences where pollution is caused by acts of third parties which gave rise to pollution (a third party could be prosecuted if traced), or accidents.

Care should be taken in investigating the pollutant's identity if a corporation is believed to be behind the pollution. A number of subsidiary companies are created as water undertakers which may mean difficulties in discovering the registered address of the company legally responsible. Where the commission, by any person, of an offence is due to the act or default of some other person, that other person may be charged with and convicted of the offence whether or not proceedings for the offence are taken against the first-mentioned person.

Prosecutions may thus take place of persons and occupiers who are unaware of leaks or discharges from their land. There is no need to prove negligence or carelessness. A person will not be guilty of an offence if a third party, such as a vandal, causes the pollution. However, not every outside cause will enable a person to avoid liability; if a particular risk could have been anticipated or foreseen, a polluter will be potentially liable if the outside intervention could have been prevented or guarded against.

All kinds of polluting matter may be covered by these provisions, including chemicals, silage, manure, fertilisers, pesticides, oil spillages and solid items such as oil drums, litter etc.

Under section 103, the time limit for bringing proceedings is extended by an extra six months from the limit normally imposed by section 127 of the Magistrates' Courts Act 1980. A magistrates' court may try any summary offence if the information is laid not more than 12 months after the commission of the offence.

Prosecution evidence

As noted earlier, it may be difficult to use information contained in registers such as those held by the NRA since it is likely to be considered hearsay. This duty can only be overcome by use of section 24 of the Criminal Justice Act 1988, to obtain original records or by subpoenaing the NRA official involved. However, in offences involving the breach of discharge consents, it is submitted that the practice set out in *Ashcroft* v *Cambro Waste Management* (1981) 1 WLR may be adopted. This establishes that once the elements of the offence have been proved, it is for the defendant to show or prove any special defence as required for the conditions of consent. The onus of proving an exception or defence will be on the defendant under section 101 of the Magistrates' Court Act 1980, such as the production of a consent which is relevant to the substance discharged.

DEFENCES

Certain defences which exist are included in section 88 of the Water Resources Act to an offence under section 85 where:

(a) the polluter has a consent under the Water Resources Act 1991 or the Control of Pollution Act 1974;

(b) an authorisation for a prescribed process designated for central control under the Environmental Protection Act 1990 is held;

(c) a waste disposal licence is held (which should have been granted in consultation with the NRA);

(d) the discharge is permitted under section 163 or section 165 of the Water Industry Act 1991 (discharges for works purposes);

(e) a licence under Part II of the Food and Environment Act 1985 is held;

(f) any other statute or order allows such a discharge.

Other defences available are included in section 89, which provides that a person will not be guilty of an offence

(a) where the release occurred in an emergency in order to avoid danger to life or health;

(b) providing that all such steps are taken as are reasonably practicable in the circumstances for minimising the extent of the entry and discharge and its polluting effects;

(c) where particulars of entry or discharge are furnished with the National Rivers Authority as soon as reasonably practicable after the entry occurs.

Other exceptions include discharges from ships and escapes from abandoned mines. Accidental releases from deposits on land or in mines or quarries which are authorised to take waste where no other site is reasonably practical and where steps have been taken to minimise any release are also exempt.

If none of these exemptions apply it is unlikely that there will be any defence. As a result, a polluter might well be advised to plead guilty and hope for a corresponding reduction in any penalty imposed, together with credit for any clean-up measures or steps which have been undertaken to prevent any repetition.

If a plea of guilty is not entered and no defence is available, defence tactics are likely to rely upon trying to find a technicality to escape prosecution. In a case where a defendant relies upon a technicality, there still may be implications for costs (see Chapter 4).

Type of pollution and evidence of samples

Special provisions apply before a sample can be admitted as evidence by the National Rivers Authority. These are set out in section 209 and are known as 'three way' procedure.

Section 209(1) states that

> 'the result of the analysis of any sample taken on behalf of the Authority [NRA] in exercise of any power ... shall not be admissible in any legal proceedings in respect of any effluent passing from any land or vessel unless the person who took the sample:
>
> (a) on taking the sample notified the occupier of the land or the master of the vessel of his intention to have it notified;
>
> (b) there and then divided the sample into three parts and caused each part to be placed in a container which was sealed and marked;
>
> (c) delivered one part to the occupier of the land or the owner or master of the vessel and retained one part, apart from the one he submitted to be analysed, for future comparison.'

This is a strict requirement – at least for the NRA. In *NRA* v *Harcros Timber and Building Supplies* (1992) *(The Times*, 2 April 1992), it was held that where the result of a sample of water or effluent was sought to be admitted in impending legal proceedings, part of the sample had first be given to the defendant, otherwise it would be inadmissible.

The situation is probably different for a private prosecution. This is important to recognise, lest a water prosecutor is faced by a defence lawyer arguing that 'Three way procedure has not been followed – my client has been utterly prejudiced and the statutory procedure ignored'. Before the court dismisses the case, it should be pointed out that the requirements only apply to proceedings commenced by the NRA. But because this would be a ripe area for an appeal – even as a delaying tactic – private prosecutors might be well advised to explain this as a preliminary point.

Subject to these restrictions, any other scientific evidence of sampling such as the effect on flora or fauna is potentially admissible, including tests from the bodies of dead fish and crustaceans.

Deposits of waste and vegetation

A person is guilty of an offence under section 90 if she/he disturbs water courses and causes or removes any deposit from a river. Under section 90(2) a person is also guilty of an offence if she/he is responsible for causing or permitting a substantial amount of vegetation to be cut or uprooted in any inland fresh waters, or to be cut or uprooted so near to water that it falls into it, and then fails to remove it.

This section does not include actions in connection with land drainage, flood prevention or navigation.

OFFENCES IN CONNECTION WITH AGRICULTURE

The harmful effects that certain modern agricultural practices may have on water quality have been acknowledged and made subject to controls contained in the Control of Pollution (Silage, Slurry and Agricultural Fuel Oil) Regulations 1991 S.I. 324 made under the Water Act 1989. These impose restrictions on the making of silage, the storage of slurry and the storage of fuel oil on farms. The regulations give rise to criminal offences which are triable either way, with offences punishable by a £2,000 fine in the magistrates' court and an unlimited fine on indictment. It is quite possible that large numbers of farms and agricultural enterprises operate without regard to these provisions.

Rules for silage storage

Under regulation 3, any crop which is being turned into silage must be stored in a silo which complies with the restrictions placed by Schedule 1. The base and walls of the silo must be impermeable and capable of lasting at least 20 years. The capacity of the effluent tank, in the case of a silo with a capacity of less than 1,500 cubic metres, shall not be less than 20 litres for each cubic metre of silo capacity. In the case of a silo with a capacity of 1,500 cubic metres or more, the effluent tank shall not be less than 30 cubic metres plus 6.7 litres for each cubic metre of silo capacity in excess of the 1,500 cubic metres. Where part of a tank is constructed below ground, it must be sufficient to satisfy requirements of the regulations without maintenance for 20 years.

Where the silage is compressed into bales it must be wrapped in an impermeable membrane or enclosed in impermeable bags and must be stored at least ten metres from any inland or coastal waters which silage effluent could enter as a result. Under regulation 3(2), if a person having custody or control over any crop which is being turned, or has been made, into silage opens any bag or removes the wrapping of any bale within ten metres of any inland or coastal waters which effluent could enter, an offence will be committed.

Rules for oil storage

Fuel oil stored on farms must be contained in tanks which comply with the requirements of Schedule 3 of the regulations. A fuel storage area must be surrounded by and within a bund. The bund must be capable of retaining within the area a volume of not less than 110 per cent of the capacity of the tank. Various requirements are laid down for combinations of tanks or where fuel is not so stored.

The bund and the base of the storage area must be impermeable and shall be designed and constructed so that through proper maintenance they are likely to remain so for at least 20 years.

Any tap or valve permanently fixed to the tank through which fuel oil can be discharged to the open, must also be within the bund. It must also be arranged so as to discharge vertically downwards and must be shut and locked in that position when not in use. Where a flexible pipe delivers fuel from the tank, it must be fitted with a tap or valve at its end which automatically closes when not in use and which is locked in a way which ensures that it is kept within the bund when not in use.

No fuel storage area, or the bund surrounding it, must be placed within ten metres of any inland or coastal waters in case of an escape.

Rules for slurry

Under regulation 4, slurry may only be stored in a slurry system which fulfils the requirements of Schedule 3, with the exception of slurry which is temporarily in a transport tanker with a capacity not exceeding 18,000 litres used on roads or on the farm. Any facilities used for the temporary storage of slurry before it is transferred to a slurry storage tank shall have adequate capacity to store the maximum quantity of slurry which is likely to be produced on the premises within a two day period.

The tanks used for storage must have adequate storage capacity for the likely quantities of slurry produced on premises and with regard to the method of disposal. Where it is proposed to dispose of slurry on the premises by spreading it on land, any tank is required to store not more than the maximum quantity likely to be produced in any continuous four month period. The person controlling the tank must have regard to the likely quantities of rainfall (including any fall of snow, hail or sleet) which may fall or drain into a slurry storage tank, during the likely maximum storage period.

Licences to extract water

The Water Resources Act of 1963 gave the occupier of the land contiguous to an inland water a right to abstract. With the privatisation of the water industry, section 24 of the Water Resources Act 1991 states that

'no person shall abstract from any source of supply, or cause or permit any other person so to abstract any water, except in pursuance of a licence under this Act granted by the river authority and in accordance with the provisions of that licence.'

Under section 52 such a licence may be varied or revoked. Applications for a licence must be advertised in the *London Gazette* and local newspaper. Objections can be made, with the familiar route of the matter going to the Secretary of State where the applicant seeks to appeal a refusal from the NRA.

Section 189 of the Act requires that a register is kept of all abstraction licences which have been granted. Details to be kept in the licences are prescribed in the Water Resources (Licences) Regulations 1965 (S.I. 1965 No. 574). These provisions do not apply to subterranean flows of water.

A licence is not required in cases involving any abstraction of a quantity of water 'not exceeding five cubic metres', providing it does not form part of a continuing operation where more than five cubic metres is abstracted. Section 39 provides that a licence must not affect the rights of existing licence holders or small abstractors who do not require a licence.

If consent is given by the NRA, not more than 20 cubic metres may be abstracted, again provided that it is not a continuous operation. Such an abstraction may be made by or on behalf of an occupier of the land providing that the water is:

(a) abstracted for use on a holding consisting of that land with or without other land therewith; and

(b) is abstracted for use on that holding for the domestic purposes of the occupier's household and/or an agricultural purpose other than spray irrigation.

If the quantity of water removed exceeds 20 cubic metres, in aggregate, in any period of 24 hours, the licence will be breached.

Consultation must take place for an abstraction licence to be granted. The procedures follow the usual format of a public advertisement in local newspapers and the *London Gazette*. Any applicant refused a licence, as mentioned earlier, may appeal to the Secretary of State and a public inquiry may be held. Issues that may be raised include the rights of any other owners of the water at civil law and the question of how a reduction in flow will affect the flora and fauna of the river and any other waters concerned.

These measures exist for the protection of individual and wider public rights. To what extent licences may be granted or refused with reference to the wider need to protect the environment or particular species of flora or fauna, has yet to be adequately tested in the courts. With the privatisation of water and increased charges for water supply, the number of companies and individuals seeking to abstract water is likely to increase.

Section 52 gives a power to the NRA to revoke a licence and to the Secretary of State to direct the NRA to draw up proposals for varying or revoking a licence.

Minimum acceptable flow

The concept of 'minimum acceptable flow' existed in earlier water legislation. Under section 21, the NRA may submit a proposal to the Secretary of State for the minimum acceptable flow along a particular river or estuary. Under section 22, the Secretary of State may direct the NRA to draw up a scheme. Such powers existed under the Control of Pollution Act 1974 but were never brought into force. In the absence of any such schemes, the NRA must consider the following matters:

- the flow of inland waters from time to time;
- the duties under sections 16 and 17;
- any water quality objectives which must be met;
- ensuring that water flow does not go below that necessary for preserving public health and
    - meeting the requirements of existing lawful uses of inland waters, and
    - meeting the requirements, in relation to those waters and other inland waters whose flow may be affected by changes in the flow, of navigation, fisheries and land drainage.

Curtailment of certain existing rights

Section 55 of the Act gives a right to the owner of fishing rights to apply to the Secretary of State for the variation or revocation of a licence where the flow of a river is threatened. However, this does not apply where the water flow is reduced because of a lack of rainfall.

CIVIL CLAIMS

It might be thought that the granting of a discharge consent would exempt a person from any legal liability for whatever substances are released into controlled waters. This is far from the case. Anyone exercising a discharge consent needs to be extremely careful not to infringe the rights of private parties – or at least those who may suffer damage as a result. At least in terms of protecting landowners, the civil law imposes a more draconian regime at common law than exists with criminal legislation. Indeed, a discharge consent in no way protects the holder from potentially large civil claims, exceeding penalties that might arise in a criminal prosecution, particularly when legal costs are added. Small businesses and negligent farmers could be bankrupted by a sizeable civil claim.

At common law a person may have a claim against anyone who pollutes any water over which they have rights. At common law, the doctrine of 'riparian rights' establishes that anyone owning land is entitled to the enjoyment of water running over, through, below and adjoining the property. The fouling of water in a natural river or stream flowing past the land of a riparian owner is an infringement of a property right of that owner, whether or not she/he actually owns the land forming the river bed.

Pollution of water over which a person enjoys riparian rights can be actionable as a tort in negligence, nuisance or trespass. Anything which changes the quality of the water is potentially actionable. This includes anything which affects the temperature of the water (see *Tipping* v *Eckersley* (1855) K&J 264). Where there is little interference with a person's rights, any damages awarded are likely to be nominal, but cost could be incurred if an order to restore the stream to its natural state is included. With increased awareness of environmental matters and the general concern about toxic substances in the environment, properties with land adjoining polluted rivers may be able to sustain claims to compensate for any fall in market value.

If procedural obstacles can be overcome, there will be a number of advantages with bringing a civil claim, not least that the standard of proof is lower (on the balance of probabilities) and otherwise hearsay evidence may be admissible. No defence is available on the grounds that others have already polluted the water (*Staffordshire County Council* v *Seisdon RDC* (1907) 5 LGR 347). In cases where the pollution comes from a number of sources, all that need be shown is that the polluter is responsible for one of them (*Crossley* v *Lightowler* (1866) 11 Ch App Case 478).

Much documentary evidence, such as the NRA register, will be easier to admit in civil proceedings under section 4 of the Civil Evidence Act 1968. Damages can be substantial but can only be awarded for actual loss, not future harm (*Pennington* v *Brinsop Hall Coal Co* (1877) 5 Ch D 769). The statement of claim should seek sufficient damages to cover the cost of putting the plaintiff back into the position that was being enjoyed before the incident occurred. This could include clean-up costs, pleaded as special damages, and the cost of restocking fish. Loss of profits (for example in a fish farm or a river leased to anglers) could also be included. Other applications for award might be losses sustained by excluding a polluted intake of water, the costs of procuring clean or fresh water supplies (eg transport costs, hire or purchase of purification equipment etc) and any other losses which flow directly from the pollution.

To a victim of pollution this may be far more satisfactory compensation than would arise from a criminal conviction and it is frequently sought in claims brought by anglers, who have led the way in water actions.

A restitution order – basically an injunction – might require the person responsible for the pollution to clean up a site as part of the relief claimed under an injunction. It should be noted that one potential drawback will be that such clean-up operations will be confined to the area over which the riparian rights extend. The court will not order activity in relation to the rights of a non-litigant.

There is no reason why a statutory nuisance should not be an alternative claim where the circumstances merit, such as persistent fouling of a river or stream. Injunctions to restrain the actual process completely may prove impossible – only the effects arising from it. Matters should, however, be brought to the attention of the NRA to consider an alteration of the consent.

Pollution of the sea

Various provisions apply to pollution of the sea, putting into effect certain international obligations. The Merchant Shipping (Oil Pollution) Act 1971 requires compulsory insurance against oil pollution for vessels carrying over 2,000 tons of persistent oil.

It should not be imagined that the threat comes purely from tanker disasters such as the *Braer*, which broke up off the Shetland Islands in January 1993. For example, in 1984, when no tanker losses were recorded in UK waters, at least ten major oil slicks were reported.[5]

The Prevention of Oil Pollution Act 1971 makes it an offence, under section 2, to discharge oil or any mixture of oil from land or from the sea. The section applies to the following waters:

(a) the whole of the sea within the seaward limits of the territorial waters of the United Kingdom; and

(b) all other waters (including inland waters) which are within those limits and are navigable by sea-going ships.

Offences can be committed by the owners or masters of vessels, occupiers in the case of spillages on land, owners of a pipeline and persons carrying out exploration of the seabed or the soil. Schedule 14 of the EPA makes certain amendments and enables foreign companies, which may own vessels, to be prosecuted. Any documents served on the master of a vessel are deemed to be served on the company.

Defences exist for an owner or master, charged with an offence under sections 1–2. It is a defence to prove that the oil or mixture was discharged for the safety of the vessel, or for preventing damage to any vessel or cargo, or to save lives. To prevent such defences being raised as a matter of course, if the court is satisfied that the discharge of oil was not necessary, it may still convict.

A further defence applies in land where the oil was contained in effluent produced by operations for the refining of oil, and where reasonable steps had been taken to dispose of the effluent and for eliminating oil from the effluent.

The Secretary of State has powers to make directions to owners and masters of vessels in the case of shipping accidents. Anyone guilty of ignoring such a direction or of wilfully obstructing a person carrying out a direction faces a fine of up to £50,000 in the magistrates' court. Section 20(1) of the Prevention of Oil Pollution Act 1971 enables the court to direct that the fine imposed may be paid to any person who has incurred or will incur expenses in removing any pollution, or making good any damage which is attributable to the offence. The court may order the whole or part of the fine to be paid to that person for or towards defraying those expenses. (Civil claims may also be brought by persons who have suffered harm.)

Under section 20 the court is also given additional powers to enforce fines by way of distress or arrestment and sale of the vessel, tackle, furniture and apparel.

Dumping at sea

A licence is required under the Food and Environment Protection Act 1985 for the deposit of substances or articles within the controlled United Kingdom waters either in the sea or under the sea-bed. The EPA has made amendments under sections 146 and 147 to extend offences to foreign ships.

Details of licences issued are kept in public registers maintained by the Ministries, formerly detailed in Schedule 4 of the Act but now repealed and replaced by section 147 of the EPA which sets out the prescribed contents of registers. Inspection is free of charge. Information included in the registers details the nature of containers and packages in which substances were intended to be deposited and the results of any toxicity tests carried out to determine if a licence should be issued, or terms under which it should be issued.

It is an offence to deposit any substances or articles without a licence

- within United Kingdom controlled waters, either in the sea or under the sea-bed –

  - from a vehicle, vessel, aircraft, hovercraft or marine structure

  - from a container floating in the sea

  - or from a structure on land constructed or adapted wholly or mainly for the purpose of depositing solids in the sea;

- anywhere in the sea by a British vessel or aircraft;

- from a foreign vessel anywhere in the continental shelf.

The scuttling of vessels is also included as a form of deposit in the sea.

It is an offence for anyone to do any of the above without a licence or cause or permit any other person to do any such thing (section

9(1)). Certain vessels, however, are exempted under the Deposits in the Sea (Exemptions) Order 1985 S.I. 1699.

A person charged with an offence under section 9(1) will have a defence if the operation was carried out for the purpose of securing the safety of a vessel, aircraft, hovercraft or marine structure or of the saving of life, and the person took steps to contact one or other of the ministers concerned.

No defence is available under section 9(4) if the court is satisfied that the operation was not necessary for one of the purposes mentioned in section 9(4A) and was not a reasonable step to take in the circumstances.

The penalties are set out in section 21 (2A), as amended by the EPA. A person found guilty of an offence under section 9(1) shall be liable, on summary conviction, to a fine of up to £50,000 and on indictment by an unlimited fine or imprisonment for up to two years. Offences committed in British waters may be prosecuted through the magistrates' and Crown Courts as though offences had taken place on land.

The licences themselves are detailed in section 8. The Minister responsible for Agriculture, Food and Fisheries must have regard to the marine ecosystem (ie the marine environment itself and the systems supported by it). Conditions and monitoring provisions can be placed in the licence. An important consideration is the possibility of other methods of disposal.

Licences can be revoked and varied as necessary, in light of developments in scientific knowledge. The number of licences granted over recent years has declined dramatically and few, if any, will currently be valid. If a licence application is refused, reasons must be given.

A right of judicial review may be available to the applicant but it will be very difficult for any third party to be involved with current arrangements. Schedule 3 lays down a right of representation for licensees and disappointed applicants with regard to the terms of licences, refusals, revocations or variations of licences. Representations must be considered by an expert committee who may allow a hearing and issue a report to the licensing committee.

Under section 6 a licence is needed for incineration of substances at sea or articles on a vessel or marine structure –

(a) in United Kingdom waters;

(b) anywhere at sea, if the vessel is British;

(c) anywhere at sea in British fishery limits, if the incineration takes place on a foreign vessel or foreign marine structure which was loaded in the United Kingdom or United Kingdom waters.

A licence is also required for the loading of a vessel or marine structure in United Kingdom waters with substances or articles for incineration at sea.

NOTES

[1] See Haworth, note 11, Chapter 1; *Halsbury's Statutes* and *Halsbury's Laws of England.*

[2] See *Environment News*, December 1992.

[3] *River Pollution – A Sleuth's Guide*, (1992), Friends of the Earth. *Water Pollution: Finding the Facts*, (1993), Friends of the Earth.

[4] See Chapter 5 – 'Natural justice'.

[5] *New Statesman and Society* , 29 January, 1993.

Chapter 10

Waste and Hazardous Substances

In the past, waste was not seen as a particular problem. Bio-degradable substances might cause a temporary nuisance but eventually would rot away to be re-absorbed into the environment without significant harm. But with the Industrial Revolution and the development of consumer society, waste and refuse have become an increasing problem. Both the processes of manufacturing industry and the products themselves generate amounts of waste which must be disposed of somewhere. In the last 20 years it has been recognised that inadequately maintained disposal systems may cause environmental damage.

Waste disposal has ostensibly been replaced by waste management – a developing field in which waste is being used for recycling, a more environmentally-sound disposal method.

Waste disposal is a matter of concern to many citizens because of its effects on health and property values. The planning of waste disposal sites is usually controversial with objections coming not only from those living in the proximity of the site (who may object even more loudly if section 61 is considered – see below) but also from those living along the routes on which waste is transported to such locations. The regulation of waste disposal is a matter largely under local government control, although the Secretary of State ultimately has the power to assume overall control in the event that an authority fails to exercise its powers (section 72).

Controversial as the issue of waste may be, there are limits to the amount that citizens can do in connection with waste disposal matters, not least because it will overlap with other areas of pollution control. For example, those who carry on waste disposal activities may have to have authorisations from HMIP. If such an authorisation is granted, HMIP must inform the waste regulation authority concerned. Any pollution which escapes into water from a site where waste is being treated may be prosecuted by the National Rivers Authority. If the operation of a waste disposal plant causes a nuisance to local residents, a prosecution may be launched against the owner for permitting or causing a statutory nuisance. Providing that citizens are involved with these decision making processes, the potential for involvement in waste disposal issues will be limited.

In terms of enforcement by criminal prosecution, it has to be noted that private prosecutions concerning waste may be both physically and legally risky. Apart from the fact that exposure to waste and hazardous substances can be dangerous in themselves, matters such as the collection of evidence may be legally risky as they could constitute offences in themselves. Interfering with substances in the waste stream is an offence under the EPA and unlicensed collection of waste substances and material will also be an offence unless a licence is held. For those involved with community activities such as waste recycling, care has to be taken not to commit an offence in breach. When dealing with waste, harm which is detected should be referred to the authorities concerned.

Environmentally concerned citizens may play an important role, beyond mere 'NIMBYism', in scrutinising the implementation of waste disposal in their area. They may also play a crucial part in reporting threats arising to the environment and human health from waste disposal sites. This could be particularly important since there is a built-in economic disincentive from neighbours and adjacent land owners to reporting such threats (see below).

The existing system for waste regulation is contained in the Control of Pollution Act 1974, being superseded by the developments in Part II of the EPA. Further changes are likely to be imposed by the EC regulations, including an important provision to lender liability.

EC LEGISLATION AND WASTE

The UK has been bound by important EC legislation since the 1970s. The EC produced the 1975 Directive on Waste, the 1978 Directive on Toxic and Dangerous Waste, the Transfrontier Shipment of Hazardous Waste Regulations 1988 and the Hazardous Wastes 1988 Directive.

The Directive on Waste (75/442/EEC) was known as the frame-work directive because it contained a coherent set of measures covering the appointment of waste regulation authorities, drawing up detailed disposal plans. In addition, a licensing system was established. The system which emerged from the EC was similar in many ways to that under the Control of Pollution Act 1974 – a rare example of UK legislation being ahead of proposals from Brussels.

A second Directive (78/319/EEC) laid the basis for controls covering toxic waste – that is waste of such a nature, in such quantities or concentrations, as to constitute a risk to health or the environment. The Directive also made provision for more complete records to be kept on the quantity and nature of waste.

Further EC legislation is expected to cover the clean-up of contaminated sites and of ground water, perhaps modelled on German legislation. Other proposals emerging from the EC on waste include lender liability for damage caused by waste.

Even with these measures there is not likely to be an end to waste disposal problems in the near future. One result of a stricter regime on waste disposal will be greater attempts at incineration, leading to increased need for HMIP control. Another problem will be the export of waste to dumping sites in the Third World. Eventually the underlying problem of waste production will have to be considered – there are faint signs that such a time is approaching.

What is waste?

A code of practice (*Waste Management; The Duty of Care*, December 1991, HMSO) is issued which states that anything which is discarded or dealt with as if it were waste is presumed to be waste unless the contrary is proven.

Controlled waste is defined by section 75(4) of the EPA as household, industrial and commercial waste. Domestic waste is excluded from the definition of controlled waste, when present on the property of the person who has produced or generated it. Waste contained in a person's own dustbin does not fall within the waste regulation scheme of the EPA while it remains on the premises.

Under section 62, the Secretary of State may identify certain categories of waste as 'special waste'. This covers waste which is particularly dangerous or poses particular problems. The current designation of 'special waste' is contained in the Control of Pollution (Special Waste) Regulations 1980, 1709.

POLLUTION BY WASTE

Under section 29(3) of the EPA, pollution by waste is taken to mean any escape of pollution from:

(a) the land on which controlled waste is treated;

(b) the land on which controlled waste is kept;

(c) the land in or on which controlled waste is deposited;

(d) fixed plant by means of which controlled waste is treated, kept or disposed of, substances or articles constituting or resulting from the waste and capable (by reason of the quantity or concentrations involved) of causing harm to people or any other living organisms supported by the environment.

The EPA 1990 extends the range of environmental matters which are to be considered by local authorities in Part II. Under section 30, various tiers of local government are to become waste regulation authorities (WRAs). These are the county councils in non-metropolitan areas and in London the authority constituted as the London Waste Regulation Authority. They are responsible for strategic planning in waste matters and the licensing of waste disposal.

Under section 30(3), district councils and London borough councils are designated waste collection authorities (WCAs). It is the WCAs which are under a duty to collect household waste and, if requested, commercial waste (section 45). They are also under a duty to arrange for the emptying of cesspools and privies, to supply receptacles for waste collection and make arrangements for recycling.

The waste is collected and disposed of under the arrangements made by waste regulation authorities set out in section 30(1). Under section 30(7), the regulatory functions and the existing disposal functions are separated. Under section 30, the existing WDAs have to split to form new Local Authority Waste Disposal Companies (LAWDCs) or pass on the task to the private sector, with the sale or lease of assets – which amounts to an attempt to privatise waste disposal (these provisions do not apply in Scotland). The tasks of the WRA become ones of planning, awarding contracts and licensing. These developments may be criticised from an environmental point of view since they create a market in waste rather than seeking to curb the creation of waste at the source. WRAs are responsible for granting licences for waste disposal sites and management licences, subject to guidance and directions from the Secretary of State. The potential for Central Government control remains considerable, with the Secretary of State being able to give directions on a wide variety of matters, including licences, the content of waste disposal plans and the inspection and modification of landfill sites.

LICENSING UNDER THE EPA

Section 35 of the EPA covers the waste management licences for persons collecting and disposing of waste. A licence is granted by a waste regulation authority authorising the treatment, the keeping or the disposal of any specified description of controlled waste in or on specified land, or the treatment or the disposal of any specified description of controlled waste by means of a specified mobile plant.

An application for a licence will be made under section 36 to the waste regulation authority which covers the area in which the land is situated; with a mobile plant, the relevant authority is the one which covers the area where the business is based.

Licences may only be held by 'fit and proper persons' as defined by section 74 of the EPA. This proviso was introduced into the law because of weaknesses in COPA where no qualifications or relevant expertise were required to hold a waste licence. With section 74, whether a person is fit and proper will be decided by reference to the activities to be carried out under the licence and by fulfilment of requirements in the licence.

Under section 74(3) a person will not be considered a fit and proper person if:

(a) she/he or a relevant person have been convicted of a relevant offence;

(b) the management of the activities which are to be licensed will not be in the hands of a technically competent person;

(c) the person appears unable to fulfil any financial requirements which will have to be discharged if holding the licence.

A relevant offence means an offence committed which is considered to be relevant, such as breaches of the Control of Pollution Act 1974 or offences involving fly-tipping.

Condition (a) may be waived and a person may be considered a fit and proper person notwithstanding the conviction. Licences cannot be issued unless there is planning permission or an established use certificate is in force. No doubt many of the convicted persons may be 'legal persons', that is companies rather than individuals. It is interesting to consider whether convicted companies would be allowed to operate as freely in other parts of public life were they individuals. The fact that such a provision was thought necessary may generate speculation about the scale of offences in the past.

There is a presumption in favour of granting a licence to an applicant, providing the authority considers the applicant to be a fit and proper person to hold such a licence. Obviously, the authority will have regard to any relevant information supplied by the public (which should also be made available to the applicant). The proposal must also be referred to the National Rivers Authority and the Health and Safety Executive to consider any representations which either body may make. A similar obligation arises where the land contained in the proposal is a notified site of Special Scientific Interest under section 28(1) of the Wildlife and Countryside Act 1981. In such a case the authority must refer the proposal to the appropriate nature conservancy body. Each body has 21 days in which to make representations.

A licence relating to the treatment, keeping or disposal of waste may be granted to a person who is the occupier of the land on which these processes take place. In the case of a mobile plant, the licence is awarded to the person who operates the plant.

The waste regulation authority may set conditions covering the activities which are licensed and precautions which are to be taken in handling the waste. In setting such conditions, waste regulation authorities are under a duty to put into effect any guidance and directions from the Secretary of State. Under the provisions of COPA, such conditions can not relate to controlling a statutory nuisance arising from the waste disposal site (see Court of Appeal judgement in *Att-Gen's Reference (No.2 of 1988)* [1989] 3 WLR 397) but the wider definition of the environment contained in Part II of the EPA. In any event, proceedings for a statutory nuisance could still be brought by an aggrieved citizen.

Variation and revocation of licences

Powers to vary licences are contained in section 37 of the EPA. A waste regulation authority may, on its own initiative, modify the conditions of the licence to an extent which is desirable and unlikely to cause unreasonable expense to the licence holder.

Typically, the licence holder may be under restrictions as to the classes of waste (eg household, commercial) that may be dealt with, conditions as to fencing and security, signposting, record keeping and the screening of the site (eg planting trees or landscaping). Certain sites may also be subject to monitoring or requirements to control vermin.

The licence holder, on payment of an appropriate fee, may also apply to have the terms and conditions of the licence altered. The WRA is required to alter the terms of the licence to the extent (in its opinion) that it ensures that the activities do not 'cause pollution to the environment or harm to human health or become seriously detrimental to the amenities of the locality affected by the activities'.

Under section 38 a licence may be revoked where it appears to the authority that:

(a) the holder of the licence has ceased to be a fit and proper person by reason of having been convicted of a relevant offence; or

(b) the continuation of the activities authorised by the licence would cause pollution of the environment or harm to human health or would be seriously detrimental to the amenities of the locality affected; or

(c) the pollution, harm or detriment cannot be avoided by modifying the conditions of the licence.

In order to vary or revoke a licence, the authority must serve a notice on the holder stating the time at which the revocation or suspension of the requirement is to take effect. An authority may also revoke a licence from a company or revoke certain parts of it where it appears that the licence is no longer in the hands of a technically competent person. This will prevent the management of a waste company passing to potentially incompetent hands.

As an alternative to revoking the licence entirely, the authority may suspend it. Such a situation may arise where a pollution problem arises through some particular activity. Where a suspension takes effect, the licence holder may be prevented from undertaking some or all of their activities. In addition, the authority may require the holder of the licence to take such steps as the authority thinks are necessary. This is a wide power and is backed up with criminal penalties of a fine not exceeding £20,000 or, on indictment, a term of imprisonment not exceeding two years.

A WRA must be careful to exercise its powers according to the EPA and any regulations issued under it. It should ensure that conditions and revocations are exercised fairly. A right of appeal arises under section 43 to the Secretary of State against the refusal of a licence.

Surrender of licences

Once taken on, the responsibilities of waste licence holders are not easily relinquished. Section 39 provides that licences can be surrendered, but in the case of a site licence the surrender will only be effective if the authority agrees. The holders of licences may be held liable, after they have surrendered licences, for the cost of any emergency work that needs to be carried out once their activities have ceased.

Breach of conditions

Where it appears to an authority that conditions in a licence are not being complied with by the licence holder, the authority may require the licence holder to comply with the condition within a specified time. If, in the opinion of the authority, the licence holder has not complied with the condition in the time set, it may:

(a) partially revoke the licence, as regards the carrying on of certain activities;

(b) revoke the licence entirely – effectively shutting down the site;

(c) suspend the licence so far as it authorises the activities specified in the licence or by the authority.

Obviously, WRAs will be prepared to act upon and carry out investigations based on information and complaints from the public.

Section 33 of the EPA makes it an offence for any person without authority to deposit, treat or dispose of controlled waste: effectively, everyone involved with physically dealing with the waste must have a licence to do so. Public registers are established containing information on waste management licences, in order that the public can check that anyone handling the waste is legally entitled to do so. There are also provisions for annual publicity.

Public register provisions

Section 64 of the EPA establishes a comprehensive public register to be maintained by each waste authority. The register must contain:

(a) current or recently current licences;

(b) current or recently current applications for licences;

(c) applications to modify licences;

(d) notices affecting the modification of licences;

(e) notices issued to revoke, suspend or impose conditions on licences;

(f) appeals against decisions of the authority;

(g) certificates of completion issued under section 39(9);

(h) imposition of requirements under section 42(5);

(i) convictions for any offence of the holder of licences granted by the authority;

(j) details of inspections or functions under section 61;

(k) directions from the Secretary of State for the Environment;

(l)   any prescribed information on the pollution of the environment.

A recently current licence is taken to mean any licence which expired during the previous 12 months and a recently current application is taken to mean any unsuccessful application made within that period.

These registers may be consulted, for example, to discover if authorities are carrying out their duties to inspect sites on which waste has been deposited and what steps may have been taken by the authorities.

A further provision for public registers is made for waste collection authorities under section 64(4). Each collection authority must maintain a register consisting of details supplied by the WRA, relating to the treatment, keeping or disposal of controlled waste in its area.

Under sections 65 and 66, exemptions to the requirement to include information are made on grounds of national security or confidentiality. Applications may be made by individuals or companies to restrict the inclusion of commercial information, unless the Secretary of State has ordered that such registers include such information.

Supervision

Under section 42(1) a WRA is under a duty to supervise licensed activities. It must ensure that the activities do not cause pollution, harm human health or become detrimental to local amenities, and take appropriate steps where such problems arise. Section 42(3) provides that any officer who is authorised in writing, may, in emergency cases, carry out work on the land or to the plant or equipment. The cost of such expenditure may be recovered under section 42(4) from the holder of the licence. Such costs are not recoverable where the licence holder or former licence holder shows that there was no emergency requiring any work or where part of the expenditure was unnecessary.

If water pollution is likely to be caused, the problems should be referred to the National Rivers Authority. If matter escapes into controlled water the occupier of the land will be guilty of an offence under section 85 (see Chapter 9).

OFFENCES

Under section 33(1) a person shall not:

(a) deposit controlled waste, or knowingly cause or knowingly permit controlled waste to be deposited in or on any land unless a waste management licence authorising the deposit is in force and the deposit is in accordance with the licence; or

(b) treat, keep or dispose of controlled waste, or knowingly cause or knowingly permit controlled waste to be treated, kept or disposed of –

   (i) in or on any land, or

   (ii) by means of any mobile plant

   except in accordance with the waste licence; or

(c) treat, keep or dispose of controlled waste in a manner likely to cause pollution of the environment or harm to human health.

Subsection (2) provides that these wide-ranging sections do not apply to household waste which is kept or disposed of within the confines of a dwelling house by or with the permission of the occupier of the dwelling.

Just to make sure that the conditions are met, section 33(6) provides that, in addition to contravention of section 33(1) giving rise to an offence, any person who contravenes 'any condition of a waste management licence commits an offence'. A person who commits such offences may, on summary conviction, be fined up to £20,000 or be sentenced to six months in prison.

Under section 33(7) it shall be a defence for a person charged to prove:

(a) that he took all reasonable precautions and exercised due diligence to avoid commission of the offence;

(b) that he acted under instructions from his employer and neither knew or had reason to suppose that the acts done by him constituted a contravention of section 33;

(c) that the acts alleged to constitute the contravention were done in an emergency in order to avoid danger to the public and that, as soon as reasonably practicable, particulars were furnished to the waste regulation authority in whose area the treatment or disposal of waste took place.

Another interesting offence is for cases of dumping from cars and motor vehicles, introduced by section 33(5). Where controlled waste is deposited from a motor vehicle, the person in a position to control the vehicle will be treated as an offender under section 33(1) as knowingly causing the waste to be deposited, whether or not he gave instructions for this to be done. Given the possible penalty (see below) this is a severe sanction.

In each of these cases an offence carries a penalty of up to £20,000 fine or six months' imprisonment; the Crown Court may impose an unlimited fine or up to two years in prison. Even more severe penalties are imposed where the offence involves special waste, where a five-year sentence is possible. This penalty turns the matter into an arrestable offence.

What is particularly striking is that the function of waste disposal is contracted out – effectively privatised. This process may be open to criticism from an environmental point of view since it creates a market and industry based upon waste. A better environmental policy might be to aim to reduce waste production and promote recycling. The measures contained in the EPA arguably do not go far enough to establish this, though some provision for recycling is made.

Waste management – duty of care

The duties placed on persons undertaking waste disposal are only part of a wider duty of care imposed at law on all those involved in waste, from its creation to its final disposal. These overcome problems that existed under the Control of Pollution Act as to who would ultimately be responsible at law for different stages in the disposal of controlled waste.

Section 34 of the EPA places a wide duty of care on persons who import, produce or keep controlled waste. (The duty does not extend to household or domestic waste.) It represents an attempt by society to place some responsibility on those who produce and handle waste – a matter which society values, as is evident by the level of maximum fines which may be imposed. Provisions covering the duty are contained in the Environmental Protection (Duty of Care)

Regulations 1991 S.I. No. 2839. Other guidance is contained in the Code of Practice (Waste Management; Duty of Care) and Circular 19/91 issued by the Department of the Environment. The Code of Practice may be referred to in court proceedings.

The duty of care has caused a considerable degree of concern – at least among those aware of its existence. In practice, many people will be unaware of it and may carry on regardless even if they are. A complacent attitude could be dangerous. The duty is imposed on any person who 'imports, produces, carries, keeps, treats, disposes of controlled waste, or as a broker, has control of such waste, to take all such measures applicable to him in that capacity as are reasonable in the circumstances'. Effectively, this covers waste from its production to its point of disposal. Each person handling the waste, in whatever capacity, is under a duty to behave reasonably. When transferring waste, reasonable steps must be taken to show that it is passed on to a responsible operator who is required to take such steps as to:

- prevent the escape of any waste;

- prevent any other persons committing the offences of disposing, treating or storing controlled waste, either without a waste management licence, in breach of conditions of a licence or in a manner likely to cause pollution or harm to health;

- when transferring the waste to make sure that

    - it is only transferred to an authorised person or to a person authorised to transport it;

    - a written description is included.

Persons who are authorised to take waste are:

- holders of disposal licences made under the Control of Pollution Act 1974, section 5

- carriers registered under the Control of Pollution Amendment Act 1989, section 2

- local authorities – holders of waste management licences from April 1993.

The regulations detail the documentation which must be maintained by the persons under the duty. The transferrer of the waste must complete and sign a 'transfer note' for the person into whose charge and control the waste is being passed (the transferee). The note must include the names and addresses of the parties, their role in dealing with the waste and the place and date of transfer.

It can be seen how wide this duty is – not only does the person have to act reasonably but also must take reasonable steps to ensure that no other person commits an offence. In essence, a person to which this section applies must take such steps as are reasonable to prevent any offence which may be committed in connection with the waste. For example, a shopkeeper or restaurant owner should check whether the person collecting the waste is properly authorised to do so.

Probably, the prosecuting authorities will pursue at criminal law those they consider directly responsible, subject to proof being available. If the prime offender has vanished, proceedings may be taken against other defendants.

CIVIL CLAIMS

In a civil claim, a litigant is likely to look for any defendant with enough money to be worth taking proceedings against.

Sections 73(6–9) of the EPA impose civil liability for damage caused by waste. Anyone who deposits or knowingly dumps waste, so as to commit an offence under section 33(1) or 63(2) and causes damage, will be liable in civil law. This statutory right to bring an action does not affect civil liability at common law but will be actionable as one of the class of torts which fall under breach of statutory duty. Proof of a conviction for such an offence may be admissible as evidence in a civil claim under section 11 of the Civil Evidence Act 1968. Defendants to such actions will be entitled to raise the defences under section 33(7).

Likely claims would cover damage to property, (eg clean-up and replacement costs) and 'claims for the death of, or injury to, any person (including disease or impairment of physical or mental condition)'. A medical report substantiating the injury will be essential to any claim. Forthcoming EC proposals will extend the scope of this liability further.

The development of lender liability claims will have a particular impact. For example, if a bank makes a loan to set up a waste disposal site (or any project involving high environmental risk) a duty of care will be imposed upon the bank. If after operating for ten years the business collapses and it is discovered that the environment has been harmed through illegal activity, the bank will be liable to pay for any clean-up bill. At the very least, this directive when it emerges will encourage any UK or UK-registered bank to undertake an environmental impact assessment prior to granting a loan.

Closed landfills

A great deal of waste is 'disposed' of by the simple expedient of dumping it into holes in the ground. This method has been recognised to have a number of problems, not least the build-up of dangerous and explosive gases through decomposition.

Figures appear not to be kept by Central Government as to landfill gas explosions; a Parliamentary Written Answer in November 1992 suggested that any such information, including deaths and injuries, will be available from the relevant local authority in whose area the landfill is to be found.

As detailed above, every WRA is required to licence and oversee conditions on operating landfills, but duties are also imposed under the EPA with respect to unlicensed sites which have now been closed.

As part of their supervisory duties, WRAs are under a duty to inspect closed landfill sites to discover, for instance, if deposits of controlled waste are creating dangerous build-ups of gas or noxious liquids on the site (section 61, EPA). An officer acting on behalf of an authority has a power of entry and if such problems are revealed the authority must monitor the site. Sites covered include any land:

(a) in or on which controlled waste has been deposited at any time under the authority of a waste management licence or disposal licence under section 5 of the Control of Pollution Act 1974;

(b) in which the authority has reason to believe that controlled waste has been deposited at any time (whether before or after 1 January 1976); or

(c) in which there are, or the authority has reason to believe there may be, concentrations or accumulations of noxious gases or noxious liquids.

Where it appears that there is an accumulation of noxious substances, the local authority must inspect and monitor the situation. In the event of a risk of water pollution, the authority must inform the NRA.

Where it appears to the authority, following an inspection of the site, that pollution of the environment or harm to human health is likely to be caused, the authority is under a duty to do such works and take such other steps (whether on the land affected or on adjacent land) as appear to the authority to be reasonable to avoid such pollution or harm. As it is a duty, the local authority may be compelled to undertake such works by way of judicial review for an order of mandamus.

It should be noted that this wide power allows a waste authority not only to undertake work on the site but also on the land of private owners who have no property rights or interest in the site but who merely own land which happens to be adjacent to the waste site. This is likely to prove a controversial measure since section 8 enables an authority to recover the cost or any part of the cost from the person who currently owns the land. The only defence to this claim is for such a person to show that the costs were incurred unreasonably (how the waste authority has exercised its duties in relation to the site could be relevant to this). In deciding whether to recover an amount of costs which have arisen, the authority shall have regard to any hardship which the recovery may cause to the owner of the land. How the waste authority exercises this discretion will be open to judicial review and will probably vary from area to area. Wider awareness of these potential financial costs for merely owning land next to a waste tip is likely to lead to increased challenges in planning applications to open such sites. They will also act as a financial deterrent to owners of neighbouring land from reporting any pollution which becomes apparent.

Planning conditions

In addition to the EPA controls, the local authority may control waste collection and treatment by means of planning under the Town and Country Planning Act 1990.

Under section 36(2) of the EPA, a licence shall not be issued for use of land for which planning permission is required unless either valid planning permission is in force or an established use certificate is in force under section 192 of the 1990 Act or section 90 of the 1971 Act.

The matter of planning permission gives the local authority, in its role as a planning authority, the right to impose extra controls on a waste disposal site. As a result, citizens will have an opportunity to make representations as part of the planning process. An authority may refuse permission or impose conditions, such as the eventual clean-up and restoration of the site.

PLANNING AND HAZARDOUS WASTES

Several proposals were made from the 1970s onwards to extend town and country planning law to the storage and treatment of hazardous substances. Problems arose from the fact that an increase in the amount of a hazardous or lethal substance stored upon land did not amount to 'development' for the purposes of the Town and Country Planning Act 1971 or 1990. Thus, such increases could escape control by planning law unless there was a material change of use at the same time or some other associated construction.

To tackle this problem, the Planning (Hazardous Substances) Act 1990 was introduced. Local authorities added to their bevy of responsibilities the task of being 'hazardous substances authorities' (HSAs) controlling the build-up of waste on land. In cases of planning not involving mineral extraction, District Councils and County Councils exercise these functions. It will be interesting to see the ultimate authority to whom these powers will pass with the threats to County Councils. London Boroughs and the surviving Metropolitan areas have the same functions and the same responsibilities for their respective urban areas.

Regulations have been made under this Act – the Planning (Hazardous Substances) Regulations 1992 S.I. 656. These regulations list the substances which are classed as hazardous, the quantities that may be kept and the procedure to apply for hazardous substances consent. The regulations also cover the form of the consents register, enforcement and fees.

The regulations for hazardous substances cover 71 listed substances but do not cover controlled waste under section 75(4) of the EPA or radioactive waste as defined by the Radioactive Substances Act 1960.

Exemptions from the need for consent are made for the temporary presence of a hazardous substance due to vehicles unloading the substance and its transfer from one vehicle to another, exempt pipes and service pipes and a 14 day exemption for the cargoes of sea-going ships which are unloaded in an emergency.

For details of hazardous substances to be found locally, an inquirer can consult the register established under section 28 of the Act. Regulation 23 sets out that the register shall be kept in six parts. It should contain a copy of every application made to the HSA (whether determined or not), details of any direction and details of any conditions imposed on the consent and any decisions of the Secretary of State for the Environment. From this the name, address and details of the consent holder may be discovered.

Other parts contain copies of every hazardous consent given to government departments, of every order revoking or modifying hazardous substances consents and directions sent by the Secretary of State under section 27 of the Act.

These regulations affect, in particular, any new business involved with the storage of dangerous waste. Businesses which are already in possession of hazardous substances (as prescribed) may claim deemed consent to hold such substances. The relevant period is the 12 months prior to 1 June 1992. Deemed consent must have been claimed from the local HSA before January 1993.

Other conditions which are required for a deemed consent are that the substance shall not be kept in a larger container than that currently existing before the relevant date and that the maximum quantity shall not, on the land or within 500 metres of it, exceed the established quantity. The only exception is under regulation 4.

Contaminated land

Under section 143 of the EPA, contaminated land registers were to have been established by District Councils and London Boroughs. While such registers are presently unlikely to emerge, contaminated land use remains an important issue in planning and development. Contamination will cover any land which is being, or has been, put to a 'contaminative use'. As a result of this definition, a site need only be suspected of having had a contaminative use to be included. Contaminated sites will include power stations, gas works, various manufacturing sites, sewage works, scrapyards, dry cleaners and slaughter houses.

The strategy of the government was to identify all contaminated land with a view to eventually cleaning up that land with appropriate technology. Once identified, such sites could be subject to clean-ups including such methods as microbial degradation, pumping and treatment of groundwater, soil extraction and soil incineration. One drawback with the register is that it will record sites which have had contaminative uses, rather than the actual pollution present.

Regulations to commence this task have been delayed by the 1992 General Election and as a result of lobbying of property groups. If established, the registers were expected to have a dramatic effect on property transactions in years to come. Owners of sites included in the register would have found the value of their land falling, though much would have depended on the type of contamination. A search of the contaminated land register would have been likely to become commonplace for any property transaction and, in cities, inclusion of land on the register would have influenced urban regeneration schemes.

Pressures placed on developers to seek non-contaminated sites are increased by a number of legal implications when applying for planning permission. Full environmental audit/site investigations may be necessary to begin development on land which is believed to be contaminated. Planning authorities may, using their discretion, set conditions to clean up a site, making anyone owning or holding land liable for some or all of the clean-up costs if development goes ahead. Liability may also arise if the contamination ever gives rise to a statutory nuisance. Under section 81(4) any expenses incurred in abating or preventing the recurrence of a statutory nuisance may be recovered from the person who is the owner of the premises. The court may apportion expenses as is thought reasonable.

Further EC legislation may yet appear to tackle the clean up of contaminated sites, and grants may become available from the government or from Brussels.

Control of Pollution (Amendment) Act 1989

The Control of Pollution (Amendment) Act 1989, which came fully into force on 1 April 1992, originated as a private member's bill to deal with the offence of fly-tipping – the transport and dumping of waste without proper registration. Section 1 of the Act makes it an offence for any person who is not a registered carrier of controlled waste to transport waste in the course of his business or with a view to profit.

Enforcement can be by local authorities and the success of such prosecutions will depend upon the vigilance of the public. Certain defences are given, including the usual provision about the transport of waste in an emergency of which notice was given as soon as practicable. Further defences are provided where, after taking all reasonable steps to ascertain whether controlled waste was involved, there were no grounds to believe that this was the case or where a person was acting under instructions from his employer.

Under section 2, the Secretary of State may make regulations to provide for the registration of carriers. Some powerful sanctions are provided in the Act, including a power to seize vehicles which are involved in illegal transport (section 6 provides powers for the seizure and disposal of vehicles used in fly-tipping). A justice of the peace may issue a warrant to a disposal authority for the seizure of any vehicle if he is satisfied that an offence under the Control of Pollution Act 1974 is taking place and that the vehicle has been involved. This power may be exercised where proceedings have not yet been brought and where the authority has failed to ascertain the name and address of the person who can identify the individual using the vehicle for the offence. Such a warrant will remain in force until its purpose is achieved. Any person who obstructs the execution of a warrant will be guilty of an offence. However, only a police officer may stop a vehicle whilst it is on the road.

Information-gathering powers and powers of entry arising from sections 91 to 94 of COPA apply to an offence of fly-tipping under section 7 of the Act.

Recycling

Although provisions are made for recycling, the term is not defined in the EPA, but provision is made under section 52 for a system of payments to act as inducement to divert recyclable materials from household waste. The recycling of waste from the materials collected by the WRA may yield a credit which is payable from the WRA, which has saved costs and expense as a result of the recycling.

Chapter 11

Habitat and the Protection of Wildlife

Britain has long considered itself as an animal-loving nation which values its countryside and natural heritage. Yet domestic legislation for protecting our natural heritage is limited and in many places seriously inadequate. The hunting of mammals remains an emotive issue, with an attempt to outlaw it in Parliament in 1992, [1] yet modern farming and developments which wipe out millions of members of non-mammalian lifeforms each year evoke comparatively little concern. Certain species enjoy protection, but many more do not. One wonders whether the attitude of legislators on species protection is a variant of the philosophy of 'One death is a tragedy – a million is a statistic.' [2] Killing a single member of a species can result in a person being summoned to the magistrates' court (perhaps after being searched and arrested) and fined or even imprisoned. But to wipe out every member of some other non-protected species through development, land drainage, pesticides and the destruction of its habitat can be perfectly legal. [3]

It is nearly ten years since the Nature Conservancy Council, then a unified body, stated that nature conservation had been a failure for the last 40 years. [4] The ten years since has compounded this disaster.

Against this depressing background, statutory agencies, environmental groups and concerned citizens are fighting a rearguard action. However, the potential does seem to exist at law to reverse much of the damage, utilising a 'twin-track' approach of both the criminal law and planning legislation.

THE WILDLIFE AND COUNTRYSIDE ACT 1981: SITES OF SPECIAL SCIENTIFIC INTEREST

Conservation is largely covered by the Wildlife and Countryside Act 1981, as amended. Unfortunately, this Act is proving seriously flawed in its ability to protect unique sites. The designation of SSSIs has far more significance in theory than in actual reality, in spite of efforts to amend the legislation.[5]

Sites of Special Scientific Interest are areas of special interest by reason of any particular flora, fauna, or geological or physiographical features. The first SSSIs were originally established under the Countryside Act 1949. At present there are some 5,576 SSSIs, covering 1,721,502 hectares of land – about 8 per cent of the United Kingdom. The definition of an SSSI has remained unchanged since the first use of the classification under section 23 of the National Parks and Access to the Countryside Act 1949. Up until 1981 such designation was under the direction of the National Environment Research Council who merely had to inform the local planning authority concerned. Many owners would have been unaware of the designation. Agricultural and forestry operations could take place, being outside the scope of any planning control.

Reports of damage continue to accumulate each year.[6] Warnings since the mid-1980s have not been heeded. Such diverse activities as ploughing, over-grazing and mountain-biking, and so-called recreations such as paint-balling war games, have all harmed different sites.

Creation of SSSIs

The duty of selecting and designating SSSIs is now the responsibility of the Nature Conservancy Councils. As noted in Chapter 2, these were originally unified in one body but, following changes under section 128 of the EPA, it has been split into three Nature Conservancy Councils for England, Scotland and the Countryside Council for Wales, which are co-ordinated under the Joint Nature Conservation Committee.[7] The aim of the present Nature Conservancy Councils is to form a national network of areas representing the highly concentrated or highest quality sites of wildlife conservation.

Section 28 of the Wildlife and Countryside Act 1981 provides that the Nature Conservancy Councils have to notify the local planning authority, the owner and occupier of the land and the Secretary of State for the Environment of any area of land which is of special interest. The notification alerts landowners to the site and objection against it can only be made when the scientific argument is not justified. If a Nature Conservancy Council ever misused its power for some reason, this would be potentially open to judicial review.

In addition to the notification, the landowner is informed of potentially damaging operations which may not be performed on the site except in certain situations. Such operations could include drainage, tree felling, pesticide spraying and the grazing of livestock. The term 'operation' was considered in *Sweet* v *Secretary of State for the Environment* (1989), a case involving section 29 of the Act (see below). The word was taken to have a wider meaning than the equivalent term used in planning law, and could include many acts (though arguably not all) which damage the flora, fauna or soil of an SSSI. If prosecutions for damage to SSSIs become more common-place, this will be a useful argument for the magistrates' court but may not necessarily be binding on future divisional court judgements. The owner or occupier of the site must give the NCC notice of any potentially damaging operation.

A period of four months may then elapse during which the Nature Council concerned may give consent to an operation, possibly with conditions attached, or it may reach a management agreement with a landholder where the operation is not carried out but compensation paid. Alternatively, the owner may just wait until the four months have expired and then commence upon the operation.

Loopholes in the system

This is how the Act currently stands, after one loophole was closed in 1985 by the Wildlife and Countryside Amendment Act. Under the original section 28, owners and occupiers could legally carry out damaging operations during a three month period in which the NCC had to consider any objections to an SSSI designation. The current section 28(2) ensures that the designation takes effect as soon as the owner or occupier is notified by the Council, although representations may still be made.

The owner of the site need only obtain planning permission from the local authority to overturn an SSSI designation. The fate of an SSSI can thus be in the hands of local politicians. Just one such example was the grant of planning permission in 1989 to the Music Corporation of America to build a theme park as a rival to Euro-Disney on Rainham Marshes in Essex. However, the development has not gone ahead, despite the reported enthusiasm of the former Prime Minister, Margaret Thatcher. In such a case there may be a possibility of judicial review by an interested person or party able to have *locus standi* to challenge the grant of permission, as with the British Herpetological Society in *R* v *Poole Borough Council ex parte Beebee* (1991) (see Chapter 5). At the time of writing, some 160 proposed road schemes threaten different SSSIs across the country.[8]

Weakness of the law

The weakness of the law is not an accident but a result of deliberate political intention. When the original bill was introduced there was great emphasis on the voluntary approach towards wildlife conservation. Despite the importance to national and global heritage (and unknown effects on other ecosystems) the legislation cannot stop damage. The problem is that, with the land in private ownership and weak legislation, the Wildlife and Countryside Act can no more stop damage to an SSSI any more than a private art collector can be stopped from throwing an old master on the fire. (Indeed, the position is even worse, since a private owner may have an economic incentive to damage an SSSI site.) The fate of Britain's SSSIs might be held up as an example of how a free market approach to environmental protection is substantially flawed.

The owner or occupier of the land (or for that matter a third party) can obtain planning permission or be prepared to wait more than four months before undertaking a potentially damaging operation. It is this feature which caused Lord Musthill to comment in the House of Lords case of *Southern Water Authority* v *Nature Conservancy Council* (1992) *(The Times*, 22 July; see below) that 'It needs only a moment to see that this regime is toothless, for it demands no more from the owner or occupier of an SSSI other than a little patience'.

For operations which go ahead without planning permission, within the four month period, there is a risk – if the operation is discovered – of prosecution but with a maximum fine of £1,000. In some instances, the fine might be negligible compared with the economic benefit derived from allowing the operation to go ahead – though prosecution costs would increase the total loss to the landowner or the person who has committed the offence. Faced with these problems, there are two possible ways an individual can use the law to protect SSSIs: either through bringing or supporting prosecutions for offences; or, alternatively, by seeking to prevent damage at an earlier stage when development plan proposals are drawn up.[9]

COLLECTING LEGALLY ADMISSIBLE EVIDENCE ON SSSI DAMAGE

Obviously, there is much that can be done by observant people in their own areas to 'police' their local SSSIs. Breaches of planning control or damaging excavations can be reported to the local authority or Nature Conservancy Council concerned with protecting the site. Since the Councils do not enjoy budgets sufficient to employ enough staff to be able to supervise sites, much will depend on information reported from the public. With an SSSI there is a good chance of being able to collect legally admissible evidence, since operations will often be taking place on open sites to which public access may easily be gained.

One hurdle that private individuals and Nature Conservancy Council investigators face is that entry on to an SSSI may be a trespass in the case of privately held land. In practice, civil actions for trespass by landowners are exceedingly rare, not least because of the difficulty in identifying the trespasser. No more than nominal damages may be awarded unless harm to the land is caused (in this instance, the last thing that an official or an environmentally-minded private citizen would want!). If entry to the land is denied by the owner, she/he has the right to expel the trespasser using reasonable force but to stay on the safe side of the law must allow a reasonable opportunity to withdraw (see *Snook* v *Marrion* (1982) RTR 321). The method by which the evidence is obtained might be raised by the defence to try and exclude it as being obtained unlawfully, although, as noted in Chapter 4, this does not automatically mean that the evidence should be excluded.

To avoid these difficulties, observations or photographic and film evidence could be made or recorded from vantage points on adjoining land, highways or public footpaths and bridleways. Section 57 of the Wildlife and Countryside Act 1981 requires the surveying department of the local authority to compile and keep a copy of a definitive map of not less than 1:2500 scale of 'all public rights of way in their area, classifying them as bridleways, footpaths or roads used as public paths'. The map must be available for public inspection at reasonable hours.[10] Evidence could be given of vehicles and machinery seen entering or leaving the SSSI, from which a court may be able to draw necessary inferences.

Where an operation is noticed, a person should make and date notes to correspond to a contemporaneous record (in accordance with details in Chapter 4), should they be called upon to give evidence. It is important to note any company names, descriptions of the persons and equipment involved and registration numbers of vehicles.

Section 69 makes directors, managers and secretaries or other analogous officers liable as well as the corporation, and these may be proceeded against personally, in the same way as with section 157 of the EPA.

Who can be prosecuted?

Any proceedings, other than by the enforcing authority, require special permission from the Director of Public Prosecutions.[11] It is possible that the Crown Prosecution Service might take over and proceed with the case in some circumstances. If a case is taken over and then abandoned, judicial review might conceivably be available of this decision not to proceed, by anyone showing *locus standi*, although chances of success would be slim.

There is also difficulty in mounting prosecutions against some persons responsible for damage, following the definition given to the word 'occupier' in the Act in *Southern Water Authority (SWA)* v *Nature Conservancy Council*. The prosecution arose from land on the Isle of Wight where the water authority and two farmers each owned part of the site. Across the land (although not that part owned by the water authority) ran a ditch which flooded. The farmers asked the SWA to dredge the ditch in 1987, despite it being a prescribed operation under the designation. This was carried out in February 1989 and SWA were prosecuted and convicted in the magistrates' court. The justices reasoned that the SWA were guilty of occupation in that they treated the SSSI as their own. On a case-stated appeal to the divisional court (see Chapter 4) this interpretation was rejected, a decision upheld by the House of Lords.

The House of Lords considered whether carrying out an operation could amount to occupation. In giving judgement, Lord Musthill held that section 28 included occupiers who were present when the original designation was made, occupiers after designation who would be deemed to be notified and subsequent purchasers of an interest in the land. However, the phrase could not extend to those merely on the land to carry out works or operations. The House of Lords held that to be an occupier included in the section, notification would have had to be formal or implied.

The House of Lords also considered whether the occupier of an SSSI could commit an offence with regard to another, adjacent, SSSI although owned by the person charged. The House of Lords ruled that the commission of the offence could only be committed with respect to the portion of land actually owned.

Since under section 28 'occupiers' and 'owners' may be liable for damaging an SSSI, third parties (whether invited onto the land or not) who may enter land cannot be caught by the offence if prosecuted solely as occupiers, as in *Southern Water Authority* v *Nature Conservancy Council.*

It has been suggested that a conspiracy [12] or offences of 'aiding or abetting' could be alternative charges, provided that the person knows that the offence is being committed and he gives assistance and encouragement to the perpetrator of the offence. For example, an owner employs a private contractor who commences a building or excavation operation on land designated an SSSI, causing damage. Criminal proceedings can be commenced against the owner but no proceedings may be commenced solely against the private contractor, since under section 28 the contractor is neither an owner or an occupier for the purposes of the section.

SECTION 29

Under section 29 of the Act, special protection is given for certain areas of special scientific interest which the Secretary of State considers of national importance. The Secretary of State may prohibit operations likely to destroy flora, fauna or geological or physiological features by means of a Nature Conservation Order (NCO). The Order lists operations which may not be permitted on a site within a three month period of notice being given to the NCC responsible. This can be extended to a 12 month ban, by offering a management agreement to buy the land or interest. A power of entry is available to a person authorised in writing to determine whether a site should be designated under section 29.

Procedure under section 29

The scheme for making an Order under section 29 is set out in Schedule 11 of the 1981 Act, with notice of the Order being advertised in the *London Gazette* and a local newspaper. Land-owners affected are served with a notice which describes the effect of the Order and includes the date on which it comes into effect and a place where its details can be inspected. A period of 28 days is allowed in which representations may be made. If there is opposition, the Secretary of State may hold a local inquiry, after which the Secretary of State's decision to revoke, amend or maintain the Order is given. A similar procedure applies where the Order falls to be revoked by the Secretary of State.[13]

Any person who is aggrieved may challenge the validity of the Order through the High Court within six weeks of the notice being made, amended or revoked, as the case may be. This follows the procedure for legal challenge within six weeks which applies under the Town and Country Planning Act 1990. The grounds of the application are that the decision was not within the powers under the Act or that the statutory procedures have not been followed and the interests of the applicant have been substantially prejudiced.

Where a Nature Conservation Order is in force, the powers restricting damaging operations are wider than with section 28. Breach of an NCO can be committed by any person; there is no ambiguity with the occupation as with section 28. A further advantage is that, unlike section 28 offences, no consent is necessary from the DPP to instigate a prosecution, so a private prosecutor is free to present information as soon as an operation contravening the Order is detected. As a preliminary step, it will be necessary to establish that the NCO is in force, which may be proved in the same way as any other Act or instrument. It would not be necessary to prove any actual harm to flora or fauna or to the site, since the order prohibits operations *likely* to cause such damage. The carrying on of the operation is the offence itself - although the issue of damage may be relevant to punishment.

The only defences are planning permission or operations carried out in an emergency. The offence of contravening a prohibition notice is triable either way and a £2,000 fine may be imposed in the magistrates' court; in the Crown Court an unlimited fine.

Under section 31, the court has an additional power to make an Order requiring the defendant to carry out operations to restore the land to its former condition as may be so specified. This is available in prosecutions both in the magistrates' court and the Crown Court. Were an Order to be made by the Crown Court, it would, on appeal against sentence, be treated as the equivalent of an Order for the restitution of property. The Order may specify a time period in which the work is to be completed. Any such order must be based on sound scientific and ecological methods; in many cases the damage may well be irreversible. Up to 1991 no court cases making such Orders have been reported. [14]

Where an Order is made by a magistrates' court, under section 31(3), the period will not begin to run until the expiration of the time limit for appeal (ie 21 days from date of conviction). Where an appeal is commenced, the time limit will not begin to run until the appeal is determined. If the person against whom the Order is made fails, without reasonable excuse, to comply with the Order, a fine of up to £2,000 may be imposed. In the case of a continuing offence, a further fine not exceeding £100 is applicable for each day during which the offence continues after conviction.

Where the person under the Order fails to comply, a Nature Conservancy Council is empowered to enter the site and undertake the restoration work themselves, recovering the cost from the person subject to the Order.

Section 31(4) gives a right to a person against whom the Order was made to apply to court for a variation or discharge of the Order. A discharge or variation may be made if it appears to the court that a change in circumstances has made compliance or full compliance with the Order impracticable or unnecessary.

Naturally, the terms of such an Order would have to be set out for the benefit of the court and only after serious consideration. Although there is no report of any such Order being imposed, the growing evidence of damage to SSSIs should certainly mean this should be given consideration in appropriate cases.

Wider evidence-gathering powers are possible for a person authorised by a relevant authority. Any person authorised in writing may, at any reasonable time, enter land designated under section 29. *Sweet* v *Secretary of State for the Environment* was an attempt to overturn a prohibition imposed by the Secretary of State following a public inquiry. The dispute arose from the fact that the Order was extended to three hectares of land which were not of special interest in themselves but were considered to be essential for the survival of the adjoining land which was of special interest. The Inspector acting on behalf of the Secretary of State considered that this constituted a single environment and was covered by the Order, a view which found favour with the divisional court, rejecting the argument that section 29 could only cover land that contained flora and fauna of interest.

Section 137 of the EPA gives a clear power to enable the Nature Conservancy Councils to acquire land which is of special interest.

OTHER METHODS OF CONTROL

Management arrangements may be entered into between the owners or occupiers of land and the Conservancy Councils. In its first year English Nature spent £5.8 million on management agreements covering over 55,000 hectares of SSSIs.[15] The usual basis of a management arrangement is the lost profits arising from a potentially damaging operation not taking place. This provides an opportunity for unscrupulous landowners to gain compensation for refusal of permission to carry out a potentially damaging operation which in reality the owner has no intention of carrying out. Ultimately, a landowner may weigh up the costs of carrying out a damaging operation against the gains from a management agreement.

It seems that an injunction could be obtained to prevent breach of an agreement, and any action could lead to civil proceedings for breach of contract. The Act enables NCCs to provide grants to individuals or groups or to non-governmental organisations.

Development plan control

As explained above, local planning authorities can control threats to SSSIs where a landowner applies for planning permission. or where an unauthorised development is commenced. In the case of unauthorised development, a stop notice or enforcement notice may be served by the local planning authority.[16] In cases where a landowner or developer is refused planning permission, an appeal may be made to the Secretary of State for the Environment. In such a case there is evidence to suggest that the contents of the Development Plan play a major part in the way in which the planning system may protect or, as the case may be, fail to protect SSSIs.[17] The strength of local planning policies is of major significance in protecting the SSSIs against development. As a consequence, involvement in the consultation stage for a development plan is important. This was a trend apparent under the pre-1990 planning system and will be all the more evident with the changes introduced by the Planning and Compensation Act 1991 (see Chapter 7).

Department of the Environment Circular 1/92 issued in January 1992, 'Planning Controls over Sites of Special Scientific Interest', and The Town and County Planning General Development Order 1988 (Amendment) (No 3) Order 1991 require English Nature to define consultation areas around sites of special interest. Such areas may extend up to 2 km from the edge of a special site. A local planning authority must now consult with English Nature where a planning application would fall into such a site.

A study of 114 planning appeals in which SSSIs had been a material consideration between 1982-92 revealed that 59 per cent of sites were threatened by building development, including residential schemes, leisure developments, caravan sites and roads. Some 31 per cent of appeals involved unbuilt development, with waste disposal and tipping being the highest category. The remainder of appeals included controlled agricultural operations and other miscellaneous works. [18]

Subsequent analysis of random samples from the data revealed a positive correlation between the strength of development plan policies and the ability of the local planning authority to resist threats to the SSSIs and other sites of nature conservation interest. But as the study concludes:

'In terms of the hierarchy of planning designations the SSSI is virtually at the bottom of the pecking order, but nonetheless it does offer limited protection to otherwise undesignated sites...in the final analysis one is therefore forced to conclude that one is limited as to the strength of the designation but it is better than no designation at all.' [19]

Other planning controls

The planning system provides various other controls for the conservation of the environment. The oldest of these are the 'green belts', the most significant being the one which surrounds London to a depth of 25 to 40 km. Additional green belts have been established in Hampshire, Cambridge, Oxford, the West Midlands, and Yorkshire and Lancashire conurbations.

Green belts effectively impose a bar on all development, with the exception of buildings connected to agriculture and leisure facilities.

National parks

National parks consist of areas of beautiful and relatively wild country with access for the public. Development may take place but subject to certain restrictions, such as building design. Areas of outstanding natural beauty apply to areas not meeting the standards of a national park. Local planning authorities may divert development out of these areas.

Protected species

The Wildlife and Countryside Act 1981, as amended by the Wildlife and Countryside (Amendment) Act 1992, provides measures for the protection of species.

Section 1(1) protects birds from being killed and their nests from being damaged or destroyed. Any person who has in his possession any live or dead wild bird or egg is guilty of an offence. This has been taken to include a golden eagle, even when stuffed and mounted as a display.

A defence is provided under section 1(3) if a person shows that the bird has not been killed or the egg has not be taken otherwise than in the relevant provisions. A person may not be guilty of an offence if it is taken outside the close season, included in Part I of Schedule 2.

The Secretary of State may establish special areas under section 3 in which it may be an offence to kill or disturb birds and their nests. The Secretary of State must give particulars of the intended Order by notice in writing to every owner and every occupier of any land included in the area concerning which the Order is made. Where the giving of notice is impracticable, an advertisement may be placed in a local newspaper instead.

The Secretary of State may not make such an order unless:

• all the owners and occupiers affected have consented;

• no objections to the order have been made by any of those owners or occupiers before the expiration of a period of three months from the date of the giving of the notice or the publication of the advertisement; or

• any objections made have been withdrawn.

Certain defences in section 4 apply in the cases of:

• the taking of any wild bird, if it can be shown that the bird had been disabled otherwise than by his unlawful act and was taken in order to tend to it;

• the killing of any wild bird if it can be shown that the bird had been seriously disabled otherwise than by his unlawful act and there was no reasonable chance of its recovering;

• any act made unlawful by those provisions if he shows that the act was the incidental result of a lawful operation and could not reasonably be avoided.

A defence is also provided where a bird is killed for

• preserving public health or public or air safety;

• preventing the spread of disease; or

• preventing serious damage to livestock, foodstuffs for livestock, crops, vegetables, fruit, growing timber or fisheries.

Prohibitions are also placed on the means of killing wild birds and the sale of birds or their eggs. These provisions have recently been extended by the Wildlife and Countryside (Amendment) Act 1992.

Protection of wild animals

Section 9 proscribes the killing or injuring of any animal listed in Schedule 5 of the Act. Certain exceptions are made and a person will not be guilty of an offence if it is shown that:

- the animal had been disabled otherwise than by his unlawful act and was in his possession for the sole purpose of tending it until no longer disabled;
- prior to killing the animal it had been seriously disabled otherwise than by his unlawful act such that there was no reasonable chance of its recovering.

An authorised person will not be guilty of an offence by reason of the killing or injuring of a wild animal included in Schedule 5 if he shows that his action was necessary for the purpose of preventing serious damage to livestock, foodstuffs for livestock, crops, vegetables, fruit, growing timber or any other form of property or to fisheries.

Protection of plants

Under section 13 any person, not being an authorised person, who intentionally picks, uproots or destroys any wild plant in Schedule 8 will be guilty of an offence.

Under section 16(1), a person holding a licence from the Secretary of State can obtain a right to carry out practices with regard to protected species for a wide range of purposes including scientific and educational purposes, conservation, falconry and aviculture, preventing the spread of disease and preventing damage to food, livestock, crops, timber and fisheries. Such licences may, under section 16(6), specify the area within which birds and animals may be killed and the methods which may be used. A period for the duration of the licence may be imposed which, in any event, must not exceed two years.

Wide powers are given to police constables to stop and search persons suspected of carrying evidence relating to an offence. If a constable suspects that a person is committing an offence under Part I of the Act she/he may enter any land (though not a dwelling house) and arrest the person concerned. A justice of the peace may also grant a warrant under section 19(3) to a constable (with or without other persons) to enter upon and search premises for evidence which is suspected as being on that premises.

Any person who attempts to commit an offence under Part I of the Act will be guilty of an offence and may be punished in the same manner.[20]

Wide though these powers may be, they will naturally depend upon the enthusiasm of the local police for carrying out these duties. Faced with a multitude of pressing concerns, they are unlikely to see these offences as a priority area and exercise their discretion not to get involved. Much may be left to private citizens or organisations such as the RSPB and RSPCA, sometimes with back-up from the police.

Any citizen sufficiently concerned about police policy in their area could make representations to the police. Under section 106 of the Police and Criminal Evidence Act 1984, Chief Constables are required to have regard to representations and comments from the public about any policing functions.

The following is a list of relevant Schedules and the areas of wildlife conservation which they cover:

- Schedule 1 – Birds protected at all times and in the close season.

- Schedule 2 – Birds which may be killed or taken outside the close season, only by authorised persons.

- Schedule 3 – Birds which may be sold if ringed and bred in captivity.

- Schedule 4 – Birds which must be registered and ringed if kept in captivity.

- Schedule 5 – Protected animals.

- Schedule 6 – Animals which may not be killed or taken by certain methods.

- Schedule 8 – (As amended by S.I. 1988/288) Protected plants.

- Schedule 9 – Animals and plants which should not be released or allowed to escape into the wild.

The Wildlife and Countryside Act 1981 (Variation of Schedule) Order 1992, which came into force on 17 March 1992, adds a further seven animal species and nine plant species to Schedule 9.

Few of the species are guaranteed permanent protection – some species may move on and off the Schedules, depending on the view of the Secretary of State. A creature can be a protected species one second before midnight on one date and lose its protection a second after midnight through such changes.

Effect on planning and development of discovering a protected species

The discovery of a protected species in a certain locality may act as a brake on any development or operation being conducted on the site. This is because the range of offences falls into the category of strict liability.

The existence of planning permission does not entitle an operation to go ahead which is likely to destroy the protected species; any work which is under way will have to cease if the commission of offences is to be avoided. This can cover the nesting sites of bats or threats to the spawning grounds of natterjack toads. Only the relevant Nature Conservancy Council or the Secretary of State may give permission for any work to continue. In practice, the existence of a protected species on a site may operate as a major obstacle that objectors can raise against any controversial development.

Protection of individual species

Certain individual species have the benefit of protection by way of specific Acts of Parliament. The Conservation of Seals Act 1970 makes it an offence to kill seals by the use of any poisonous substance or by any firearm with a muzzle energy of not less than 600 foot-pounds and a bullet weighing less than 45 grains.

A closed season exists under section 2 for the killing of grey seals between 1 September and 31 December. For other common seals a closed season exists between 1 June and 31 August. Any person who kills or injures a seal in these periods commits an offence. Prosecutions may also be brought for attempts to commit offences under section 8.

Section 1 of the Badgers Act 1973 makes it an offence to wilfully kill, injure or take badgers. Section 2 creates offences to:

(a) cruelly ill-treat any badger;

(b) use in the course of killing or taking, or attempting to kill or take any badger, any badger tongs;

(c) save as permitted or under the Act dig for any badger; or

(d) use for the purpose of killing any badger any firearm other than a smooth bore rifle.

Restrictions are also placed on the selling and possession of live badgers and the marking and ringing of badgers. Powers to stop and search persons suspected of offences are available to the police. A further Act has since been passed to ensure the protection of badgers. The Deer Act 1991 replaces the Deer Act 1963 and provides for a close season for killing deer.

Tree preservation

Although the cutting down of a tree appears to be outside the definition of development, details of tree preservation orders are contained in Part VIII of the Town and Country Planning Act, but at present such orders may only be made where the authority considers it 'expedient in the interests of amenity' (section 198, Town and Country Planning Act 1990).

A local authority may make an order prohibiting the cutting down or the lopping or topping of trees without its consent. Such orders do not apply to trees which are dead, dying or have become dangerous, or to work done under an Act of Parliament or to prevent or abate a nuisance. In the absence of one or more of these special circumstances or consent from the local authority, an offence will be committed.

The offences are committed where a person, under section 210, in contravention of any tree preservation order,

(a) cuts down, uproots or wilfully destroys a tree, or

(b) wilfully damages, tops or lops a tree in such a manner as to be likely to destroy it.

These are strict liability offences, it not being necessary to prove that the person who damages the tree knew of the preservation order (*Maidstone Borough Council* v *Mortimer* (1980) 43 P & CR 67). Care will have to be taken, however, in proving that the order exists by producing a certified public record.

A tree is considered to be 'destroyed' if it ceases to have any amenity or be worth preserving and if a competent forester would conclude it ought to be cut down (See *Barnet LBC* v *Eastern Electricity Board* (1973) 2 All ER 319).

It is for a defendant to show on the balance of probabilities that one of the defences available applied to any action which falls under section 210. A fine of up to £20,000 is possible in the Crown Court. The magistrates' court can impose the statutory maximum or twice the value of the tree. In imposing the fine, the Court is entitled to consider the profit or financial advantage that the person may have obtained by destroying or damaging the tree and set the penalty to take this into consideration.

Trees in conservation areas

Further power to control the cutting down of trees in conservation orders has been given in section 211. Effectively, the same offences as exist under section 198 may be committed in respect of trees in a conservation area, regardless of whether any preservation order has been imposed (although the Secretary of State may disapply the effect of section 211 in certain cases). Defences available cover,

- that he served notice on the local planning authority of his intention to do the act in question (identifying the tree);
- that he did the act in question
  - with the consent of the local planning authority in whose area the tree is or was situated
  - after the expiry of the period of six weeks from the date of the notice but before the expiry of the period of two years from that date.

BIOTECHNOLOGY AND THE RELEASE OF GENETICALLY ENGINEERED ORGANISMS

An area which is going to be increasingly important with growing legal ramifications is genetic engineering. Ever since the concept developed there have been concerns voiced about the moral and ethical implications, and not least the environmental implications of genetic engineering. To some, biotechnology is a science to be promoted because it (purportedly) offers a world of plenty. We are right, if experience teaches us anything, to be sceptical about such promises. The same was said about atomic energy and a good many other areas of science which have been misused. At the same time as feeble efforts are being made to preserve existing biodiversity and even to catalogue what species we already have on this planet, it seems a most questionable matter to be trying to create new life-forms artificially.[21]

Just one of many risks is the possibility that the ecological balance of an area may be upset by the introduction of a genetically created organism. This has happened in the past with natural creatures which have been released into a different habitat.

The public debate on biotechnology has scarcely begun in the UK, and there has been little public participation in the making of legislation.[22] Regulation of genetic engineering has existed since 1978 (leaving aside the Biological Weapons Convention and the Biological Weapons Act 1972 which was signed in 1972 against germ warfare), largely under the remit of health and safety. EC legislation is likely to overtake any initiatives that the UK may generate.

The most detailed regulations are the Genetic Manipulation Regulations 1989 S.I. 1810, made under the Health and Safety at Work Act, which cover harm to human beings, and the Genetically Modified Organisms (Deliberate Release) Regulations 1992 No. 3280 which came into force on 1 February 1993 and cover harm as defined to any organism. These bring into force the provisions on biotechnology contained in the Deliberate Release Directive 90/220/EC. This should have been brought into force in UK law on 31 October 1991 but an extension was granted to the UK for compliance.

Genetically modified organisms are covered by Part VI of the EPA, which provides powers to minimise damage to the environment from the escape or release of the products of biotechnology.

The term organism covers any acellular, unicellular or multicellular entity (in any form) other than humans or human embryos, and articles consisting of 'biological matter'.[23] Biological matter is defined as ' tissue or cells (including gametes or propagules), or sub-cellular entities of any kind capable of replication or of transferring genetic material'.

The Secretary of State may impose prohibition notices on persons who may be involved in importing, acquiring, keeping, releasing, or marketing genetically modified organisms, if it is considered that such organisms may involve a risk of damage to the environment.

There is a register maintained by the Secretary of State under section 122 of the EPA. In the case of an application for a consent, regulation 17 requires the following information to be included on the register:

- the name and address of the applicant,
- a general description of the genetically modified organisms,
- the location where they are to be released,
- the general purpose behind the release,
- the foreseen date of release.

The register should also give details of methods and plans for monitoring the organism and for emergency response. An evaluation of the environmental impact must also be included and either a list of conditions imposed on the release or the reason why a committee appointed under section 124 has advised why a consent should not be granted.

Consents may be granted and limitations may be imposed subject to the Secretary of State. An application for a consent to release genetically modified organisms must be made in writing to the Secretary of State and must be made either:

- for one or more releases of one or more descriptions of genetically modified organisms on the same site for the same purposes within a limited period or
- for one or more releases of one description of genetically modified organisms on one or more sites for the same purpose within a limited period.

Under regulation 8, a person who makes an application for a consent to release genetically modified organisms must publish an advertisement concerning the proposed release. This must be done between two and four weeks after the date of acknowledgement of the receipt of the application. The advertisement must be published in a newspaper or newspapers 'circulating in the areas likely to be affected by the proposed release'. This puts the judgement as to the area to be affected solely with the person making the release.

The notice must contain the name and address of the applicant, the general description of the organisms to be released, the location and general purpose of the release and the foreseen dates of the release.

The person seeking consent for the release must also notify the owners of any sites affected, the local authority, the relevant Nature Conservancy Councils, the Countryside Commission, the NRA and the Forestry Commission. In a case relating to human health, no release may take place without the consent of the Health and Safety Executive.

Where a release has obtained a consent from the Secretary of State, the effects of the release do not amount to harm for the purposes of the regulations.

Wide powers are given to inspectors to carry out investigations and obtain information on the modification of organisms. Sections 122–123 establish public registers for information; such, however, is the competitive nature of biotechnology that commercial enterprises may seek exemptions on the grounds of protecting confidential and trade secrets.

Section 118 creates 15 different offences which may be committed, including contravention of section 108 and section 109. These include: contravention of prohibition notices, failure to inform the Secretary of State of the keeping of organisms, and release or marketing of organisms without a consent.

Other legislation which may be relevant is the Animals (Scientific Procedures) Act 1986. The production of genetically engineered vertebrates will be an offence unless the licensing system is observed. The Act controls any experimental or scientific procedure which may cause a protected animal distress, pain or lasting harm. However, obtaining the necessary evidence could be very difficult.

NOTES

[1] Private Member's Bill introduced in February 1992.
[2] A remark attributed to Joseph Stalin.
[3] For a general outline of conservation see Denyer-Green, (1983), *Wildlife and Countryside Act 1981: The Practitioner's Companion*, RICS.
[4] NCC Report, June 1984, reported in ENDS 114/July 1984.
[5] Halliday, Richard, (1992), *An Evaluation of the SSSI Designation as Protection Against Development*, Private publication.
[6] Rowell, T. A., Dr, (1991), *SSSIs - A Health Check*, Wildlife Link, December 1991.

[7]   See Chapter 2.
[8]   Hatton, Carol, of the World Wide Fund for Nature (WWF); broadcast on *The Natural World*, BBC Radio 4, 28 February 1993.
[9]   Halliday, op. cit.
[10] See also sections 15, 36 and 37 of the Highways Act 1980.
[11] Currently Barbara Mills, QC.
[12] Jewell, T., (9 October, 1992), 'Conservation and Crime', *New Law Journal*.
[13] Halliday, op. cit.
[14] Rowell, op. cit.
[15] *English Nature First Report* 1991/92.
[16] See Chapter 7.
[17] Halliday, op. cit.
[18] Ibid.
[19] Ibid.
[20] See *Stone's Justices' Manual*.
[21] Acharya, Rohini (1992), *Intellectual Property, Biotechnology and Trade*, ACTS Press, Kenya/Netherlands for some of the issues.
[22] There are exceptions. For the work of the Green Alliance see 'Who's Who in European Anti-Biotech', *Biotechnology*, December, 1992.
[23] See the EPA.

Appendix 1

Sources of Information

Sources of environmental law grow ever more varied each year. For the ordinary citizen, the key thing is to be able to find a way through the mushrooming range of books, journals and legislation to find the relevant information.

LAW REPORTS

These are the different law reports, referred to in this work. The year is the date the case was written up in the report (not necessarily the date it was heard) and the number is the page reference:

The All England Reports (All ER)

The Queen's Bench Reports (QB)

Weekly Law Reports (WLR)

Appeal Cases (AC)

The Justice of the Peace Reports (JP)

New Law Journal (NLJ)

Estates Gazette Case Summaries (EGCS)

Appeal Reports (App Rep)

A number of magazines also carry law reports, such as:

Journal of Planning and Environmental Law – (JPL) Published by: Sweet & Maxwell, Northway, Andover, Hampshire SP10 5BC.
Solicitor's Journal – (Sol. Jo.) Published by: Longman, 23-27 Lamb's Conduit Street, London, WC1.
The Times, The Independent and *The Guardian* all carry daily law reports which are usually reported in greater detail in the main reports.

PRACTICE AND PROCEDURE

For information on practice and procedure the works referred to in Chapter 3 are invaluable:

Magistrates' Courts – *Stone's Justices' Manual*, referred to in the text.
County Court - *County Court Practice*.
EC Legislation – Haigh, Nigel, *Manual of Environmental Policy, The EC and Britain*, looseleaf publication by Longman.
Barnard, D., *The Civil Court in Action* is a useful guide on civil procedure.
Emins, C.J., *Criminal Law and Procedure*, published by Financial Training and Services, Butterworths.
Directory of Courts 1992-93, published by Shaw & Sons, lists the addresses of UK courts.

BOOKS ON ENVIRONMENTAL LAW

Garbutt, John, (1992), *Environmental Law: A Practical Handbook*, Chancery, is a useful book designed for solicitors.
Whose environment is it anyway? (1992), Law Centres Federation Environment Project, is a wide ranging summary of environmental law for progressive lawyers.

ENVIRONMENTAL PROTECTION

The Control of Pollution Act 1974 covered the old system of environmental protection and is being replaced by The Environmental Protection Act 1990, now the main source of further regulations. The following regulations have all been made:

The Environmental Protection Act 1990 (Commencement No. 5) Order 1991 S.I. 96.
The Environmental Protection Act 1990 (Commencement No. 6 and Appointed Day) Order 1991 S.I. 685.
The Environmental Protection Act 1990 (Commencement No. 7) Order 1991 S.I. 1042.
The Environmental Protection Act 1990 (Commencement No. 8) Order 1991 S.I. 1349.
The Environmental Protection Act 1990 (Commencement No. 9) Order 1991 S.I. 1577.
The Environmental Protection Act 1990 (Commencement No. 10) Order 1991 S.I. 2829.
The Environmental Protection Act 1990 (Commencement No. 11) Order 1991 S.I. 266.
The Environmental Protection Act 1990 (Commencement No. 12) Order 1991 S.I. 3253.
The Environmental Protection Act 1990 (Modification of section 112) Regulations 1992 S.I. 2617.

The Environmental Protection Act 1990 (Authorisation of Processes) (Determination Periods) Order 1991 S.I. 513.

The Environmental Protection Act 1990 (Amendment of Regulations) Regulations 1991 S.I. 836.

The Environmental Protection Act 1990 (Applications, Appeals and Registers) Regulations 1991 S.I. 507.

The Environmental Protection Act 1990 (Controls on Injurious Substances) Regulations 1992 S.I. 32.

The Environmental Protection Act 1990 (Controls on Injurious Substances) (No. 2) Regulations 1992 S.I. 1583.

The Environmental Protection Act 1990 (Controls on Injurious Substances) Regulations 1993 S.I. 1.

The Environmental Protection (Determination of Enforcing Authority etc) (Scotland) Regulations 1992.

The Environmental Protection (Duty of Care) Regulations 1991 S.I. 2839.

The Environmental Protection (Prescribed Processes) (Amendment) Regulations 1991.

The Environmental Protection (Prescribed Processes and Substances) Regulations 1991 S.I. 472.

The Environmental Protection (Prescribed Processes and Substances) (Amendment) Regulations 1991 S.I. 614.

The Environmental Protection (Waste Recycling Payments) Regulations 1992 S.I. 462.

The Financial Assistance for Environmental Purposes (England and Wales) Order 1992 S.I. 654.

The Financial Assistance for Environmental Purposes Order 1992 S.I. 682.

The Highway Litter Clearance and Clearing (Transfer of Duties) Order 1991 S.I. 337.

The Litter (Animal Droppings) Orders 1991 S.I. 961.

Litter Control Areas Order 1991 S.I. 1325.

Advisory Committees on Hazardous Substances Order 1991 S.I. 1487.

Advisory Committees on Hazardous Substances (Terms of Office) Regulations 1991 S.I. 1488.

Genetically Modified Organisms (Contained Use) Regulations 1992 S.I. 3217.

ENVIRONMENTAL ASSESSMENT

Regulations covering projects where environmental assessments are required include the following:

Town and Country Planning (Assessment of Environmental Effects) Regulations 1988 S.I. 1199 as amended by the Town and Country Planning (Assessment of Environmental Effects) Regulations 1992 S.I. 1494.

Environmental Assessment (Scotland) Regulations S.I. 1221.

Environmental Assessment (Salmon Farming in Marine Waters) Regulations 1988 S.I. 1217.

Environmental Assessment (Afforestation) Regulations S.I. 1241.

Harbour Works (Assessment of Environmental Effects) Regulations 1988 S.I. 1336.

Electricity and Pipeline Works (Assessment of Environmental Effects) Regulations 1990 S.I. 442.

PLANNING

The Department of the Environment has produced a useful series of *Planning Policy Guidance Notes* of which number 12 (Cost £8.00) is one of the most useful, covering development plans.

For practitioner works, *The Encyclopedia of Planning Law*, Butterworths, looseleaf volumes, 1992 edition, is the most useful.

PLANNING LEGISLATION

Town and Country Planning Act 1990.

The Planning and Compensation Act 1991 (Commencement Order No. 1 and Transitional Provisions) Order 1991 S.I. 2067.

The Planning and Compensation Act 1991 (Commencement Order No. 2 and Transitional Provisions) Order 1991 S.I. 2092.

The Planning and Compensation Act 1991 (Commencement Order No. 3 and Transitional Provisions) Order 1991 S.I. 2272.

The Planning and Compensation Act 1991 (Commencement Order No. 4 and Transitional Provisions) Order 1991 S.I. 2728.

The Planning and Compensation Act 1991 (Commencement Order No. 5 and Transitional Provisions) Order 1991 S.I. 2905.

The Planning and Compensation Act 1991 (Commencement Order No. 6) (Scotland) Order 1992 S.I. 71.

The Planning and Compensation Act 1991 (Commencement Order No. 7 and Transitional Provisions) Order 1991 S.I. 334.

The Planning and Compensation Act 1991 (Commencement Order No. 8) Order 1992 S.I. 665.

The Town and Country Planning General Development (Amendment) Order 1991 S.I. 1536.

The Town and Country Planning General Development (Amendment) (No. 3) Order 1991 S.I. 2805.

The Town and Country Planning (Enforcement Notices and Appeals) (Amendment) Regulations 1991 S.I. 2804.

The Planning and Compensation Act 1991 (Commencement Order No. 9 and Transitional Provisions) Order 1992 S.I. 1279.

The Planning and Compensation Act 1991 (Commencement Order No. 10 and Transitional Provisions) Order 1992 S.I. 1491.

The Planning and Compensation Act 1991 (Commencement Order No. 11 and Transitional Provisions) Order 1992 S.I. 1630.

The Planning and Compensation Act 1991 (Commencement Order No. 12 and Transitional Provisions) Order 1992 S.I. 1937.

The Planning and Compensation Act 1991 (Commencement Order No. 13 and Transitional Provisions) Order 1992 S.I. 2413.

The Planning and Compensation Act 1991 (Commencement Order No. 14 and Transitional Provisions) Order 1992 S.I. 2831.

The Planning and Hazardous Substances Act (Commencement and Transitional Provisions) Order 1991 S.I. 725.

The Planning (Hazardous Substances) Regulations 1992 S.I. 656.

The Town and Country Planning Appeals (Determination by Inspectors) (Inquiries Procedure) Rules 1992.

The Town and Country Planning (Control of Advertisements) Regulations 1992 S.I. 666.

The Town and Country Planning (Control of Advertisements) (Scotland) Regulations 1992 S.I. 666.

The Town and Country Planning (Crown Land Applications) Regulations 1992 S.I. 2683.

The Town and Country Planning (Enforcement) (Inquiries Procedure) Rules 1992 S.I. 1903.

The Town and Country Planning (Fees for Applications and Deemed Applications) (Amendment) Regulations 1991 S.I. 1817.

The Town and Country Planning (Fees for Applications and Deemed Applications (Amendment) Regulations 1992 S.I. 1982.

The Town and Country Planning (Fees for Applications and Deemed Applications (Amendment) (No. 2) Regulations 1992 S.I. 3052.

The Town and Country Planning (Development) Plan Regulations 1991 S.I. 2794.

The Town and Country Planning (Structure and Local Plans) Regulations Rules S.I. 2038 1992.

The Town and Country Planning (Inquiries and Procedures) Regulations Rules S.I. 2039 1992.

The Town and Country Planning General Regulations 1992 S.I. 1492.

The Town and Country Planning General Development (Amendment) Regulations 1992 S.I. 609.

The Town and Country Planning General Development Orders have been amended six times as follows: 1991 S.I. 2268 (No. 2), S.I. 2805 (No. 3), 1992 S.I. 658 (No. 2), S.I. 1280 (No. 3), S.I. 1493 (No. 4), S.I. 1563 (No. 5), S.I. 2450 (No. 6).
The Town and Country Planning (Modification and Discharge of Planning Obligations) Regulations 1992 S.I. 2832.
The Town and Country Planning (Simplified Planning Zones) Regulations 1992 S.I. 2414.
The Town and Country Planning (Use Classes) (Amendment No. 2) S.I. 657.

WATER

Legislation: the principal Acts are:

Water Industry Act 1991
Water Resources Act 1991
Land Drainage Act 1991

Statutory Instruments:

Control of Pollution (Registers) Regulations 1989 S.I. 1160.
Water Consolidation (Consequential Provisions) Act 1991.
The Bathing Water (Classification) Regulations 1991 S.I. 1597.
The Water Supply (Water Quality) (Amendment) Regulations 1991 S.I. 1837.
The Water (Prevention of Pollution) Code of Practice Regulations 1991 S.I. 2285.
The Private Water Supplies Regulations 1991 S.I. 2790.
The Merchant Shipping (Prevention of Oil Pollution) (Amendment) Order 1991 S.I. 2885.
The Surface Waters (Dangerous Substances) (Classification) Regulations 1992 S.I. 337.
The Trade Effluents (Proscribed Processes and Substances) Regulations 1992 S.I. 339.
Friends of the Earth have also published two useful booklets:
River Pollution – A Sleuth's Guide (1992)
Water Pollution: Finding the Facts (1993)

PARLIAMENT AND PARLIAMENTARY PROCEDURE

Publications from the Government are mostly available through HMSO outlet: HMSO Publications Centre, PO Box 276, London SW8 5DT.
Dod's Parliamentary Companion.

Erskine May's Parliamentary Procedure.
and a useful pocket-sized guide, *Vacher's Parliamentary Companion.*
Green Alliance Parliamentary Newsletter, 49 Wellington Street, London
WC2E 7BN (071 836 0341).

BOOKS

Bell and Ball, (1990), *Environmental Law,* Butterworths.
Hughes P., (1993), *Environmental Law.*
Tromans, The Environmental Protection Act 1990: text and commentary, Sweet & Maxwell.
Encyclopedia of Planning Law, Sweet & Maxwell.

MAGAZINES

Environment Information Bulletin, Eclipse Group Ltd, Industrial Relations Services, 18-20 Highbury Place, London N5 1QP. 071-354 5458.
Environment Law, Brief Legal Studies & Services Ltd, Unit 1, Hainault Road, Little Heath, Romford, Essex RM6 5NP. 081-597 7335.
Environment Law, Bates Wells & Braithwaite, 61 Charterhouse Street, London EC1M 6HA.
Environment Now, Brodie Publications Ltd, 11-13 Victoria Street, Liverpool L2 5QQ.
European Environmental Law Review, Graham & Trotman Ltd, Sterling House, 66 Wilton Road, London SW1V 1DE.
Environmental Risk, Euromoney Publications Plc, Nestor House, Playhouse Yard, London EC4V 5EX.
International Journal of Marine and Coastal Law, Graham & Trotman Ltd, Sterling House, 66 Wilton Road, London SW1V 1DE.
Environmental Law Monthly, Monitor Press, Rectory Road, Great Waldingfield, Sudbury, Suffolk CO10 0TL. 0787 78607.
nawdc news, (National Association of Waste Disposal Contractors), National Association of Waste Disposal Contractors Ltd, Mountbarrow House, 6-20 Elizabeth Street, London SW1W 9RB. 071-824 8882
Water Law, Chancery Law Publishing Ltd, 22 Eastcastle Street, London W1N 7PA. 071 323 2386.

INDEX

INDEX OF STATUTES

INDEX OF STATUTORY INSTRUMENTS

INDEX OF CASES